The Life of
An Ordinary Bloke

by

The Barra

Copyright © 2020   John Manson Barraclough

All rights reserved. No part of this publication may be reproduced, distributed or transmitted in any form or by any means, without prior written permission.

John Manson Barraclough (The Barra)

The Life of an Ordinary Bloke by The Barra -- 1st ed.

First Published 2020 by M.C. Sutton,
139/218 Bishop Rd, Beachmere, Queensland, Australia

Editor   Chris Sutton

ISBN 978-0-6483106-6-4

Dedication

*I have written these words for my wife
and three sons,
as a record of our lives to date.*

Acknowledgements

I must thank the following people for their encouragement, help and support;

Sandra Cavanagh, for suggesting that I write this. It came about during a 'happy hour' when we were all discussing things past.
Sandra said, "You guys have done so much, you should write a book about it all." So here it is.

Lyn Barraclough, for jogging my memory from time to time.

My late sister Risè. I have referred every now and again to the work she wrote on the history of our family, which she called "The Barracloughs of Opunake".

Annie Hartland and Ron Byrne, who did the first editing of this work (mainly fixing my spelling mistakes).

Angela Jordan, for her proof reading. She did a tremendous job.

Chris Sutton, for her help in editing and publishing, as well as general advice in getting this book to its final stages. She turned it from a bunch of words to a proper biography.

Thank you, for reading this. I hope you enjoy the yarn.

Contents

Prologue	6
Chapter 1 - In the beginning	10
Chapter 2 - The Learning Years	17
Chapter 3 - The Teenage Years	22
Chapter 4 - Growing Up	42
Chapter 5 - The Married Thing	53
Chapter 6 - Finding our feet	58
Chapter 7 - Time for Adventure	68
Chapter 8 - Bigger Adventures	89
Chapter 9 - The Challenges	106
Chapter 10 - Bigger Challenges	119
Chapter 11 - Different Challenges	132
Chapter 12 - The Biggest Challenges.	151
Chapter 13 - The Best Challenges	170
Chapter 14 - The Pinnacle	189
Chapter 15 - Enjoying Life.	222
Epilogue	263

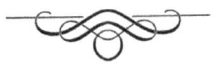

Prologue

I come from a long line of butchers. My Great Grandfather, Lawford Stroud Barraclough, was born in Rose Street, Collingwood, Victoria in 1856. He moved with his parents to Nelson, New Zealand, where he was educated and learned the butcher's trade. It was in Nelson that he met and married Anne Curran. They had four sons and three daughters.

Lawford was in the meat trade as a butcher and a farmer. He founded his butchery business in Patea in 1882 and transferred it to Hawera 6 years later. He lived in the centre of town. He also farmed 150 acres at Turamona, near Hawera, and another 46 acres in connection with his business.

Lawford was a member of the Hawera Borough Council for two terms and was prominently connected with the Borough from the year 1888. He was Captain of the Hawera Fire Brigade for several years and for twelve years, a member of the *H Battery* in Nelson under Captain Pitt (who at the time was Attorney-General of New Zealand). He rose to the rank of Lieutenant.

Later, he was a member of the *Hawera Mounted Rifles*. In 1890, he was superintendent of the Sunday school and laid the foundation stone for the Methodist Church... and thought he owned it.

Lawford founded Barraclough's butchery in Hawera. Later, it was run by his son Manson, followed, after the war, by his nephew Mannie (Harry's son).

Lawford was often generous to the Maori people and would go up the river to Tikikaworo's camp and chop up meat for the hangi. On one occasion, the chief gave him a carved walking stick as a gift. This was later handed down to his son Manson, who then handed it on to his nephew, Harry's son Manson (Uncle Mannie). His eldest daughter, my cousin Lois Aitchison, now has it.

Manson was good to his customers. He supplied meat to the Hawera Hospital, gave meat once a week to the Salvation Army, even gave some to those in need. At the local A&P shows, he would provide the bullock, sheep and pigs for the *Guess the Weight* competitions.

One year he bought a massive roan coloured bullock from Bourne's in Waverly. It was so large that when it was to be weighed at the abattoir, it was too big to fit into the crush. The next day he got some of the butcher boys from the shop, went out to the abattoir and cut it up. He gave it to some Maori people he had rung earlier in the morning.

A little bit more on Lawford, as researched by Linda Barraclough in Australia. Linda provided the following information.

Linda's grandfather, Luke Barraclough, had a brother Henry, born about 1827 at Wibsey near Bradford in Yorkshire. Both were the children of James Barraclough and Hannah Carter. He may be the Henry Barraclough whose record shows an arrival in Victoria, Australia, in 1848 aboard the *Tasman*, with his wife Mary. Her maiden name is given as Dove and her place of origin as *"A native of Clickerton, Yorkshire"*. Henry and Mary married in 1846 at Dewsbury, West Yorkshire. The records show Henry's birthplace as Wibsey, which is correct if he is Luke's brother. With them was their daughter, Selina Tasman, born aboard the ship. Selina died, aged 9 months, in 1849.

Divorce was not available in Victoria until 1861. On the 24th January 1853;

- Henry Barraclough married Mary Ann Fletcher. Joe Wright witnessed their marriage.
- Mary Barraclough neè Dove married Joe Wright. Henry witnessed their marriage.

The double ceremony took place at the Independent Congregational Church in Melbourne, and Henry Hison witnessed both marriages.

In 1853 Henry's brother, Luke arrived in Victoria as a single man. He met and lived with Susannah Hignett, and they had a child in Melbourne. Henry and Luke both worked there as brick makers. In 1855, Luke and Susannah married at Ballarat, where they lived. Henry witnessed the marriage. Henry and Mary Ann's children, born in Melbourne, were:

- Henrietta, born 1854, Victoria, died aged one year in 1855.
- Price Fletcher, born 1855, died in 1857, in Melbourne.
- Lawford Stroud, born Collingwood, Melbourne, 1857,
- Hannah, born Brunswick, Melbourne, Victoria 1859.

The birth certificate states Lawford was born in Rose St, Collingwood, which was also the family address. Henry was a brickmaker, and previous children were Price Fletcher and one daughter, who died in December, 1855. Their mother, Mary Ann Fletcher, is given as a native of Staffordshire.

The records show that, by 1860 Henry and his family lived in Castlemaine, where Henry's occupation was given as a *"medical botanist"*. Their son Henry James was born in Castlemaine, in 1861.

This was a time of tension between doctors and herbalists. In April 1862, Henry was alleged to have mal-administered to a woman, Mrs Lillycrap, who died in childbirth while having her twelfth child. Dr Thomas McGrath made allegations against him and, despite two subsequent trials, Henry was acquitted. During the evidence, it transpired he was a brickmaker working in Melbourne, where a Melbourne herbalist trained him.

There are no further records of Henry and his family until 1870, when they appear in the New Zealand records. It is in New Zealand, in that year, that Henry and his wife have their last child, Hebe. Henry is practising as a doctor and the family believes he had been a trained doctor.

He then disappears from the New Zealand records. Through the years, the family believed he had died when Hebe, was *"quite young"*, but no official record of his death, nor a death or burial certificate, had been found. There *is* a death record for Mary Ann Barraclough neè Fletcher in Nelson, New Zealand, dated 1880.

However, Australian death records show that a Doctor Henry Barraclough died in 1890 in Boggabri, NSW. He was unregistered and does not appear to have had any qualifications.

In 1886, he was listed as having lived there for the past 10 years and having practised for twenty years in Australia. On his death, he left everything to his housekeeper, Bridget McNeil, who provided the information for the death certificate.

Little is known about Henry's parentage, other than that his father was thought to have been called Henry, and he was said to have been born in Bradford about 1828. However, he is said to have had three daughters; names unknown, and his wife's name had been Mary Dove.

This information, particularly the name of his wife provides strong evidence that this Henry, and the Henry who appears in the New Zealand records are the same person.

If I may, I also include a piece from
"The Barraclough Biographies".

The Bronte's Barraclough clock
(Courtesy of The Bronte Parsonage Museum)

"The Clockies of Dollymore" Haworth.

For many years from the late seventeenth century, the Heatons, living in what in those days must have been a truly isolated farmstead, carried on a thriving trade as clockmakers. Inevitably, as is the way of country-folk, they were dubbed the "Clockies of Dollymore", and when the secrets of clock making were passed down to the Barracloughs, the name went with them.

The Barraclough strain was introduced into the Heaton Family when Jonas Barraclough of Horton, married Martha Heaton.

Their son was taken as a boy to "Dollymore" to be taught clock making by his uncles, and it was the descendants of Jonas and Martha Barraclough who went into Haworth and further afield.

From the Bradford Telegraph and Argus, Saturday, May 17, 1958.

Courtesy Mick Marshal of Essex.

Another piece from the ***"The Barraclough Biographies".***

The coming centenary commemoration of Charlotte Bronte's death (31st March 1855), has reminded a colleague, of a conversation he had some years ago with the late Mr Herbert Barraclough, then head of the Leeds firm of Jewellers, Messrs Z Barraclough and Sons, Ltd.

Mr Barraclough represented the fifth generation of a famous family of clockmakers, whose first shop was opposite the Black Bull at Haworth. Barraclough has then specialised in the making of grandfather clocks and huge affairs they were, containing enough mahogany "to make a dining-room suite" said Mr Herbert Barraclough, whose sister possessed one of these massive timepieces made a few years before Charlotte Bronte died. Mr Barraclough recalled a boyhood visit to the Haworth shop when the face of the village idiot pressed against the window gave him a fright. Amongst others who peered into that window was the Rev. Patrick Bronte; he would often pause for a moment to get the correct time.

From the Yorkshire Life Vol 1X, No 3 March 1955.

Courtesy Mick Marshal of Essex.

A few years ago, I went onto the website of Christie's of London. They had a Barraclough Grandfather clock for auction. The reserve price was £7,000.

Chapter 1 - In the beginning

I was born John Manson Barraclough on 11th June 1945, in Hawera, New Zealand, the second son of Frederick Stroud Barraclough and his wife Mavis June Barraclough neè Lovell, who married on 28th June 1941.

Mum gave birth to me in my Great Uncle Manson's home at 29 Argyle Street, Hawera. I am not sure of the reason for this, however, it is the reason for my middle name being Manson.

Very soon after my birthing day, we all went home to 6 Tasman Street, Opunake, which was 26 miles to the north, on the slopes of Mt Egmont, (later to be renamed Mt Taranaki.) It boasted one of the best beaches on the Taranaki Coast. This is where I spent the next sixteen years of my life.

My mother's parents were Frank Woolsey Lovell, and Emily Jane Lovell, (neè Henderson). They were married on the 9th August 1917. We called them Nana and Poppa. They managed a sheep farm, on the Upper Glen Road, Manaia. They both loved their garden and I remember that they grew berries; cape gooseberries, red currants, black currants, raspberries and more. These were grown in the orchard they developed, where apples, plums, nectarines, and kiwi fruit also grew. Nana did a lot of preserving and jams of fruits from the orchard. She was also a great cook. My sister Risè liked the jelly sponges, which were as light as a feather. Dad's special was cream puffs, and Nana always had a fresh batch made every time we went down to see them, which was about monthly. Before all of that, Poppa was a sheep shearer, and went over to Australia at the ripe old age of 25. He was there for about 4 years before returning to New Zealand to marry.

Poppa was a cheese maker. He started in the Park Vale Cheese Factory in Carterton and it was was there he learnt all about cheese making. Later he was to move to Balance Cheese Factory south of Woodville, and then on to Newbury, Palmerston North, where he became Manager. He showed the cheeses at the agricultural shows. They called the cheese *"Silver Leaves Cheese"*. The next move was to Parewanui, south of Bulls, then on to Tutaenui, north of Marton, where he won the Lonsdale Challenge Cup in a dominion wide competition in 1936.

In 1938, he moved up to Taranaki and the Kina Road Cheese factory. In 1939, they decided to go dairy farming and for the next four years they milked cows, until changing again to manage the sheep farm for Jack Campbell, on the Upper Glen Road in Manaia.

On retirement in 1958, they moved to 6 Burns Street Hawera, and started setting up their gardens all over again. Poppa had the vegetable garden. It was always full of beans, peas, cabbages, and everything else that was in season. Poppa's greatest joy was his flowers. In the sheltered part of the garden were the chrysanthemums. There were rows of them, each one staked. Nailed to the top of each stake was one of Nana's old preserving jar lids, with the name of the flower. Another of Poppa's favourites was the dahlia. He had a special dahlia plot up the side of the house.

Both Nana and Poppa became members of the Hawera Horticulture Society. Each year at the Dahlia Show, Poppa would win a few trophies. When he was in his 80s, he scooped the pool and won the New Zealand Dahlia Society's Bronze Medal for a fine specimen of *A. J. Parker*, a giant decorative. Two days before this particular show, Poppa had a fall and injured his ankle. Despite this, with the aid of crutches, he was able to gather his blooms and stage his dahlias. While he was always busy growing dahlias, he still had time to breed one of his own. It was a lengthy process, and it had to be grown in other gardens to make sure it was of good quality. A friend of his, a Mr Mason from Fielding, grew one and was pleased with the outcome. He wanted Poppa to name it so that he could register it for him. He named his dahlia *Frank Lovell*. It was a large yellow cactus variety. Unfortunately, all this excitement was too much for him. He died on the 4th February 1970. (This was Lynette's and my third wedding anniversary.)

My Nana & Poppa meeting our son Marc, not a month old.

My father's parents were Harry Wakefield Barraclough and Florence Hilda Barraclough (neè Meyrick). Grandad Pop, as he was known to us, lived in King Street Opunake. Harry was the third son of Lawford Stroud Barraclough. Florence died in 1947 when I was 2 years old.

Harry was the butcher in Opunake, his son Fredrick, my Dad, worked with him. The other son, Bob, took over once Harry retired and Fredrick left. Harry also opened butcher shops in Pungarehu, Rahotu, and Okato. He bought some land just north of Opunake and on this built an abattoir. It supplied the meat for the four shops and processed about twenty sheep and five cattle a day. It was a big business. In the early days, he brought stock up from Waverly to Auroa on the train, and then drove them along the road through the town to the abattoir.

My elder brother had been born on the 13th November 1942. He was named Frederick Hilton Barraclough, but called Hilton by all.

On the 12th September 1947, my sister arrived via the Opunake Cottage Hospital, Risè June Barraclough. The name Risè (Pronounced Ree say) came from a singer that my father had heard while he was serving in New Caledonia during the Second World War. Anyhow, Dad was taken with her enough to name his first and only daughter after her. The singer was Risè Stevens, who was born in New York City on 11th June 1913. (11th of June is also my birthday). She was a Mezzo Soprano and sang with the Metropolitan opera in NY from 1939 for over 2 decades. She died on the 20th March 2013, aged 99 years.

The three kids

A few words on our town Opunake, if I may. My sister Risè researched the following when she wrote the history of our Barraclough Family.

Sally Karena was not a sports person, but a people person. She was very involved in the community, and for her efforts, they awarded her the QSM, Queens Service Medal. Sally was born in 1906 and died 9th November 1994, aged 88 years, and is buried in the Opunake cemetery.

Mary Hickey was born in a thatched whare (small Maori hut) on 13th April 1882, where the Cottage Hospital is today. She was the first European girl to be born in the town and the first pupil teacher there. In 1925, she achieved the distinction of being the first woman in Australasia to be awarded a Doctorate in Literature. She became Mother Mary St Domitille and taught for 20 years in Christchurch. They awarded her the OBE for her work in education; she died 20th June 1958.

Blanche Stevenson lived on Watino Road, with her husband. They cleared the flax covered land, and turned it into a dairy farm. She developed a 3-acre garden, complete with an orchard and apple trees imported from Scotland. Amongst the flowerbeds they built a tennis court. With Blanche's extensive knowledge of horticulture, in 1940 she was awarded a Fellowship of The Royal New Zealand Institute of Horticulture, an award she treasured for the rest of her life. Blanche died on the 9th November 1965 and is buried at the Lizzie Bell Cemetery at Pihama.

Sporting greats to come from Opunake were Graham Mourie and the great Peter Snell.

Graham Mourie was Opunake's best Rugby player. He became Captain of the *All Blacks* in 1977 to 1983. They released an autobiography entitled *"Graham Mourie – Captain"*. This book gave an insight to all the exploits of the *All Blacks* under the leadership of the young Opunakean.

Peter Snell was born in the same hospital as Risè, the Opunake Cottage Hospital. Peter was best known for winning three Olympic gold medals at the Rome Olympics in 1960 and at Tokyo in 1964.

At one time he also held the world record for the fastest mile, which he ran at Cooks Gardens in Wanganui on the 27th January 1962. I had gone down to this meeting with my parents and a friend Len Henderson. People talked about this great achievement of Peter's for years. There was a saying after the meet, "I was there".

The following is an extract from Wally Ingram's book. (Wally is a noted New Zealand Sports Commentator)

> "One of the best stories that followed Snell's great mile run at Wanganui came, naturally enough from his proud mother. "He was a 9lb baby and was a holy terror", she said. "Even as a little fellow, at least as a youngster" – for Peter was never little – he was full of energy and, because of this, his mother saw that he had plenty of honey and glucose in his diet. So, like another famous New Zealander, Edmond Hillary, with Sherpa Tensing, the first to conquer Mt Everest, Peter Snell has been a good advertisement for New Zealand Honey. "I used to buy honey in 60lb tins," said his mother, "and he just piled it on his bread. In addition, he was a great boy for taking glucose in his drinks, but Peter Snell was fortunate to be born into a sport loving family. His mother, who is 5ft 2in, was a champion athlete of her college in the Wairarapa district; his father, who stood 6ft 1in, at his best, was more than good at cricket, and Peter's elder brother, Jack, knows what it is to make runs and take wickets".

Peter was nine when he left Opunake, the town whose athletic fame at that stage had been in giving New Zealand a better-than-ordinary pole-vaulter, Fred Barraclough.

In the early thirties, Dad started getting serious about athletics and was competing in the 100 and 200-yard sprints at a provincial level. He then started doing the long jump, and the hop, step and jump. He was very good at these, but he really enjoyed and excelled in the pole vault, so much so that he won the New Zealand championship in 1934-35, 1937-38 and 1938-39.

Dad vaulting during a practice session

The long jumper

From my sister's collection of Dad's Memoirs.

In those days they did vaulting using a bamboo pole. This was rigid, and did not flex like a modern pole, therefore the technique was to work on the pole to get your feet in the air, then push upward while you are upside down. I guess you can tell that I enjoyed it as well. I got to the heights that Dad achieved back in the thirties but, of course, they were jumping a lot higher in the sixties.

I don't remember many of my first five years, except for one Christmas present being a big red fire engine. It had an extension ladder that you could wind up, which could turn 360 degrees. At the top of the ladder was the attached hose and nozzle. It had a water tank and a big rubber ball. By pushing the ball you could make the hose squirt. The harder you pushed, the further the hose sprayed.

I also remember walking on water, but at the time, did not understand the significance. It was a freezing winter's morning. I was playing in what was a puddle, except that it had a half an inch of ice on the top, and I found I could walk on it if I was careful.

I do know that in those first five years, my father renovated our home, turning it from a small green weatherboard cottage into a much larger three-bedroom home with a sunroom in the front. It had a large lounge room with a big open fire. I remember enjoying evenings in there and being very cosy. In the winter, the family would listen to the request session on the radio, while knitting woollen jumpers. Only Dad would not be knitting, as he would be reading.

There was also a big living room and kitchen, with a serving bar out to the meals area. I shared my bedroom with my brother, or he shared it with me, I am not sure which. Opposite our bedroom was the bathroom, laundry, and toilet. We could boast that we had one of the first flushing toilets in town.

Outside the back-door dad had built a big pergola between the house and the garage/workshop and of course mum had it planted with all sorts of greenery.

The house had a stucco finish and was painted a very light grey.

The house is still standing today and has been turned into a B&B. It has had a few coats of paint and is now a different colour, and the gardens are not the same as my Mum had it back then, but the basics are still the same.

This was our house at number 6 Tasman Street.
Photo taken in Feb 2002.

Chapter 2 - The Learning Years

I started Primary School in 1950, a tiny, shy, nervous little boy. Miss Fordyce was my teacher. I remember Miss Fordyce very well, but I don't remember any other of my primary teachers.

Many, many years later, my mother-in-law met Miss Fordyce in England, while they both were on a touring holiday. They were talking, and my mother-in-law mentioned that her daughter had married a young man from New Zealand, and his name was John Barraclough. Miss Fordyce replied, "I taught a John Barraclough when he was in primary school".

I remember little else about primary school. The introduction to book learning was something different and I don't think I got what it was all about, because I never really succeeded at it.

I remember, when I was about seven or eight my Mum enrolled me in dance lessons. As Mum liked tap dancing, and we had a very good teacher in town by the name of Jean Mackillsy, I learned to tap dance. (I think the spelling of my teacher's name might be wrong, but it's near enough). She was from Ireland so was good at tap dancing. I think the lessons went all right and at the end of the year, there was a big concert held in the local movie theatre. I remember, when the dancing was all finished, they called a few kids up on stage for a prize giving. I was one of these unfortunate few to get a prize. It was a string of sausages, but filled with sawdust not meat. I think it must have been the booby prize. I could never work out what I was supposed to do with them.

One weekend we all went down to Carterton, where Mum had an Auntie. It was a Saturday morning and us kids, along with some from next door, were playing cricket on the back lawn, all was good until I hit one a bit hard, and it sailed straight through the neighbour's window. I went over and apologised and said I would pay for it. I didn't know how I would do that, but I had said it, so now I was committed. I thought that I could get an advance on my pocket money, from Dad. Later in the morning we all got cleaned up and we were off to the races; Mum and Dad, me and Mum's Auntie. Mum put ten shillings each way on a horse, because she thought it looked pretty good. I thought this was an opportunity to help pay for the window, so I asked Mum if I could have two shillings and sixpence worth (i.e. 25%) of her bet. She agreed, so we all waited for the race, and some return on the money we had bet.

Mum was having a little luck as the day went, and continued to have a bet, and I continued to have my 25%. However, at the start of the last race I didn't quite have enough for the window. The last race saved me, as Mum had put a pound each way on this horse and I thought I also had to have part of that, so paid out my money to get my 25%. The horse won the race and paid twenty pounds for the win. How good was that? When we got back to Mum's Auntie's place, I went straight next door and paid for the window. I got some change back, as they said it would not take all of my winnings to get it fixed. That day was the first time I had ever been to a racetrack, and it was also my last.

During that weekend in Carterton, I also met my Great Grandfather, on my mother's side, Thomas Henderson. He was 95 years old and still very fit as he used to walk everywhere. He lived on his own in a big old house on about a half an acre of land. He built a chicken shed way down the back under some big cypress trees. He did this so he would have to walk that far twice a day.

At Intermediate School, for Forms 1 & 2, my teacher was Jim Munro. He was into Maori culture, and we were lucky enough to get a reasonable understanding of the Maori people. He taught us their history, including the migration in 1315, through to the present; including the wars, both tribal and against the British, the treaty of Waitangi, signed in 1840 with the British and the notorious Maori Honi Heki, who chopped down the flagpoles (I think five times), and became a bit of a legend.

The other thing I remember he taught us was efficiency. He would give groups a task, usually things that we would do, or should do, around the house. Against each task he would ask us to put the times we took to complete each one, so that the group with the lowest time would take the honours. Then we compared each group member's results to get the best time possible. The task would then be compared by the class, as an open discussion, to get the ultimate time. This exercise stayed with me, and I still, practise it with most things I do.

I walked to school every morning, with a Maori boy, Barry Simmons, nicknamed Sam. Why Sam? I have no idea. He was my age, and we were in the same class all the way through our schooling. Sometimes we got into a bit of mischief on the way home, but I won't talk about that.

On Sunday mornings, I took Mum and Dad an early cup of tea, and they would have this before getting up. One particular morning, after delivering the tea, I went out of the back door and stopped. There was a kitten sitting on the doormat. It looked up at me and meowed. I bent down and picked it up, and it didn't mind at all, so I took it up to Mum and Dad, and said, "Look what I found, can I keep it?"

The answer was, "Take it outside, it will be full of fleas". I took it outside. Dad followed me and got some flea powder. With that job done, I asked again, "Can I keep it?" "I suppose so, until we find its proper owner." I never looked for an owner, and I don't know if Mum or Dad looked for an owner, but I kept the kitten.

I had to come up with a name for the kitten, and I thought about this a lot. When I looked at the kitten's face I could make out the letter "M" on her forehead, and I thought that it was significant. Why, I didn't know. On the Saturday preceding this event, I went to the Saturday matinee at the local theatre. The movie was a comedy about some gangster bloke, by the name of Mugsy G Fogillmire. It must have been that Sunday night in bed in the middle of the night, it came to me, the kitten's name would be "*Mugseedo*". She would be known around the house as Mugs.

Mugs fitted into the family well. She would even rub up against Hilton's leg and that was something. Mugs was a good cat and stayed with us for a long time. But she had one major problem, she was just about always pregnant. This did not worry me too much but was a problem for Dad who had to do something with the kittens.

Mugs and one of her families

It had to be around 1960 that Mugs disappeared. She had just had another litter of kittens. I was away on a hockey tournament. When I got home, the reality hit.

About three weeks later, on Sunday morning. I had just taken Mum and Dad their cuppa. I was walking into the kitchen and there stood Mugs, dirty and skinny. I picked her up and took her up to show Mum and Dad.

They were shocked, and I asked could she stay this time. The answer from both of them was "Yes!" Soon after, we took Mugs to visit the local vet. No more kittens.

I found out many years later that Dad put Mugs in a bag with the kittens and gave the bag to another person to dispose of. The person took the bag, miles up the road, under the mountain, and threw the bag into the river. As he watched the bag slowly sink, he saw Mugs poke her head out of the bag. He saw no more. It took her three weeks to find her way home. She had to cross several roads and at least two rivers, but she made it. She had earned her home.

In the 50s we went camping at the Opunake beach. Dad had a big, 12 feet by 12 feet tent. I think it was an old army tent that Dad must have bought as army surplus. At least, it was the right colour. Back then, I thought it was big.

It had a wooden floor made up of panels 3 feet by 4 feet, so they had to be carried down to the beach as well. Mind you, home was only 5 minutes from the beach, and the trailer did the carrying. The tent had four rooms around the centre pole. Mum and Dad used to bring their double bed down, along with the wardrobe and the cot for Risè.

Dad was still working in town and would commute each day from the beach. We had a lot of fun and spent most of each day in the water or lying on the beach in the nice warm black sand.

The sand was black because of the amount of iron in it. A few years later, a company set up a smelter up the coast, where they produced pig iron. The beach was so safe you could swim no matter what the tide. These were good times, and we made the most of them.

Opunake Beach

When I was a little older, Dad gave me five shillings to get a crayfish down at the wharf. The wharf, now derelict, was once used to tie up the ships that exported the cheese produced at the milk factory, as well as flax harvested from around the district. The flax was the raw material for making ropes.

However, the old breakwater on the seaward side was a very good cray fishing ground. I remember one diver telling me, "They are sitting there like chickens on a perch". When the divers had all the crayfish they wanted, they would sell one to me for the five shillings. The cray was so big that I could just fit my hand around its back. I would ride my bike home as fast as I could, with one hand on the handlebars, and the other holding this big flapping thing.

All that was left of the old wharf in 2011.
The breakwater is on the right.

Chapter 3 - The Teenage Years

When I was about 12 years old, I started going to church on a Sunday with Mum. She and Dad had me christened in the St Barnabas Anglican church in town. Dad's family was of the Methodist faith, but I guess he missed that one back then. Mum didn't go every Sunday, but I kept going. Eventually I was confirmed. Why? I can't remember.

I also started going to bible classes each Friday night. I believe the reason for this was the fact that the Vicar's daughter was also going and she was a bit of all right. When I started High School, and started studying science, it created a conflict between what I was being taught at school and what I was being taught at bible class. I raised the point with both teachers. I gave up bible class not long after. I guess in my mind, the scientific theory outweighed the theological one.

We played Rugby in Forms 1 & 2 and represented our School against other teams around the Mountain. I was playing full back. Barry was in the back line, as he was very quick on his feet. I remember we were practicing rugby one lunchtime when somebody passed me the ball. I headed for the try line. I was just about there when Barry tackled me. He drove me into the ground and we both ended up in a heap. I found, when I got up, that the skin on my kneecap had peeled off and was rolled up at the bottom of the kneecap itself. It earned me six stitches and a couple of days off school.

We were lucky enough that our family could go on a holiday every year around Christmas time. Around 1957, we were heading for the Bay of Islands. My brother and I decided that we needed a bit of pocket money, so we collected beer bottles from around town and sold them at the local hardware store. Why a hardware store? I don't know, but they paid the money, and I was too young to ask questions. However, there was a problem.

The shop had a front step about 150 mm high, and this little boy, with arms full of beer bottles, tripped over it. Throwing my hands out in front to protect myself, I managed to slash my left wrist on one of the broken bottles. I had never seen so much blood in my life (not that my life had been very long at that stage). They carted me off to the local doctor, and he got it all back together with only four stitches.

All of this meant that I went on holidays with an arm all bandaged up and no pocket money.

One holiday I stayed with my Uncle Cyril and Aunty Phillis (Aunty Phillis is my Dad's sister) in New Plymouth. (They later moved down to Palmerston North).

Uncle Cyril was a pilot instructor and flew out of Bell Block Aerodrome. He had worked in this job for quite some time, as he has been an instructor during the war. He was flying Tiger Moths in New Plymouth, an ancient bi-plane. However, the art of flying was much the same, in any aircraft, unless, of course, in a very modern jet fighter or one of those aircraft with the propeller on top. (In these aircraft, things happened much, much faster).

I was lucky. When I was the ripe old age of thirteen, my Uncle Cyril took me up for a flight in the old Tiger Moth. I cannot explain the feelings going through me on that flight. It must have been that adrenalin stuff, but I did't know it then. I was thinking about the plane, and how it operates, and the "what if's" I should be feeling. All the time knowing that he was still in control of it.

Then he said to me, "It's yours, John". I knew what this meant and took the stick and flew the aircraft.

What else is there that could top that in the eyes of a 13-year-old? I was in another world; banking the aircraft from right to left, pulling back on the stick to gain a bit of altitude. Man, this was so good!

When Uncle Cyril said, "Come around onto a heading of 160 degrees, John." I had a good idea that this was to bring the aircraft around onto the heading required for the landing. It was at this point that I said,

"Uncle Cyril, the aircraft is yours".

Even at that age, I knew my limits. But I have regretted handing it back to him. I have landed a plane many, many times, in my dreams, and never crashed. I was so over the moon that I remember little of the rest of the day, or the week, or the whole time I was flying the aircraft.

In February 1959, I started high school. They put me into an engineering class, Form 3E, as I was not much of an academic student. I did not mind this, as I enjoyed engineering and building things using my hands. Schoolwork in high school seemed to be a continuation of primary school and did not interest me too much, apart from technical drawing and engineering practice. I also enjoyed General Science and topped my class in this and Tech Drawing throughout high school.

After a while, a couple of students began picking on me. I guess it was because I was a bit smaller, and it got to me a bit, so I went up to one of those kids, a big student for a thirteen-year-old.

His nickname was Bull. I asked him how he got so big. The answer he gave was that he used chest expanders. I asked if he had some old ones he wanted to sell. He did. After asking and receiving the money from Dad, I got my chest expanders, and started working with them, with more enthusiasm than I was giving to my schoolwork. It must have done something as no one ever picked on me again.

In sport, I gave up rugby and went to hockey, mainly because it was quite a bit faster. The first year was a year of learning the new game. I also took up archery and gymnastics. With a lot of practice, I made the school gymnastics team. Our coach entered the team in The Taranaki Gymnastic Championships. For a small country school, we did very well to take out the junior teams prize, and I got a third in the individual overall and a first in the horizontal bar.

Certificates from the championships

June 1960 saw me turn the ripe old age of fifteen. It also saw the start of the second year of high school, Form 4E. Academically, I did not achieve a whole lot. Technical Drawing and Science were still good but the rest I needed to catch up on.

Sport was a little different. I made the school team for .303 rifle target shooting. This was as part of the military training we did. If I remember rightly, training was once a month for an afternoon. I was in the Air Training Corps (ATC). I chose this because I liked aircraft and flying. Anyway, I represented the school in the provincial championships.

In hockey, I made the First Eleven, also the tournament team going to Levin for the annual national championships. In athletics, I won the pole vault, setting a new record. I guess I should have done well, as Dad coached me and he was a three times national champion back in the thirties.

I continued with archery but did not achieve too much. I also continued with gymnastics but despite more training found it harder, as I was getting a little taller and the routines were a whole lot more difficult. I guess I was losing my agility as well. Our coach did not enter the team in the championship that year, as he said we were not quite up to standard.

I did my pole vault training in the backyard at home. Dad knocked up some uprights, and we used bamboo for the crossbar. The pole we used first up was one of Dad's that he had used in the thirties, but this soon had to be replaced, as Dad thought it was getting unsafe. He knew a farmer, Mr Maxwell, out near Rahutu, who had a big clump of Chinese Bamboo, and my first pole came from there. We cleared part of Mum's garden of flowers and piled up some sawdust to cushion my landings. My run up was along the back lawn, then I placed my pole into a tapered wooden box and if I held on tight, up I would go. A few times my run-up was not fast enough, and instead of going up and over, I would go up and just come back down, landing on my bum on the wrong side of the crossbar. One time I came down on the wrong side of the crossbar and my heel hit the side of the box. Later this caused the bone to grow on my heel, so the doctor put it in plaster for six weeks. It was fun on crutches!

Our coach for gymnastics and hockey was Brian Hurle who was also our form teacher that year, a nice chap for a teacher, and we got on fairly well. We were talking one day, and he mentioned that he had to commute to New Plymouth each day. That night I talked to Mum about this, and she suggested I ask him if he would like to board with us. I mentioned this to him and he went to see Mum. Now we had a boarder in our home.

This was all good. I had to do more homework, but the other benefits were good. Brian had a degree in both Engineering and Science and flew as a navigator in Lancaster bombers for the Royal Canadian Air Force in WWII. I once asked him, why the Canadian Air Force? He replied that he tried the RNZAF and could not get in, so he went to Canada.

Brian came along on a couple of our holidays. One of these was to the Bay of Islands again, but this time it was much better as Brian towed his boat, which also doubled as his accommodation. It was a cabin cruiser powered by a very powerful V8 engine. He took the family out around the Bay of Islands, which meant that we could see much more than by just going on the tourist boats.

A couple of years later, when we all went for a tour of the South Island, Brian did not take the boat. He took the Morris Minor he used for most of his commuting. It was not a standard Morris Minor. It was fitted with an "Alta" cross flow head conversion, giving the little Morris twin carburettors, and a not very standard exhaust system. All of this made it go very well. On this trip, Mum and Dad invited Trish Reid along as company for Risè. Trish was the daughter of Bob Reid, who was Dad's Subaltern in the army and his best man at Mum and Dad's wedding. We all had a very good holiday.

In 1961, we entered the hockey team in a big hockey tournament. They played the tournament in two centres on the North Island and two on the South. From this tournament, they picked a team from each island to play off in the final.

> **50 YEARS AGO – 1961**
>
> Opunake High School boys hockey team was unbeaten at a Levin hockey tournament. The team was: A Corbett (captain), R McCandlish, G Phillips, J Carr, G Rowe, J Barraclough, B Martin, B Rowe, A Harding, W Dyatt, D Colson, G Boyd and R Heslop. A Corbett, R MCCandlish and G Phillips were selected to play for a tournament side against Horowhenua colts. G Phillips was selected to captain the North Island team to play the South Island.

A news clipping out of the local newspaper

To play in the tournament, we first had to get there. As it turned out, Brian Hurle had a 1938 Ford Pickup with a canopy on the back. Brian built seats down each side and this became the team transport vehicle. Dad had a good size trailer, and that carried all the team baggage. As for the tournament, we were all billeted out to families around Levin. I was billeted to a nice family in Otaki just south of Levin.

Our team comprised some very good players and some not so good smaller kids. With a bit of grit and determination we made it to the finals and had to play off against Hamilton Boy's High School. These were big hairy-legged boys, almost adults, but we beat them 1-0. To top it off, three of our players made it to the North Island team, to play against a representative Colt's team, and later the South Island. In addition, they selected Graham Phillips as the Captain of the North Island team.

Hockey Team
Yours truly is second from the left back row,
Graham Phillips is third from left

The Team Transport

Around 1960, I had a friend, Paul Coltart. He was a boy from across the street who I knocked around with a bit. He was a year older than I, but it didn't seem to make a lot of difference. In the school holidays, we decided we could go camping up on the mountain. We knew of a place on the Wiremu Road that was a good camping spot. The Wiremu road is a ring road that goes around the mountain on the western side.

If we went up the Eltham road for about 5 km then turned left onto the Kaweora Road and went another 10km, to the Wiremu road and turned left, it was about 1km down the road on the right. It was all uphill; I mean up the side of the mountain.

After getting permission from our parents, we loaded up the bicycles. Early on Saturday morning, away we went. We got to the spot mid-afternoon. It had been a long haul up the slope of the mountain.

We pitched the tent up on the fringe of the cleared area, so we were into the bush a fair bit. We found a rise in the ground and put the tent on that, as best we could. We fashioned a drain around the perimeter, in case it rained. You would never know up there. There is a saying about Mt Egmont (Taranaki), if you can see it, then it is going to rain, if you cannot see it, then it is already raining. We then set to finding firewood, got a good fire going, and fried up some dinner. Our parents had given us a lot of stuff, so we ate our fill. The night closed in very quickly. We thought it was smart to get into the sleeping bags. We heard some thunder in the distance. It was getting closer. We started counting the time between the lightning and the thunder. Every second is a mile, which was what we worked to. It began to rain, and everything was working fine. The lightning was getting loud, a real crack to it, then the thunder. We got down to not even one second between lightning and thunder, which meant that it was on top of us, and really going to town. The tent stayed standing, but the surrounding drain was not quite big enough. We had some drying out to do next morning. We had the bedding out of the tent and over some branches.

We were trying to get the fire going when my Dad arrived. "You guys OK?", he asked, "Of course" was the answer. "Good I'll have a cup of tea, with you, and then go home".

We dried the bedding in the sun during the day, and got things right for the coming night, which was uneventful so we had a good night's sleep. The next day it was a pack-up and head for home. We hardly had to pedal going home as it was downhill all the way.

I mowed the lawns for Grandad Pop. He had a good Masport drum type motor mower so it wasn't so bad. The hardest part was the front lawn. It had a big slope on it down to the front fence. If I took it easy, and it was dry, it was okay. If the grass was wet, the mower would just slide down the hill. I had to mow around the slope and not straight up and down. After I had finished the lawns, we would sit on the veranda and talk about my schooling, not a subject I enjoyed. One day we were talking, and he said that his initials HWB actually stood for Harry's Wicked Boy. He would tell me about the trotting horses he used to have, he called one Twice Worthy. His brother Manson also had trotters, down in Hawera, but that was a while ago.

Grandad Pop had a black Citroen car, one with the gear change on the dashboard. He asked me to drive him up the coast one day (this was after I had my licence), and I remember him saying to me, "It will go faster than that boy!" I was already doing the 60mph speed limit.

Granddad Pop was on his own after his wife Florence died in 1947. He had housekeepers to keep house and do the cooking, etc. The first one was a refugee. I think Grandad Pop assisted with her transportation from Poland. Her name was (hope I get the spelling right on these names) Edvida Moshos. She had a daughter, and her name was Yvonnegillia. I was about 16 when Edvida's husband managed get out of Poland and come to New Zealand, He stayed at Grandad Pop's place for a little while before the family decided to move down to Wellington.

Grandad Pop had to get another housekeeper. Her name was Mrs Ivy Duck. She worked for Pop for a long time. I can remember going around there once and she was really telling him off about something. However, they generally got on well. Later on, when I was about 18, I looked up the Moshos family in Wellington. They were doing very well and enjoying life, Yvonnegillia had turned into a beautiful girl, a little younger than I was. Maybe that's why I went around a few times. Edvida also gave me my first cup of Turkish coffee. I remember it was very sweet and only in a tiny cup. Another time I mentioned that I was going home for the weekend. Straight away Yvonnegillia asked if she could come, to see how much had changed. I looked at Edvida, and she nodded that it was okay. The next weekend, I went into town and picked her up, and away we went. It was a good weekend. I showed her all around Opunake and past Grandad Pop's place. She remembered it and Pop. (Pop had died in 1961).

I thought I needed extra pocket money, so I took on a paper round, delivering to half of the town. It was good discipline, getting up at 05.30

every morning, and doing the paper round before school. It was also good for the fitness having to do all this bike riding. My bike was a hand-me-down from my brother, but had three speed gears, and that helped against the headwinds.

One day towards the end of the year, Brian lent me a motor for the bike. It was a 25cc Italian make called *Mosquito*, and it fitted under the crank with a roller driving on the back wheel. I didn't know myself, roaring around town in the middle of the road, flinging papers left and right. One morning, I went to get the bike and found a flat tyre. Dad came to the rescue, and hooked up the trailer, and away we went. I knelt in the trailer with the papers, Dad drove down the middle of the street, looking in rear vision mirror for my signalled directions. The next morning, people were standing by their front gates waiting for the paper. I did not know what was happening, so I stopped and asked. Their answer was that everyone had slept in on the previous morning, because I was not on the bike. They were all using the bike with its little motor as their morning alarm.

I have few memories the early years of growing up with brother Hilton, except that he hit me on the head with a hammer when I was about 10 years old. (Maybe that explains many things.) Later on, though, we did a few things together. When I was about 15, I went fishing with him. He is a very good angler both in rivers and the sea, even to this day. I would be the carrier and just sat on the bank and watched him. Maybe that's why I don't enjoy fishing now; I think it's a waste of good time.

I remember Hilton and I going to fish for whitebait, using a net made of flywire cloth, around a metre in diameter. We rode our bikes to the Opunake Cemetery, hid the bikes behind a hedge, and walked through the cemetery and across the paddock behind. After half sliding down the riverbank, we were there. It was only a small stream, but few people went there. Consequently, we could get some good hauls. Many times we would have several buckets full. If the fishing was a bit slow, we went up the riverbank on the other side, to an old Maori Pa, (a village) named Te Namu. We walked around and found the tunnels that were all over the place. There was a spit of land jutting out to sea from the Pa and separated by a deep channel. This piece of land was called Te Mamu Iti. It was the place where the tribe went when attacked by another tribe, an ideal place to defend, as they erected high barricades of small diameter timber all around the perimeter of the flat land. All but a small area fell to the sea, with a steep cliff. It was interesting just to wander around and find some overgrown tunnels, most of which had collapsed.

We also went to get paua, (or abalone) as well as sea anemones, or sea eggs. The paua were in water, about knee deep, when there was a low tide on a full moon, and we pushed them off the rocks with a sharp blow with the heel of our hand.

If this failed, it was out with the knife. We shelled them by pushing our thumb into the thin end of the shell, and the paua would pop up, then we put the other thumb across the thick end of the shell. All the innards would stay in the shell, leaving us with the flesh only. Before going home, we ate the sea anemones on the shore by breaking open the shell and scooping out the flesh with our finger. The paua we took home to Lilly. Lilly Ratahi, a Maori girl, was our housekeeper, and she made the best paua and whitebait fritters you could ever eat. We would all have our fill with some in the fridge for later, and Lilly would take the rest home for her family.

Once a week, in the evening, I went out with my brother Hilton. We caught a lift from Ivan Fake, a chap who lived over the road from us, to a place called The Oaonui District Hall, about 10km north of Opunake. To get to Oaonui, you crossed the Namu River. There they had an indoor rifle target shooting range for .22 calibre rifles. The range was 25 yards, and they mounted the targets under the stage. This was good, and I enjoyed it. We shot for a maximum score of 100.10. To get 100 points you needed all 10 shots to be in the bullseye, but miss the inner bull. To get the extra .10 you needed 10 *centered* bullseyes; right in the inner bull, which was about a quarter of an inch in diameter. I shot in the mid-nineties. My highest ever score, I think, was 97.6. Hilton was a better shot than I, but then I was only a little kid.

We went rabbiting. I followed him, because he had the single shot .22 rifle, and I didn't even have a shanghai. Later on, he bought a Gevarm semi-automatic .22 calibre. That meant I could carry the old single shot. With the target shooting I was doing, he knew that I was a reasonable shot, so sometimes he would just point in the rabbit's direction, and the rest was up to me. The farmers gave us permission to shoot on their property, just to clear the rabbits out. We walked for miles some Saturday mornings and got as hungry as. Then we crossed a paddock that the farmer had sown with swedes or turnips as stock feed. We helped ourselves; just peeled them with the pocketknife, and into it.

One day, Hilton decided to build a boat. He wanted it flat bottomed, with a punt style bow on it. He aimed to use it for fishing around the rivers and lakes near home. He wanted the flat bottom so he could drag it over sand bars and things. The punt-type bow was there because it was easier to build.

When he finished it, he put it on the lake behind our home. It went well for a flat-bottomed boat. He only had one set of rowlocks so I couldn't row, which was good. The other good thing? There were no leaks.

After that first trial, Hilton decided it needed more speed, so he went about fitting it with an inboard motor. I think he got hold of a lawn mower motor from somewhere and in it went. He made a propeller for it out of some fat galvanised sheet he had and pop-riveted several of these together. I don't know how he put a pitch on it. (I was just a little kid and knew nothing).

Because I used to follow him everywhere in those days, I was down at the lake for the trial of the new prop. He pull-started the motor, and off he went, just putting around at idle. Now it was time for the real test. He opened the throttle. Unfortunately, the boat did not respond. He rowed ashore, and pulled it up on the sand, to find that the prop had folded up.

At dinner that night, Hilton told Dad what had happened. "Well, what are you going to do now?" Dad asked. Hilton replied that he would have to get a proper prop. Brian Hurle who was also at the dinner table, said that he thought he had a prop that should do the job, and he would get it at the weekend when he went home, and so he did. Hilton fitted the prop, and we were off down to the lake. Hilton allowed me to go along for the test run. It all went very well. The boat could get up a good speed, fast enough for what he wanted. He thanked Brian for the prop and asked how much he owed him. Brian replied, " Just give it back when you are finished with it."

Hilton & I in his boat

The lake behind our home was originally a natural hollowed depression that grew vegetables for the local constabulary back in the mid-1800s.

Around 1899, people first began to talk about filling it with water from the Waiaua River and piping it to a power station down on the southern end of Opunake Beach. Soldiers who had returned from the First World War deepened the depression. They used pick and shovels and wheelbarrows to do the job and make it the size it is today. They finished the job in about 1921.

Hilton and I trapped opossums in the bush. Some really stupid people before us (the pioneers) introduced opossums to New Zealand. In fact, every four-legged species in New Zealand was introduced at some stage. There were no native four-legged animals ever in New Zealand.

Anyway, back to Opossums. Because of the damage they did to the native bush, the government put a bounty on them. For a 'token', which was a strip of opossum skin, taken from down the back, nine inches long and two inches wide that included both ears, they paid a bounty of two shillings and sixpence. Therefore, for a couple of kids, this was good pocket money. I was only the helper, so I didn't get much, and Hilton said I didn't need much.

Later on, Hilton found that it was much more lucrative to get the complete skin of the opossum. The fur trade was paying big money for good skins. He screwed some clips onto the stock of the old single shot .22, and these clips held a hand torch. He fitted a more powerful globe to the torch and ran two wires to a battery he carried on his back. The torch was then zeroed in so that the sights of the rifle were set to the spot beam of the light, at a distance of about twenty feet, or the height of the foliage in the trees. It was just a matter of walking through the bush at night, with the rifle pointing up into the foliage; as soon as you saw the twin red eyes of the opossum, you pulled the trigger. This worked so well that we would get up to one hundred and thirty opossums before ten o'clock.

Then it was into the skinning of them. I watched Hilton do it a few times, then I had a go. The first one was a bit of a mess, but then I got better. I concerned myself with making a good job of it rather than how quickly I could go. We buried the skinless opossums and put the skins in a hessian bag until the following morning. Then we went home and crashed until morning. Next morning, it was a matter of tacking the skins tight onto a board, so they could dry. After tacking the skins out, we rubbed them with salt. This helped to dry them. There were some great colours amongst the skins. Some fur was blue, some red, and others every colour in between.

When I went to high school, Hilton went down to the South Island to do some tree planting, with a bit of shooting on the side. He showed me one day, when he came back for a break, the tusks of a wild boar. When they were put together, they formed a perfect circle of over six inches diameter, well, maybe not perfect, but damned close. He said the beast weighed just on four hundred pounds.

Hilton, in his time, did some track cutting on Mt Egmont (now Mt Taranaki). There are walking tracks all around the mountain, which are used a lot during the summer. He worked with a chap by the name of Brian Ogilvie, who was later to be his best man. They had all of the western side to do.

His job entailed clearing the tracks of all the last season's new growth, and repairing any washouts and general damage caused by the rain in winter. He later found a job with a guy named Peter Wisneski, as an apprentice carpenter, as Hilton was not into too much bookwork stuff. He let that side of it go, and concentrated on the practical. He was good at that.

Mt Taranaki, or as I knew her, Mt Egmont

Hilton saved and bought a house in Eltham, so that when he married the young girl he had just met, they would have a home to go too. Her name was Leonie Anglesey, and they married on 15th April 1967.

When we went down to visit Nana and Popa, Hilton and I would sometimes go down to the creek below the old dairy and try to catch some eels. The creek was very fast flowing and therefore all the eels were silver bellied, and very good eating, as different from the mud eels that were in small dams and tasted very muddy. The eels would also go to Lilly, because she did the best smoked eel you could find anywhere.

Hilton fished for Kahawai, down at the tailrace of the power station at the beach. The tailrace discharged the water from the power station on the extreme left-hand side of the beach, and we would walk out along the rocks for about 100 metres. The waves coming in would be big rounded hills of water traveling into the shore. Hilton used a medium weight spinner and cast out across the incoming waves. When the Kahawai were "running" (a term for when there is a hell of a lot of them), you could see them surfing in on the waves. On one particularly good morning, we had to carry 40 of them home. Well, not all the way home, as he would give a lot of them away before we got there.

Down below our home was the Waiaua River, a very stony river, as were most of the rivers around the mountain. It had a big horseshoe bend in it, and behind the river was a big area where the river flooded years ago. It was full of willow trees, and we used to muck around there after school. One day there were some other older kids down there who did not seem to know that this was our play place, so they tried to make us go away somewhere else. It became a bit of a stand-off as to who would prevail.

I was hiding behind a big tree and stuck my head around it, to see where the opposition was. Bang! My head was thrown back, and I fell to the ground. My face hurt like buggery. I put my hand up and, when I looked at it, found it covered in blood. Somebody yelled out that I had been shot, and they called a truce. I remember running for home with my hand covering my face.

For a long time I thought the bullet had fallen out while I was running. Mum was at home and patched me up. The iodine stung a bit. She asked what had happened. I told her. Dad arrived home about half an hour later, so the story was told again.

Dad wanted to know who had the slug gun. I told him it was Brendan Griffith. Dad was not happy. He got in the car and left. An hour later Dad arrived home having paid a visit to Brendan Griffith's father and given him a piece of his mind. He'd also taken the air rifle and delivered it to the local police officer, Jack Ward.

Some years later, I found out that the lead slug pellet had not fallen out. It is still in my face to this day. If it had been half an inch higher, I would have lost the sight in my left eye.

On 5th September 1960, while still a student, I attained my driver's license. Dad said he would teach me the basics, and my lessons started about a month before the actual day of the test. Our family car was a Vanguard Space-Master, made famous because it had a Ferguson tractor engine in it.

When the day came to do the tests, the local policeman, Jack Ward, said I had to do the written test first. If I failed that, there would be no driving. I must have passed OK, because he came back into the room and asked me where I had left the car. I said, "Out the front." Then he asked, "How did it get there?" "Mum put it there, and now she's doing some shopping" I replied. "Well, that's all right then. As long as you didn't park it there. Come on, get in and take me down to the beach."

This I did without incident, "Take us out onto the sand, John." I did as he requested. "Drive across the beach and get up to 30mph, then stop as fast as you can without skidding the wheels." I complied.

When we had come to a stop, he got out and inspected the tyre marks on the sand. He got back in, saying nothing, "Now drive up the hill." Again, I did as I was told. As we came to a pedestrian crossing, half way up the hill, Jack said with some urgency. "Stop, there is somebody coming onto the crossing!" I couldn't see anybody on the crossing, but I stopped any way. "Apply the handbrake and take it out of gear," was the next instruction. "Now let's go back to the office."

I drove back and parked where the car had been parked before. Mum was standing out the front, and as we went inside Jack said, "Good morning Mavis." Mum told me later that he winked at her as well. Once inside he wrote out the licence and gave it the official stamp. He turned to me and said "Well done John. You keep driving carefully and don't get silly. I don't want to have to clean you up one dark night down the road." "Thank you sir, I will remember." I replied.

Near the end of the 1960 school year, we were swimming down in the Waiaua River. The local council had installed rock cages to stop the river from eroding the banks when it flooded. They anchored these in place using old water tanks filled with rocks and concreted over the top. We found that it made a great diving platform. If we dived downstream, the water was nice and deep. All was good. Except one day when I was on the tank about to dive in, I was clowning and lost my balance. Instead of falling downstream, I went out and landed head first into a sandbank that only about two feet of water covering it.

I stood up, but my head flopped forward, so I put my hands around my head and lifted it up to the correct position and let it go. This time it tried to go back, but I grabbed it just in time. All this time I was spitting out sand, my mouth, eyes, and ears were full of it. I kept holding my head this time, as I staggered downstream to where Brian Hurle was swimming. He saw me coming and rushed to help. He said to keep holding my head while he picked me up in his arms and carried me home.

To get home he had to carry me about a kilometre, but also up a very steep riverbank, which was around twenty metres high. I remember, as he was carrying me through all the trees, the sun coming through looked white, and all the shadows were pitch black. Brian got me home and laid me on the bed. He stuffed rolled up towels around my head so I could not move it. Mum was home and immediately rang the doctor. Before he arrived, he had called the ambulance, and both arrived together. After his inspection, it was off to the hospital. His implicit instructions were not to exceed 30 mph (60kph) for the 40-mile trip to the New Plymouth Hospital.

The first thing they did at the hospital was to X-ray my neck and shoulders. They found three crushed cerebral vertebrae. All the gymnastics I had been doing, and the use of my chest expanders to strengthen my arms, shoulders and neck had saved me from paralysis and a wheelchair. I often think back to what might have happened if Brian had not been there. The doctor discharged me from hospital after less than a week, with no brace or support. As it was very close to school breakup, I did not go back, but stayed home and got my neck stronger.

After the neck incident, we changed our swimming place to the tailrace that fed the lake. A dam across the Waiaua River, diverted water along this tailrace to the Lake Opunake. The tailrace was good to swim in, as the current made it good for training.

For a long time, my neck never really gave me a problem, apart from my being limited in some things I could do, well I thought it limited me. I didn't do some things that I probably could have. However, in 1972, I started having some problems with it. I was in a lot of pain that would come and go. I went to our doctor in New Plymouth, and he referred me to a specialist.

The specialist happened to be the same guy who had seen me when I first had the accident. I had some X-rays, to see what had happened since then. He found the original ones, taken at the hospital twelve years before. The specialist said the neck had mended quite well. He also said that he was going to Auckland the next week to speak at a conference. He would now use my neck and how it had mended as his subject. I said, "That's very good, but what about me". He told me that three vertebrae in my neck had been badly crushed; the lower two had fused together, with fragments around them, and this left a large gap to the third and upper of the vertebrae, which had many fragments around it. He said that the only real, permanent solution was a spinal fusion.

It would have to be done in two operations, and each would have me on my back for six months. I told him that this was out of the question, as I was married with two small children. I could not afford to be off work for that long.

He told me that in that case I should have cortisone injections into the neck, and that should give me a few years of relief. "When can I get this done", I asked. "I can do it all now," was the response. I didn't hesitate. "So, let's go."

He got me to sit on the side of the bed, so that he could work from the other side. He then prepared for the injection. I noticed he had a needle, about three inches long. It was then I started to get worried. He walked around the bed and got behind me.

"There are a couple of things we have to do here." He said, " The first is that you have to be very, very still, and I have to make sure I get this in the correct place".

He wiped my skin with something that deadened it and then proceeded to thread the needle through my neck and into my spine, to the correct spot. He kept saying to me, "Hold still John. Hold still."

I could feel the needle touching the bone, withdrawing a little, then going deeper. The needle stopped for a moment, then started again, a little deeper, and stopped again. Then I could feel an increase in pressure in the area. I felt the needle retracting. The doctor said, "That's good I'm happy with that." "Thank God that's over!"

He replied, "Hang on a minute John, there's another one to go yet". After the next one, I was buggered from just holding myself so still for so long. The nurse came in with a cup of tea and a biscuit. I sat there and enjoyed both. The tea was good, the biscuit not so good, but I ate it anyway. The doctor had finished, and we sat down for a chat. He simply explained that the injection would not last for life, and that I would eventually have to have some more, or an operation. I thanked him, and that was that.

When we were on the farm, around about 1986, I had some more problems, but they were caused by me trying to protect my neck. Milking cows did not help a whole lot. It caused me to have terrible headaches. The doctor in Tatura referred me to a physiotherapist who practised pressure point therapy. She taught me how to relieve the headaches, and massage the neck muscles. So, I was back on track again, and had no further problems until about 2018.

I met a guy at high school by the name of Doug Allen. He lived out at a place called Pihama, about ten miles south of home. His parents owned a dairy farm, and Doug's elder brother worked the farm, as his Dad had retired. Doug's grandmother lived alone, opposite his parent's place, and there was a stream below her house. Doug and I went through her place and down to the little stream below to fish for eels. There was a real big one in this hole. A cliff over the water made it hard to get the bait to where he was. We never caught the big one but got plenty of smaller ones. These were the days when I would ride my bike out to his place and stay for the weekend.

Late in 1960, Mum & Dad moved out of town and onto a forty-acre dairy farm. Things were getting a little difficult for Dad to have so many chickens. At one stage there were about 360, inside the town area.

Moving also meant closing down *The Garden and Bookshop*, the business that Mum and Dad had started about six years before. In the shop they sold what the name said; all things to do with the garden, from plants and seedlings to fertilizers and insect sprays. I can't name them all. There were also books, magazines, newspapers, school stuff, pencils, pens, and, because Dad was a great reader of books, he set up the largest privately owned, lending library in the whole of Taranaki. Mum ran the shop and did her floral work. When things got a bit hectic, we would all buck in and help. Dad remained working at the telephone exchange, and the shift he was on would dictate when he could work at the shop. Mum had some casual workers giving her a hand. They found that opening the library in the afternoons suited all.

Now that Mum and Dad were milking some cows, the milk had to go to the factory on the north side of Opunake down by the Namu River. Dad told me that now I had my licence, I could take the milk down before I had to catch the school bus. Each morning I would put the trailer onto the car, pick the milk up from the milking shed and go off into town, and down to the factory. I would back the trailer up to the hardstand where a chap would come and roll the cans of milk off the trailer and tip the milk into the weighing vat. This all done, it was back home, drop the car and trailer off at the shed then get ready to catch the bus for school. Mum would clean the milk cans ready for the night milking.

I started in form 5E in 1961, and schoolwork was much the same, still a lot of work to do. Sport was another challenge altogether. Once again, I made the school teams, for .303 rifle target shooting. We represented the school in the provincial championships again.

I did all right. At the end of the 100 & 300-yard rounds I was in third place, and went in the 600-yard and last round with a bit of a good feeling. But I bombed out and came home with nothing. Later in the year I made it in the team of four going to the army base at Trentham, near Wellington, to shoot. It was quite an experience shooting at targets 1000 yards away. One would take one's shot then lean over to the telescope and watch the bullet travelling down the range to the target. It was interesting to watch the effect that the wind had on the bullet as it travelled, making it wave from left to right until it hit the target. The range had flags every 100 yards down its length, so when you were sighting the target you could compensate for the wind.

In hockey, I made the first eleven again (no tournament this year though). In athletics, I won the pole vault and set a new record. Gymnastics was disappointing, I tried, but my confidence was gone. I was subconsciously trying to protect my neck all the time.

I could no longer do somersaults during my floor routines. It was the same for the horizontal bar. I decided that if I couldn't do it properly, I wouldn't do it at all. Therefore, I took up swimming; I found that swimming helped my neck by building up the muscles in my neck and shoulders. At the school sports, I achieved a 1st and set a record in the 33.3yds, a 2nd for the 66.6yds and a 1st in the 100yds, taking 6 seconds off the record and setting a time that was to last quite a few years.

Our form teacher was Danny Hazlegrave, a wee Scotsman with a very strong accent. He had attained his engineering skills as a ship's engineer in the British Merchant Navy. Towards the end of the year, he took four students on a trip down to Wellington, to visit engineering companies and show us what the outside world of work was all about. For us country kids, it was a revelation, as they say. Out of it, after further correspondence with these companies, I was lucky enough to score an apprenticeship in Engineering Drafting, with a company named Freighter - Lowe Ltd. Another student, Ivan Reader, also got an apprenticeship in fitting and turning. A note on Ivan Reader; he was a runner and I remember in the last high school sports, at fifteen years of age, he ran the mile in four minutes five seconds. It was only a few years before that the four-minute barrier had been broken. So, for a student from the country, this was very good.

Form 5E Opunake High School 1961
Barry Simmons, back row left   Ivan Reader centre back row
The Barra second from right front row

Chapter 4 - Growing Up

I left school on 8th December 1961, aged 16 years and 5 months. I received the results for the School Certificate exam, which everybody sits when leaving school in the fifth form. I failed in English, and as they required a pass in this subject for the award of the School Certificate, I failed. My academic schooling had never been very good, all the way through. I guess I was never taught how to learn. That is something that everybody must know how to do, and if you do not know, you must be taught, or you will never achieve.

I started my apprenticeship on 5th March 1962. Ivan and I boarded in 54 Ava Street Petone near Lower Hutt. Mrs Dann was our landlady, and she ran a tight ship, as they say. After a year or so with Mrs Dann, we moved to a flat where we had to cook our own meals, etc. The owners of the property were Mr & Mrs Hulse, nice people.

Work was a challenge at the start and daunting. We both got nicknames, mine being "Moo", and Ivan's being "Fat". How this came about, I don't understand. After about 12 months on the job, our boss, Jim Howarth, a very nice guy, and very smart, called me in for a chat. He suggested that I change my apprenticeship from Engineering Drafting to Fitting and Turning. His reasoning was that I would gain better training on how things worked together and a better overall knowledge of engineering. Therefore, in July 1963, my apprenticeship changed accordingly. This did not stop me from being called into the drawing office to do the occasional bit of drawing.

Towards the end of 1964, I was once again called into the drawing office and asked to do some work. Jim had designed a four-post garage hoist, the first in New Zealand. His design drawing was a general assembly of the complete unit on one AO drawing sheet. He asked me to make detailed drawings of all the individual parts. This took me a month or so, and plenty of asking questions. I would take a fair bit of stuff home, so I could get things in the right projection. I made a few mistakes, but what an experience! I think Jim was reasonably pleased with the results.

After leaving home at the ripe old age of 16 years, I had to pay out four pounds a week for board, and I only earned five pounds eight shillings and sixpence as a basic wage. It made things a bit tight. However, in the first three months, I managed to have forty pounds in the bank. I am not sure I ever managed such a rate of saving ever again. It was time to go home for a long weekend. I booked a seat on the Wellington-New Plymouth Express.

Mum & Dad met me at the Hawera Station for the drive home. Mum and Dad now lived on the farm. They actually moved there when I was in my last year of high school. It was a forty-acre dairy farm, and they bred up a pedigree Jersey herd. It was good to be home. Brian Hurle was still boarding with Mum and Dad out on the farm. It was good to catch up with him as well. He told me that weekend that the next time I came up, he would have a car for me to drive back and forth to Petone. As you can imagine, it wasn't very long before I was home again, and true to his word, the car was parked in the driveway.

It was a 1938 Morris Eight. It ran very well, but Brian warned me it had a 1947 model crankshaft and pistons fitted to raise the compression ratio. This gave it a little more go. The downside, he said, was that after 10,000 miles the carbon buildup made the pistons hit the cylinder head. Therefore, the cylinder head had to be removed, and the combustion chamber decarbonised. Who cared? This was better than a bike. I returned the bike motor to Brian on the next trip home. Later on, I fitted twin carburettors and a free-flow manifold to the Morris, which lifted the top speed to 74 mph. Scary stuff!

When I was seventeen, on my annual leave, or as we called it back then Christmas Holidays, I was home with Mum and Dad on the farm. I thought I would go to see Doug Allan, one of my schoolmates. We first met when we started high school and went through school together. Doug was a year or two older than I, but that didn't seem to matter. I drove out to his parent's farm, out near Pihama. He said he was off to the inaugural Grand Prix up at Pukekohe. (This was the first time at the Pukekohe circuit. It used to be held at Ardmore, which was an airfield.) He had another guy going with him, but I can't remember who it was. He was leaving on Friday morning. David Young, another schoolmate, was also going. If I wanted to come, I could go with David as he wasn't leaving until after work, which was 4 o'clock on Friday. Doug and David were both doing apprenticeships as motor mechanics. When I got home, I rang Dave and jacked it up for Friday arvo.

Come Friday afternoon, and we were on our way. David had a Morris Mini at this stage, but, of course, he had removed the cylinder head and fitted oversize vales, along with a port and polish, and shaved the head a bit, to get a little more compression. On the outside of the engine, he had fitted twin inch and a quarter SU carburettors.

We were purring along. About an hour north of New Plymouth was a range of quite steep hills, the highest of these is known as Mt Messenger. We got to the start of these, and David said "Hang on!".

As the first corner approached, David put his foot a little further down on the accelerator. We flew around this corner and went straight into the next. This is when I saw the best driving I had ever seen. His right hand was firmly on the steering wheel, while his left hand danced around from the steering wheel to the gear lever and onto the handbrake. His right foot firmly planted on the *Go* pedal, and the left foot pumping up and down, he double-declutched his way through the gearbox. As he came up to a sweeping right-hand bend, he changed down a gear and pushed a little harder down on the throttle at the start of the corner. He gave a flick on the wheel, with his right hand, and, at the same time, yanked on the handbrake. This locked up the rear wheels. The back slid out to the left, which is what David wanted. The little mini was now pointing at the apparent middle point of the corner and that is the way it stayed, all the way through the corner, by him balancing the accelerator, the steering wheel, gear lever and handbrake. It was out of one corner and into the next, all the way to the top. The precision of his driving was unbelievable! I sat back, held on like buggery, and just enjoyed the experience.

We went up Mt Messenger faster, I think, than had ever been done before, or would ever be again. I congratulated Dave on his driving skills as we were sedately going down the other side.

We arrived up at Pukekohe, after dark and found Doug in the campground, opened a beer, and had a chat for a while before crashing into bed. I don't know where I slept, and I didn't care. I just slept very well. Next morning, we went downtown and had some breakfast, then dropped the car back at the camp and walked over to the track to watch the day's practice sessions. Bruce McLaren was the fastest of the day, and we were looking forward to the next day and some good racing. Bruce had retired during the race, and so did most of the other drivers. I think only about seven finished the race, which was won by John Surtees. Sad to say, a few years later an intoxicated driver killed David Young. When he was just 21 years old, on his way home from work, Dave's Jaguar was T-boned. He left behind a wife and young child.

Around that same time, I caught up with my second cousin (our Dads were cousins), Brent Purser. He lived at home with his parents in the Hutt Valley. He introduced me to some of his friends and we went to motor races, air shows, and stuff.

Once Brent asked me if I would like to go down to a place called Curious Cove, a holiday place in the Marlborough Sounds, at the top of the South Island, which catered for young people, I mean teenagers. They had all sorts of activities and things to do. I said, "When do we leave?"

Not long after, we were off. On a childhood holiday with Mum and Dad, I had crossed the Cook Strait on the overnight ferry to Christchurch. But this was my first "grown up" trip across the Cook Strait and into the Sounds. We had a good trip across and good weather. We were there for a long weekend, so went down on the Friday night, to Picton, then onto a launch that took us back up the Sounds, getting to the camp about ten o'clock. Next day we just mucked around and got to know a few people. There was a dance that night, with girls and things; some good music. I did not do any dancing. I had done none of that before, and I guess I was too shy to ask any of them for a dance anyway.

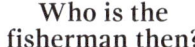

Who is the fisherman then?

The next day it was fishing. Some of us got onto a launch and went out into the Sound, almost out to the heads and Cook Strait. I don't know if it was luck or what, but I managed to get a good catch. We gave everything we caught to the Camp Kitchen, and we had good old fish and chips for dinner that night. Curious Cove was later turned into an Outward Bound School.

Brent and I went up to Levin a couple of times to the motor racing. Once we went up to an air show at the Ohakea Air Force Base, Colin Bamford and Jim Woods came as well. It was a good day. I had been to Ohakea before, when I was about 13. Mum and Dad had taken me and another young friend named Richard Marks, down to the 25th Anniversary of the RNZAF. It was a very good but long day, as we had driven down and back in the one day.

In those days, I was mad keen on aircraft and flying, and wanted to go into the air force when I finished school. Around the middle of 1965, Brent went over to Canada for 12 months to stay with a guy by the name of Brian Cardiff. Brent and Brian met when Brian was holidaying in NZ.

1965 came, I turned 20 years old, and 1965 went. I had given the Morris 8 back to Brian Hurle, and purchased a 1961 model Morris 1000 estate wagon. My very own woody wagon. (However, I did no surfing in it.) It was not long before I had built a twin carb manifold for it, fitted twin carburettors, and an extractor manifold. Now I could go home for long weekends with a radio and a heater. How good was that?

Ivan and I had moved away from Mr and Mrs Hulse, and their flat, to go into a house that Ivan had found after talking to some guys he knew. This was at 6 South Street, Petone. It wasn't a bad place. We had the whole house, which we shared with two other guys. This was good as it helped in reducing the rent. Ivan and I shared an enormous bedroom.

We had some good parties at Number 6 and the beer flowed very well. Somebody kept track of the consumption for a week. It totalled 32.5 gallons. There must have been some mid-week parties. We stayed in that flat until around mid-1966, when we moved into London Road, Koro Koro, on the hills to the west of the Hutt Valley. It was at the house opposite Number 6, that I lost my virginity to a girl who was boarding there, I remember thinking "Is that all there is?" Later on, she did the wrong thing and that was the end of that, but it's another story for another time.

Barra   Colin   Brent   Jim

I completed my apprentice on the 15th March 1966. Once again, I failed the academic side of it. I had no problem with the practical. I think, from that time on, I subconsciously began to remember more of the detail about things, and to think about how things really worked, and why they worked the way they worked.

I stayed on with Freighter-Lowe, and I was now working in the fabrication shop, where they built petrol tankers for bulk delivery and farm delivery. The farm delivery tankers had hydraulic driven pumping equipment, and it was a good job to get it all assembled in the confined space. But I still thought there must be something different for me out there somewhere.

While I was doing my apprenticeship, I went to the movies a few times and a film I saw six times in total was *West Side Story*. Why I went that many times, I don't know. I guess I must have liked it. I took my Mum on one occasion. She enjoyed it, asking me if that was the way it was in America. I knew she liked musicals as she had travelled down to Wellington a few years before to see *South Pacific*. I also took sister Risè to see it, but she was not that impressed. I remember a scene in it where a chap is sitting on a pipe fence that had no wire beneath, and fell off backwards, but hooked his legs around the pipe, and swung around until he could let go with his legs and land on his feet in a standing position. This was the exact move I had done back in 1959 when I had won the horizontal bar competition at the Taranaki Gymnastics Championships. I sat on the bar with my arms out, fingers together and hands open, and my legs straight; legs together, and toes pointed. I held the position for three seconds to prove balance and control, then fell backwards to swing around and drop to a standing position, arms still out. That was the finish of the routine.

Brent arrived back in NZ, and on 29th May 1966, which was a Thursday, called me to ask what I was doing the next day. I said I was going to work, as usual. He then asked, "Why not take the day off and come with me up to Palmerston North for the day?" He had promised to take two Aussie girls he met on the boat up north. I said, no, I couldn't do that, and that was that. After hanging up I thought about this offer and decided, "Why not?" So, I rang Brent back and said, "Pick me up".

The next day, 30th May, Brent and I went off into town in his light blue Volkswagen to pick up these two girls. We arrived at the place they were staying and parked. We weren't waiting long before a girl came out to the car and said good morning to Brent and myself, then, after chatting with Brent for a minute or so, went back into the flat.

She had shoulder length hair, very wavy and full-bodied. She was very good looking and filled out the jumper she had on very well. Brent said, "That is your blind date. She was just checking you out, before we go." I remember looking at those nicely shaped legs in her tight slacks and the tight little buttocks, and at that moment, I think I was smitten, as they say.

The girls came out. A tall blonde-haired girl named Shirley Manley lifted the front seat of Brent's VW so that Lynette Jean Watson could get in beside me in the back. Shirley jumped into the front seat. She and Brent were a thing already. They had met on the boat from Australia.

To cut a long story short, we went up to Palmerston North as Brent had promised, then it was back to Wellington in the late afternoon. We went for dinner, then took in a movie. The movie was *Goldfinger*. After the movie, we showed the girls the wonderful night-lights of Wellington, as viewed from Mt Victoria, and dropped the girl's home at 03.00 hrs. I saw a lot of Lynette after that first day.

Shirley   Brent   Lynette   Barra

On the 28th June 1966, my Mum and Dad celebrated their 25th Wedding anniversary. It was a good opportunity to celebrate my 21st birthday at the same time. Therefore, we booked the town hall, and about half the town enjoyed the party. Lynette and I went up home in the Woody and I had the pleasure of introducing her to my family.

Mum's and Dad's 25th

After the party, I had to show Lynette the sights of our little town, which meant that we got home a little late. I remember walking into the house as my Dad was leaving to milk the cows. We had a simple conversation like, "Morning Son." "Morning Dad." I went to bed, and he to the cows. It was a good weekend, and the family liked Lynette very much, a bit like me, I guess.

Lynette got a job with New Zealand Motor Distributors in Wellington and worked with a girl named Pat Goldstiver. Her husband, an Aussie electrician, had started his own business called NZ. Plant Maintenance. Through the girls talking, I found out that Dick was looking to employ another pair of hands. I went to see him one Friday after work and got myself a job. It was a good change of work.

A couple of months later, Dick asked if I knew anything about cable cars, I said no, to which his reply was "Well you had better get some knowledge on them". He had sold one to a chap in Oriental Bay. So out with the pencil and paper once again and I designed a cable car carriage, and the rail set up it required. Dick took the drawings to a Civil Engineer to get the footing and structure correct, and away we went. Dick sold another two of these around Wellington.

Back to the courtship of Lynette. We had a constraint. She was living in Wellington, and I was in Petone, about 15 miles away. I travelled into Wellington every day, to work for Dick, and she was also working, so it was not that practical to see each other every night. However, we made up for it by using the telephone. Some nights we would spend hours talking to each other. The subject matter would change all the time and include everything.

Friday nights after work, I would go to a sauna just around the corner from Dick's office, I would spend about an hour there, having a spa and soaking in the pool. After all of this, and a change of clothes, I went up to where Lynette was staying with Diane. We would go out for dinner sometimes, but mostly stayed at home and cooked. We would just lounge around and talk. Most of all we just enjoyed each other's company. I would not go home during the weekend. We would just lie in each other's arms, talking about anything, until we fell asleep. The courtship was going well; I was really starting to fall for Miss Lynette Watson.

Lynette and Shirley were flatting with Diane Stewart in Diane's parent's home while they were overseas, as Diane wanted some company. We all got on well and had some good times. Diane's boyfriend was a chap by the name of Tony Eagelton. He was a musician and had a group named *Tony and the Initials*. Tony was a lot of fun, always there with a joke, or something funny to say. The group played Thursday to Saturday at the Caltex Lounge. This venue was above a Caltex service station, hence the name. The group used to pack in the crowds, as they played all the modern songs of the time.

**Diane, Tony, Brent, Lynette (later to be Mrs Purser).
The Barra, Lynette.**

On one occasion, we all went out for dinner to a place called *The Pines*. It was a good night; a band played light type dinner music. Tony met a friend of his there by the name of Garth Young. They had a good chat. As the group playing was leaving the stage for a break, Tony went up and talked to them for a minute, and I took it from the body language, that they all knew each other. Anyway, the band left, and Tony went over to Garth and whispered in his ear. Next thing, Garth was on the piano and Tony on drums. We were entertained for the next hour by these two guys, and they were good, really great. It all turned into an evening of memories, and meeting people, and laughter, and joking. Somehow, and I can't remember how, our group was saying goodbye and good night to all these people as we were leaving via the kitchen, and it was 2 o'clock in the morning.

Brent and I took the girls on a trip to show them Taupo and Rotorua. Just north of Taupo, at a place called Wairakei, there is a very large geothermal steam project. In those days it supplied one sixth of New Zealand's power. At Wairakei, there was a place called the *Honeymoon Pool*, it was a thermal bath, set in the natural bush, with the water coming down a little stream at just the right temperature. It was very private, just the thing for honeymooning couples. That didn't include us, but we had a swim, anyway.

A place of note at Rotorua was the Rotorua Town Baths. We did not tell the girls before, but they found out soon enough, that the baths were divided into Men's & Women's. The reason for this? The bathing was nude only. The girls never forgave us for this bit of fun. We went back to Wellington via Mum's and Dad's, then back to the grind.

Lynette & I doing the dishes

Things were going very well between Lyn and I, so well if fact, that, at the end of August 1966, I went into Wellington one Friday night after work, and met Lyn by the railway station. That was a central place for us to meet, and I could get parking. In New Zealand at that time, there was late night trading on Friday. This left the weekends free. It was a good setup. Back to the Friday night, the little girl and I were on a mission. We were on our way to buy a diamond ring for her to wear on her left hand. Yes, Lyn and I became engaged after knowing each other 3 months.

On the 10 November 1966 Miss Lynette Watson had a special birthday. She had reached the age of 21. This was special, so Brent and Shirley, Lyn and myself went out for dinner, to the *La Scala*. It was a good night and a good meal, the wine wasn't too bad either. To this day, I suspect that Miss Watson had a little too much to drink. I looked over to Brent, and gave a signal, and he agreed. However, all was good, and we all had a great night. I enjoyed the feeling of this girl leaning on me for support and giggling at nothing in particular. At the end of the dinner, I paid the bill, and we went out to find the car. The cold air hit us like a hammer, and instantly this little girl on my arm stiffened and was cold sober once again. Bugger!

Chapter 5 - The Married Thing

We set the wedding day for February 4th 1967. In late December, Lyn left to go back to Australia to prepare for the big day. She went back on the *Achille Lauro*, the same ship she had arrived on. Therefore, from the 29th December, we were apart. I remember a grey-headed Maori chap started singing *Now Is the Hour* as the ship was leaving the dock. He sang in Maori, and his voice was better than anything I had ever heard. The crowds became silent to listen. It was one of the most memorable and moving things of my life so far. It even brought a tear, though that might have been the sight of my loved one going away.

I flew to Australia in early January. I had saved enough for the flight and a bit of pocket money. I remember the flight cost fifty-two quid. The big day was 4th February, 1967. My Mum and Dad and Risè came over from New Zealand as well. Risè was to be a bridesmaid, along with Shirley. My best man was Peter Burr. I had hoped that an old friend, Doug Allen, could help me out, as I had done the same for him a year earlier, but he couldn't come from New Zealand. My groomsman was Jerry Clark, Lynette's long-time friend. As it turned out, Doug and his wife Judy made it across at the last minute. The wedding was great.

The Big Day

It was a day only Melbourne could dish up. 104 degrees in the old scale, around 40 C. I remember walking into the church, not knowing anybody, with a best man who didn't know anybody, and a groomsman who came from out of town. We were literally walking into a big room full of strangers. I stood there with rivers of water running down my back. I was wet through. Everything was made worse because the driver of Lyn's car said she should be twenty minutes late. It was just as well I did not know this until much later. When my bride-to-be came up beside me, I relaxed a lot and was just happy to have her by my side. Not good words for a bloke to be using, but that is the way it was.

Our vows taken, we were man and wife. We then had to meet all the relatives. I felt very alone amongst many strangers, apart from the hand I held in mine and my Mum and Dad in the distance. They were feeling the same. I will always be grateful to Lyn's Uncle Ian, who approached and befriended them, and made them feel welcome, as I will always be grateful for the woman beside me.

We finally left the reception and headed off in the little mini we had hired. As we were leaving the reception, somebody pushed his or her arm in the back window of the Mini. In its hand was a box of confetti, which they emptied, all around the inside of the car. We had booked our first few nights at a Beaumaris motel. On our way to Beaumaris, I pulled in at a wayside stop and bought a couple of drinks. I walked in and the lady serving said to me, "I know where you have been." I asked, "How do you know?" "By all the confetti falling off you." She replied.

We got to our motel and fell in a heap. We drank a couple of gallons of water. It had been so hot, and we could not shed any clothing. That evening, we went for dinner at the restaurant and ordered a bottle of champagne. At the end of our meal, we still had half a bottle of bubbly left, which we took up to our room. We spent the rest of the night sitting up in bed, sipping on bubbly and reminiscing on the day that had been.

We had arranged for a group of us, including Doug and Judy, Chris and Neil Ormsby, and Peter Burr & Shirley Manley, to meet the next morning down at the beach for a swim.

Our honeymoon was a train trip up to Albury and Howlong, staying a few days with Jerry and Jan, then onto Sydney to catch the *Achille Lauro* back to NZ.

Lyn, Judy, Peter, Chris, Shirley, Neil, Doug.

(Note: On 30th November 1994, the Achille Lauro caught fire after an engine explosion and finally sank off the coast of Somalia.)

We got back into the old routine without too much delay. Back to the same jobs, but now we could live together, so we minded a house in Poto Road, Normandale, up on the western hills above the Hutt Valley, while the owners were overseas for a six-month holiday. Brent and Lynette came around and relaxed with us, or had dinner or something. Shirley didn't come back to NZ after our wedding. Brent got back together with his old girlfriend from school, Lynette Johnson. I don't think Brent really ever got on with Shirley, as she was quite moody.

It was a year of weddings. My brother Hilton and Leone Anglesey married on the 15th April 1967, in Eltham, and settled down there in a house that Hilton had bought before the wedding. My sister Risè and Philip Cross married on the 19th August 1967. Yes, that means that Mum and Dad got rid of all their kids in one year.

When we left Poto Road, we decided to go up to New Plymouth to live. We rented a house on Vivian Street, close to the city centre. I got a job with Cambrian Engineering, working in the tool room and doing some drafting work. Cambrian was a production-engineering firm that employed around fifty people and manufactured a diverse range of products. They had thirty plus Capstan and Turret lathes, and about six automatic lathes in the machine shop. The fitting shop was just that, and they did all the assembly work in there. The tool room had two cylindrical grinders, two tool and cutter grinders, along with a near-new Dean, Smith & Grace centre lathe. They had an electroplating shop and a foundry, casting in both ferrous and non-ferrous metal using the latest induction furnace. I found it a great place to work, as there was a wide variety of work to be done. I enjoyed the production side and the planning that went into some work to have all parts arriving for assembly at the same time.

Brent asked me if I would be best man for him, as he and Lynette would do the right thing and get married. Their wedding was on the 3rd February 1968, one day short of a year after Lyn and I. Brent had two of his schoolmates as groomsmen, Jim Woods and Ross Baker, good guys, and we all got on well.

In late February 1968, we decided that we should go and work in Australia to save some money, then come back and buy a home. We arrived in Melbourne and stayed with some of Lyn's good friends, Kris and Neil Ormsby, who were living out at Waverly. We went out and bought a car from Bob Jane. I knew of this person from his motor racing, however, that did not make any difference in our decision to buy a car from their yard. It was a 1960 XK Falcon. I thought at the time that this thing was not standard as it had twin exhaust pipes and a very different sound from the engine. We drove it back to Kris and Neil's and the thing had used three quarters of a tank of fuel. On investigating beneath the car I found a fuel leak. I rang Bob Jane's yard, told them about the problem. I said that I would come in the next day to get it fixed, which I did, and they did, and we were all happy.

We rented a flat in South Oakleigh. I got a job with Cyclone KM Products as a fitter and turner. It was quite close to where we lived and was convenient.

In January 1969, I changed jobs to work with Silcraft Industries, as a toolmaker, and Lyn got a good job with Colourtex Fabrics as an assistant to one of the managers. All went well. Doug and Judy came over to Australia and paid us a visit. They told us that they were going up to Benalla to work for a while. They would do the same thing as we were doing.

While working at Silcraft Industries, I woke one morning to find my hands were all red, and as itchy as. My mouth felt as if I had burnt it on coffee that was too hot. I needed to see a doctor. We had not been to see a doctor at this stage of the trip. I remember Dad saying before we left NZ that our family doctor in Opunake when I was a kid, Dr Phillip Cassin, was now practicing somewhere in Melbourne. I got the phone book and starting looking, and sure enough there he was, not far from Silcraft. I got Lyn to ring and make an appointment for me. She could get to a phone and I could not. At work that day, I found that if I put my hands in very hot water it was actually some relief.

The next day, I saw Dr Cassin. He remembered me from Opunake and, of course, asked after Mum and Dad. He then asked what my problem was. I explained it all to him. He thought about it for a moment, then said, "This is a strange coincidence, but I have just finished reading about your condition in a medical journal. You have the classic symptoms of hand, foot and mouth disease". For a minute there, I thought I had grown another two legs. He went on to say, "There is nothing you can take for it. Take a Disprin now and again when it gets bad, and it will go away in about 10 days". I thanked him, but I am not sure for what. He was correct, and a week later it had all gone, never to return.

The news came that the little girl was pregnant. So, back to New Plymouth we went, arriving in December 1969. We rented a flat on Carrington Street. I had put the old faithful Falcon on a ship and transported it to Auckland. This meant another trip up to Auckland to pick it up. However, because it was not registered in NZ, I had to go through the whole process of a *Warrant of Fitness*, something every vehicle owner has to do in NZ every 6 months. Anyhow, I got all of this done, and then started on the trip home to New Plymouth.

Chapter 6 - Finding our feet

Marc Jason Barraclough

On the 12th January 1970, Marc Jason Barraclough was born. This was when the big learning curve started. Now, Lyn's job was to find us a house to buy, as we had saved enough in Australia. She found a brand-new display home that had just come on to the market. Therefore, on taking out a second mortgage, we owned ourselves a brand-new home.

I got a job back with Cambrian Engineering, doing what I had before we left for Australia, plus any projects that would come up. The Managing Director of Cambrian Engineering was Tony Smales, a gentleman of the old school.

One of the special projects that came up was chrome plating aluminium. They were manufacturing a part in aluminium and thought it would look better chromed. I was now working full time in the electroplating department and after some time I achieved the results I was after. It took a while, with a lot of experimentation, but I got there. Another project was to do the tooling for the first pressure sprayer. We had the 4 litre plastic bottles made outside, but made the pump and spray wand in-house, as well as doing the screen-printing of the bottles.

The sales manager had the idea that we could manufacture the steels that butchers use for sharpening their knives. I had to set up one of the older capstan lathes, to profile turn the 375mm long and 18mm diameter bar.

I then machined up and hardened three knurls, and set them up onto a three-jaw chuck on another lathe, and attached them to air rams. This made them slide into contact with the steel, now held in the capstan. It moved back and forth, powered with an oil controlled air ram.

As the steel moved in the knurls would retract and index for the next cut. I found that the knurls could not make an impression on the tough steel, and I had to modify them by making a cutting edge, cutting the steel rather that rolling the knurl along it. This all worked well. The steel was then surface hardened in a salt bath and finished by a flash of hard chroming giving a satin finish. A moulded plastic handle, with the Cambrian name on it, was screwed on and the job was done. I still have one of the first ones off the assembly line and use it all the time.

There were many little, but very interesting, jobs that came my way while I was working there and I enjoyed it very much. One chap who worked there was an apprentice by the name of Brian Smith. I was to become a bit of a mentor for him. When I finally left Cambrian, Brian was in the last six months of his apprenticeship, and had already passed his advanced Trade Certificate. By the time he finished his trade he would also attain his NZCE. (New Zealand Certificate of Engineering). This gave him only another two years for a Degree in Engineering, that he hoped to complete in one year. I often wonder what his future held.

Another chap who worked there was a setter on the automatics. I can't remember his name, but he had a commercial pilot's licence and every winter he would go across to Australia and fly charter aircraft throughout the Aussie outback.

In 1971, my dad decided that he would shout himself a 60th birthday present and qualify for his private pilot's licence. There were a few chaps from around town, who had the same idea, one of whom was a local farmer who lived up the Ihia Road. They used one of his paddocks as a landing strip, and organised for an instructor to fly down from New Plymouth and put them all through their paces. Dad was very proud of the fact that he had achieved his goal, but only ever flew again one more time.

The house demanded a lot of time on the weekends and whenever there was a spare moment. I had to build a double garage, and on the side of that, a patio area. It was a raised block of land, with about 3 feet from road to lawn, so all around had to have something to retain the bank, being a corner block just meant more retaining wall.

The little girl found that she was pregnant again. On 12th March 1971, Tracy Lee Barraclough was born.

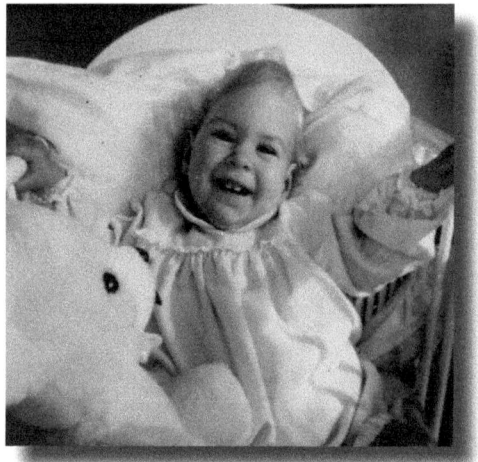

Tracy Lee

We thought something was wrong when, as soon as she was born, they took her away and Lyn could not see her. The gynaecologist came to me and asked if I could have a chat with him, in his office. He told me that Tracy had Spina Bifida. He explained all the ramifications that went with this problem. He explained that her spinal cord, instead of being a cord inside the vertebrae, was lying flat outside the vertebrae, this would mean that she would never walk. The way he was talking, it seemed that in a roundabout way he was actually asking me what they should do about the problem. I asked him if Tracy was still alive, and he said that she was. I then said to him, "Then that is the way she must stay." He said "Thank you".

The surgeon who operated on her back did a tremendous job. His name was Dr Ian Hanson, and we were always very grateful for his work. They later transferred Tracy Lee down to Wellington to have a shunt fitted into her head by drilling a hole through her skull. This was to drain off the excess fluid down into the stomach, as it would not drain naturally because of the spinal damage. It would normally be a self-draining unit they fitted, but in case of blockages, we could operate it as a pump. The problem is known as hydrocephalus.

Lyn went down to Wellington with Tracy. It was a tough call for her on her own, so I went down as well. I cannot recall where I stayed, but Lyn needed a shoulder while we were waiting at the hospital. While we were both in Wellington, Paul, and Margret Wadesworth, who lived quite close in New Plymouth, looked after Marc. They had a young boy named Craig, and he and Marc played together quite a bit. Paul was a member of Round Table.

I joined The New Plymouth Club of *Round Table New Zealand*. It was a service club founded in England, I don't know when. We had some good times doing service work around town, and plenty of social events as well. One of the big projects was carried out by a small group of five guys. They gave us the task, with all the backing we would require, of setting up and running New Zealand's inaugural Billy Cart Derby. It was later to become an annual event and was taken up by other clubs around the country. New Plymouth had the perfect venue for it, having the main street on a big hill. Therefore, it was a matter of getting Council approval and assistance for closing the main street on a Saturday morning.

I was given the task of cart design. Sounds big, but I cheated, and with a bit of research found that the Americans had a Billy Cart Derby, and it was a really big thing, so the specifications where already there. I corresponded with the Americans and they sent over all the specs and wished us the best of luck. The day was a great success. The storekeepers actually did better trading with the street closed to traffic, and it turned into nearly a full day event. There were donated prizes for place getters, and the club member's wives ran raffles.

We flew over to Australia every year for Lyn to catch up with her parents. Her dad was not keeping the best of health. One Boxing Day, we flew over and got onto a plane that been put on especially to bring Kiwis home for Christmas, so going back there were only six passengers, and four of them were our clan. One hostess kept Marc amused, and another looked after Tracy. Lyn and I had a great trip.

In the latter half of 1972, Lyn's Dad took a turn for the worse and was in hospital. We decided then that we would pack up and head to Australia to live. It also happened that Lyn was pregnant again, so if we were going to go, it would have to be sooner rather than later. On 28th of October 1972, we arrived in Melbourne and headed down to the farm at Birregurra. Lyn's Mum and Dad had sold the dairy farm at Timboon and now had a small cattle property there.

We started looking around to find a home to buy. In the meantime I walked across to a sawmill next door to the farm to see if there was any work. At the mill they asked what I did, I said I was a fitter & turner. They asked if I had ever sharpened a saw blade. I said no. They told me to have a go at one that was clamped up ready for sharpening, they would test it the next morning. If it was any good, I had a job. The next morning, I had a job, and was now a "Saw Doctor".

We went out and bought a car so we would have transport around the place. It was a Ford Cortina TC. It was average but did the job.

Later on, we were on our way back to Geelong when, after an almighty bang, we had no forward motion. The motor was still going and the wheels still turned, so the only thing in between was the gearbox. It was still under warranty, but they tried to tell me I had selected first gear while I was doing 100kph. I informed them I had been driving since I was fifteen, and I was not silly enough to do that. They replaced the gearbox, and we were mobile again.

Now it was house-hunting time, and after a fair bit of searching we looked at a house that was not even on the market. We liked what we saw and bought it. The address was 24 Elliott Ave, Highton, which is a suburb of Geelong. I needed another job, as it was too far to go to Birregurra every day. I found a job as a tool sharpener in the tool room of the Ford Motor Company. This was an afternoon shift job, so I started at 3 o'clock in the afternoon and finished at 11 o'clock at night.

After a month or so, I got another job as well. This was doing much the same thing, with a bit of machine work and some welding. I started at 08.30 in the morning and worked until 14.00. This gave me 6 hours. I then had my lunch, went across the road and started at Ford. I did this for 6 months or more and did not mind it too much. The money was good.

Ford had a program whereby employees could buy ex-Ford executive cars when they became available. One day, I noticed a car advertised on the notice board. It was a 1972 XA Falcon wagon, with all the mod cons; V8 powered with mag wheels, the price was $3,200. Like, who would not buy that? Therefore, I put in for it and as it turned out we got it. I sold the Ford Cortina I had purchased when we arrived in Australia, so now we had a car big enough for the family.

On 8th March 1973, I had to rush Lyn to the maternity hospital in Geelong, as the time had come. I was sitting out in the corridor when a nurse rushed out of the delivery room and grabbed another bassinet. I asked if all was good and she held up her hand in a V-for-victory sign, at least that is what I thought. She said, "No, there are two!" My reply was "There'd better not be!" Unbeknown to me, Lyn overheard this and was a bit upset, actually more than a bit. Lyn had been under three doctors, in two countries, and not one had picked that she was having twins.

Enter Geoffrey Wakefield Barraclough, and Anthony Wakefield Barraclough, identical twins. All sorts of things were running through my mind, but I thought, "No. One day at a time."

For a while, Lyn managed very well, looking after three children in nappies and all under two years old. Actually, the kids were good, and all got on well. Tracy was progressing with her problem. She always had a smile on her face.

They inducted me into the Apex club of Barwon-Geelong on the 7th March 1973. Actually it was more of a transfer, as Apex and Round Table where affiliated. They were a good bunch of guys, and they did some valuable charity work. Dinner parties were good for Lyn to attend and got her out of the house. I was heading the list for "Father of the Year", simply by having the twins. However, it was not to be, as a guy called Bill Jackman, was presented with triplets, so he got the honour.

Around May 1973, brother Hilton took his only ever plane ride, and his only ever time out of New Zealand, when he and Leone came to Australia to go over to Perth to visit Leone's brother or sister. On the way home, they stopped off at Melbourne to pay us a visit. I think I picked them up from the airport. They stayed a couple of days with us. Somehow, we all fitted into the house.

One afternoon Hilton said "Let's go to the pub and have a drink." We went to the Waurn Ponds Hotel, just south of Geelong on the Princes Highway. We were having a quiet drink and were playing a bit of pool, when this very loud, half-drunk guy came up to us talking a bit of rubbish, but very loudly. He said to Hilton, "Do you want to play me in a game?" Before Hilton could answer, the guy slapped a $20.00 note on the side of the table. My brother is never slow when money is around, so put his hand into his pocket, and pulled out a twenty saying, "Well I won't be needing this after tomorrow", (they were heading home the next day). He placed the twenty on top of the other one. Then this bloke, (no, that's an insult to Blokes, I'll call him a Turkey) said to Hilton "You can break, mate". Hilton said, "Okay" and set the table up. I thought to myself, "This'll be good."

Hilton broke the balls and having got one in off the break, he proceeded to clear the table. The Turkey stood there with his mouth open. After Hilton had potted the black ball, he moved around the table and quickly put his hand down to cover the notes, and then said to the Turkey, "Want another game, double or nothing?" The Turkey closed his mouth and left. Hilton said to me, "I don't like loud mouths".

In July 1973, Lyn and I had talked about this problem of having kids. It seemed we only had to shake hands with each other, and it turned into another pregnancy. Therefore, it was off to the man who did the snip, snip thing, and it turned me into half a Bloke.

On 11 July 1973, I received a phone call from my brother Hilton to tell me that our Dad had passed away from a heart attack. I was shattered. This was not supposed to happen. He had not even seen his new grandsons. I jumped on a plane and went home as quickly as I could. It was a sad time. Dad was a very well known in the community of Opunake. He had worked on the Opunake Telephone exchange for 14 years, and had come into contact with many people. His sporting achievements in the late thirties, his work as the President of the Opunake Athletic Club for several years and in training youngsters meant he was very well known. He was president of the Opunake Hospital Board and a member of the New Plymouth Hospital Board. He was also a member of the Opunake Power Board and of the Opunake County Council. During WWII Dad was a Captain in the New Zealand Army serving in the ASC. He served in New Caledonia. I remember him saying one day that his best investment had been in buying a mini tanker trailer that could hold, I think, 150 gallons. It was refrigerated. He hired it out around the countryside for when people were having a party.

Mum and Dad had sold the farm and bought the Oeo Hotel eighteen months earlier. He had really enjoyed his life as a publican. After the funeral service, we were all having a drink at Mum and Dads' pub. A

Maori elder came up to me while we were having a drink and introduced himself. His name was Joseph Pu. I realized that I had gone through High School with his son Joe Pu. Joseph asked if he could say a few words to the gathering. I said "Of course, but the place is packed, and there is a fair bit of noise."

Joseph started with the words, "Excuse me, " The whole pub fell into immediate silence. He started by stating that I had given him the permission to say some words about his old friend Fred Barraclough. He then went on to talk about the lives the two of them had as youngsters, and growing up with school, and sports, and of his latter life. At the end of his talk, I was all choked up. I was so proud of my old man.

Frederick Stroud Barraclough now lies in the Lizzie Bell Memorial Cemetery on the Puketapu Road, Pihama, just south of Opunake.

(A note – exactly thirty years later, to the day, in another country, a Great Grandson would be born, Brendan Stroud Barraclough.)

One day in early 1974, I met a guy who told me that there was a vacancy with NSK Manufacturing. I went and had a chat with them and got a job running the tool room. All was good. NSK Bearings of Japan owned the Company. They manufactured single row deep groove ball bearings in a small factory in Geelong. The Company had a Japanese Manager, Jim Najima, a very nice chap. There were also two Japanese technicians, one of whom was Tatsuo Tazo, or Ted for short. I can't remember the other one. There was also an Australian administration guy there by the name of Graham West.

Ted and I got on fairly well, and our families got on well. Ted's wife's name was Noriko, and she was an exceptional cook. Typical of Japanese women, Noriko always walked two paces behind Ted. It was a huge surprise when one day we were sitting around and Noriko asked Ted for the keys to the car.

Ted and me

He looked at her with shock, and asked why? She replied that she and Lyn were going for a drive. Ted was so dumbfounded that he just handed over the keys. Noriko and Lyn went and got in the car. Noriko backed out of the garage and off they went. I went over to Ted, helped him pick his jaw up off the ground, and told him, that Noriko had been taking lessons, and passed her licence test a week ago.

She never walked behind Ted again, saying to him, "Look at Lyn and John, they walk side by side. They even hold hands." Ted just shrugged. He knew he was beaten and that his life would never be the same again.

At one stage, we were having problems with one of the large centreless grinding machines. I removed the bearing housings and scraped and re-adjusted the bearings, then reassembled it all. My report stated that it would not last very long. A completely new spindle housing was air freighted out from Japan. It was complete, and must have weighed nearly 1.25 tonnes. They also flew over a technician from the manufacturer's assembly line. For the next ten days I worked with this chap. He could not speak English. I could not speak Japanese. Yet we both communicated with a common engineering language, and it all worked very well. He showed me how to scrape a flat surface, with the tools he had brought with him.

They were a set of scrapers of different shapes but all with long handles. Each blade and handle was about 300 mm long, with the handle being ornately carved. They almost looked too good to touch. At the end of the job, with Ted translating, he thanked me very much, for my assistance and presented me with a bottle of Japanese Sun Tory Whisky. This is a very nice whisky and I enjoyed every drop.

I went back to school again in April 1974. I was hoping to complete a supervision certificate that would help me get up into basic management. This meant studying at night at the Gordon Institute of Technology in Geelong; two hours a night, two nights a week, for two years. It was a very worthwhile and interesting course.

The family took a holiday over to Adelaide. I think it was a month or so before Christmas of 1974, when the twins were about 18 months old. We piled up the Ford, hooked up the Sun Wagon caravan we had just bought, or borrowed, and away we went. Tracy stayed behind and had her own holiday staying at a special care facility that was part of the hospital. We had a great holiday, but it was cut short as Geoffrey got a boil on his bum and was not happy. On the way home, I pushed it a bit and the big Ford returned 14 miles per gallon.

Two weeks later, I sold it to a car yard for $4000.00, then went around the corner and bought a brand-new Mazda 929 wagon, for $3700.00. A good deal and we had some money in the bank. At this stage, Lyn didn't have her driver's licence. She said the Ford was like a big boat. Now, with the Mazda, there was no stopping her. I did not mind too much. Since the twins had arrived, I had done all the grocery shopping, only buying what was on the list, which was the rule. Now she could do it herself. However, after a couple of times, I got the job back, as it was too stressful for her.

A neighbour who lived over the back of us, Robert Ubergang, together with another chap, had a small business on the side blowing and cutting floral foam. It is called Oasis and because it absorbs water, florists use for flower arranging. I "blew" the foam in one-metre square blocks in a mold lined with paper. After they were cool, I cut them up into a house brick size, pack them into boxes and sent them to a wholesale florist. I did this work after I knocked off at NSK. I went over to the factory and got into it. At around ten o'clock, I headed for home, some dinner and a shower. I did this in the evenings when I wasn't going to night school. I would never make a fortune at it but it was a bit more income.

I used the car to go to work each day, but this meant that Lyn could not go out. I bought a motorbike, a 125cc twin cylinder Suzuki. The tacho was red lined at 17,500 rpm, and I used to enjoy taking it there. It sounded fantastic.

One day I was on my way home from work, in a light rain, being a good boy and obeying all the rules. As I came up over a rise, there was a stop sign at the road on my left. The car that was stopped at the sign moved off in front of me. I had nowhere to go but into him. I left the bike in his rear mudguard and did a bit of gymnastics over his boot, landing on the road, and tumbling along it for some distance. I stood up and turned to face the car I had hit, and saw that the car that had been following me before the collision was now coming straight at me. My reaction was to jump, as the car swerved to avoid me. I went up and over his front left-hand mudguard.

I went back and fronted the guy who had pulled out in front of me. He was an old bloke. I don't think he should have been driving or really knew what he had done.

The bike cost me a new set of front forks. After that, I changed the way I went home.

Chapter 7 - Time for Adventure

At Christmas 1975, we went to Philip Island for a holiday. We stayed in a caravan, but I can't recall pulling one with the Mazda. Tracy stayed behind again in the special care facility. The Tazos came to visit as they were close by on their holiday. During our stay, Lyn was reading a Woman's Weekly magazine and found an article on a town in the Northern Territory. There was a photo of a beach, and the article called this place "paradise". It was the town of Nhulunbuy in Arnhem Land. Nhulunbuy was a mining town. The mining company was Nabalco; they mined bauxite. They had a one-million-ton-per-year alumina processing plant. Lyn said to me, "Let's go there. We can drive up there and you can get a job, and we could be in paradise."

We came home and looked at the map of Australia. At the top of Arnhem Land was Nhulunbuy. The airport was called Gove and was built for coastal defence at the start of WWII. They named it after William Gove who died up there. In February 1976, after much pestering, I wrote a letter to Nabalco, asking them if there were any jobs for a fitter and turner. I included my resumè and all the rest. About three weeks later, I saw an advertisement for a supervisor in the workshops up there. I thought, "This is for me." And applied. Another three weeks and a telegram arrived. "Please present yourself and wife at our office in Sydney for an interview and please prepare for an overnight stay. Travel tickets available at Qantas desk Tullamarine Airport, 07.00 departure."

We arrived in Sydney, and by lunchtime both of us had been interviewed. I had to spend four hours that afternoon doing Chandler and McCloud aptitude tests. Which of course left Lyn to do shopping. She enjoyed that. Spending the night in Sydney, we walked down Kings Cross that evening, and decided that we did not need to do that ever again.

Another three weeks and another telegram came. "Please prepare yourself for interview on site and two nights stay, required tickets at Qantas desk Tullamarine Airport, 07.00 departure." I received another telegram before I left and it read, "Please meet our Renè Biber at Cairns Airport." By this time it was Easter of 1976, and so off I went. After the flight to Sydney, then Townsville and Cairns, I got off the plane and went into the lounge. After a few minutes, a chap came up to me and asked if I was John Barraclough? It must have been easy to recognise me, being the only one with a suit on, as no one else was wearing one.

He introduced himself as Renè Biber, the superintendent of the workshops. Then, unbeknown to me, he started another interview. After a while, it was on to Gove. The plane arrived at about five o'clock that evening. The personnel officer, Robin Dudman met me. He took me to *Gove House* and showed me my room for the next two nights.

Next morning he met me, and we drove around the town, then out to the mine and had a quick look. There was not a lot to see. We went out to the plant and had a very quick look and he told me that others would show me the plant in detail. We went into his office for another interview. By this time, it was time for something to eat, so off to the canteen. After a bite, it was over to the workshops where I met Dirk Krause. Dirk spent the whole afternoon with me, showing me all aspects of the workshops and the different departments. He also gave me a good tour of the plant. The size of it blew me away. Dirk delivered me back to Robin, who dropped me back at *Gove House*. He said he would pick me up in the morning and take me to the airport.

This left me with not a lot to do. I walked over to the *Walkabout Hotel*, bought a six-pack, and took it back to my room. At about six thirty, there was a knock at the door. It was Dirk. He came in, and I offered him a beer, which he declined. He said he thought that he would come and tell me, before I got on the plane, that I had the job. He then asked when I could be on site to start. I was a bit blown away. I said it would probably be a month. I had a house to sell and a whole lot of other stuff to be sorted out. He reminded me that the company would come in and pack up the house, and car, and ship it all to Gove, and they would unpack it all up there. I thanked him as he left.

Next day it was the airport and home, arriving in the evening. When I broke the news to Lyn, she could not believe it at first. I told her I was still getting over it as well. Then began the packing up and selling part of it all.

On 7th April 1976, I received my Supervision Certificate, after two years of night school.

At the beginning of May 1976, I tendered my resignation at NSK and, soon after, left to get ready for Gove. I sold the Mazda and bought a secondhand Nissan Patrol. It had big sand tyres on it and I thought they might be handy. I kept doing the floral foam until about the middle of May, then gave it back to Robert to continue production. The house went on the market and was sold in a couple of weeks, which was good. The removalist came in. *Wilson Carriers* was their name. They had, I think, three guys.

In the one day they packed up all the stuff that would go to Gove. They left us with a survival kit, which was the basic stuff you needed to live. They said to leave the kit, and they would pick it up after we had gone.

They did not take the car, as we still needed transport. When we were ready to go, we drove to Melbourne and dropped it at their yard, then got a taxi to the airport. We flew to Brisbane for a few days, hiring a car and staying at a motel. The next day we drove to Bribie Island to catch up with Mrs Edwards. She was a wonderful lady who had looked after Tracy when we wanted a bit of time off. She and her husband had retired from Geelong to Bribie a couple of years before. After our stay in Brisbane, it was off to Gove.

On the 6th June 1976, we arrived in Gove and Dirk was there to meet us. He was a bit taken aback when he saw Tracy and her wheelchair, however we all fitted in his 4x4, and he delivered us to our new home. It was a four-bedroom home, quite big and spacious. A survival kit was waiting for us, as was food in the pantry and refrigerator. Somebody had been shopping for us. We had some basic dinner, and then it was off to bed. In the night, Lyn and I could hear this noise coming from the kitchen. I went to investigate and found big tropical cockroaches running all over the kitchen floor. I looked in the pantry, found some spray, and just about emptied the can on them.

Dirk picked me up in the morning, and on our way to work pointed out the bus stops that I could use next morning. Lyn was left at home with the kids. I think somebody came around and explained a few things about the place, like how to catch the bus to school, shopping and all those things. Lyn found it almost impossible to get Tracy on to the bus, having to carry Tracy on board and then get the chair on board as well. After a week or so, she said something would have to change as she couldn't keep doing it. I explained this to Renè my boss, and he said, "Come with me." We went over to the garage and met a guy who lived in Mallee Close, which was situated about halfway between the kindergarten and the school. This guy was leaving at the end of the week, and the house would be vacant. Rene suggested that I write a "Greenie", which is an inter-office memo. He said I should explain the problem we had and the solution, then send it to Robin Dudman. I did this and Robin gave me a ring, and we talked more about it. Apparently, they put us in that house because there were four bedrooms. I said that down south we only had three. It was done. A week later, we moved house again, and this time it was great, all the kids could walk to school and kindy. Lyn walked the twins to the kindy, and Marc pushed Tracy to the primary school.

It was some time after this, and after we had left Gove, that I was talking with Jock Adams who used to be the superintendent of the personnel department in Gove. We had come to know him and his wife Shelas fairly well in Gove, through their neighbours John and Marie Thomas. We visited them on the outside a couple of years later, and it was then that he said, "You know you could have asked for anything then". I asked, "What do you mean, Jock?" and he continued, "The tests you did in Sydney, before you even got to Gove, put you in the top 3% in the country for mechanical aptitude. They were not going to let you go." I said I did not know that. He said, "No, they paid for the tests, and they kept the results."

Around November 1976, Marc was playing on a Jungle Gym, (I think that is what we call them). Anyhow, he fell and broke his arm. At the hospital, they said it was quite common for newly arrived kids to fall or trip, etc. They put it down to the start of the Wet and the winds. I think Marc enjoyed having his arm in plaster, it was something new.

Marc again, a couple of years later, was playing with a friend, Kale something, and they went up Mount Saunders, a big hill at the back of town. Why I don't know. It was getting late, and suddenly Marc realized he should have been home quite a while ago. He jumped on his bike and off he went. He did not have to pedal, as gravity did a very good job of getting him moving. In fact, it was too good, and Marc could not handle the speed or the gravel. Both Marc and the bike wound up at the bottom of Mount Saunders in a tangled heap. He untangled himself from the twisted bike and took stock of his condition. It was not pretty. He had skin missing from everywhere. The gravel rashes were just that, full of gravel. He picked up the bike and wheeled it home. It was no good giving him a hard time about being late and all the rest. Just by looking at him, I knew he had learned a huge lesson. All I said to him was, "Into the bath." Lyn went with him and ran the bath, and he very slowly lowered himself into it. I gave him about five minutes then went in with the iodised salt container. I started pouring the salt into the bath and told him to mix this in. He did not dare to disagree. When the salt started to work, I could see he was putting on a very brave face, and so I said, "That will stop the infection." I then added, "It's this or you go for a swim down at the beach." He never went back up Mount Saunders again.

I think it was close to Christmas of 1976 that Lyn decided that she had to get out of Gove. I believe it was the isolation. The only way in or out was by air. Yes, you could drive, but only for four months of the year. For the rest of the time, the water level in the Goyder River was too high.

It made crossing out of the question. So, she booked flights for her and the kids, and away she went down to her parents in Victoria. She booked for a three-week stay, but said that after one day she wanted to come home. After three weeks, she and the kids headed home. It was not an easy job with three young boys and Tracy in a wheelchair. However, the boys were good and with their help, they all got home. Later, she told me to remind her of that trip if she ever had thoughts of doing that or something similar again.

It was late in 1977 that the idea of having a swimming pool in the backyard was first brought up. We decided to go ahead. The first step was to write a "Greenie" to ask if it was possible. We were lucky in one way. We had vacant land behind us, so that eliminated one possible problem. Anyhow, we received permission to build it, but it had to be a portable pool, and there were a few minor conditions. I think we bought the pool when we were out on annual leave. (Every year the company supplied free air travel back to the place you were living when you were hired. this was one of the perks of being on staff, and was very handy sometimes.) Clark Rubber was the place of purchase, and I think the length of the pool was 27ft. Digging out for the pool was a big job and even the neighbour's kids gave a hand. I think they wanted to make sure they would be able to swim in it. A week later, the pool was finished, and ready to be filled. It took a while as we only had a garden hose, which we left on overnight. The pool was was full the next morning. The water was a blue that I had never seen before. In addition, it was a clear as crystal, as they say, and this was before any filtering.

Dave and I in the rubber duck

On opening day, we banned the kids until the afternoon. This gave me plenty of time to inflate one of the yacht's dinghies and launch it in the pool. I invited our neighbour Dave Lambert over and we both spent a relaxing time drifting around the pool, each with a very cold beer in his hand. At one minute past twelve, the kids came from everywhere, jumped in the pool and capsized the dingy. Dave and I deserved that. We all had a great afternoon.

Great afternoons, great evenings, and greater nights - we had them all in our backyard. I had a big BBQ on one side. It had an aluminium plate 12 mm thick, acquired from the fab shop. I made the BBQ using old fire bricks from the kilns. We brought them from the tip where the works dumped them after they were replaced in a shutdown. There was an area that we could spread out and peg down a tarp. This was the dance floor. My Technics Hi Fi System at 50 watts per channel supplied the music. It carried to most of the town on a good night. When things got too hot from all the dancing, it was into the pool. For special occasions, we would fly in porterhouse steaks. (A company named *Tancred* flew frozen meats all over the Territory).

My work as a Maintenance Supervisor in the mechanical workshops, involved supervising tradesmen in the reconditioning of manual and control valves used around the plant. I counted them one day and there were over five hundred manual valves alone. The aim of the department was to have a minimum number of valves reconditioned and ready for use at any time, night or day. The plant ran 24/7 and maintenance in the plant also ran 24/7. Our department only ran 8 hours a day. One of the biggest problems we had was the supply of spare parts. As the throughput of valves increased, the parts supply decreased. Therefore, to get on top of this problem I had to rewrite the store's inventory levels, to match what we needed. I also had to do relief work in other departments when their supervisors went on leave. This included supervising the fitting & machine shop, automotive workshop, fabrication & welding workshop, and the specialised equipment crews such as pumps and heavy drives.

In July 1978, the Company advised that it was going to set up a new Maintenance Planning Department. I thought that this might suit me, so I applied for one of the three positions being offered. I scored one of those positions and I was to be responsible for the mechanical and electrical preventative maintenance planning, as well as major shutdown planning. Renè told me later that they were hoping that I would apply, as the company wanted me to be part of that team.

This was a challenging job. There were three maintenance planners, and we planned all the maintenance for the plant, both mechanical and electrical. We planned the daily activities for over seventy tradesmen and their offsiders. There were weekly meetings with the Supervisors where they would receive the new plan. This plan gave them their activities for the next week, plans for the next four weeks in advance, plus the week that had just gone, which was marked up at the meeting. The jobs that did not get done for some reason or another would reappear the following week.

I kept a running log on every pump and every valve, when it should come off line for maintenance and if it needed a bowl or wear ring replacement. When I say I kept a log, there were of over three hundred pumps and over five hundred valves in the plant. Each was logged as to when their maintenance was needed based on the manufacture's recommendation and its past history. The system we used was based on a similar system Renè had used when he was involved in the maintenance programs of Swiss Air a few years earlier. It was all manually done as there were no computers for us to use. Not that we knew how to use them anyway.

Once I calculated that a particular pump set should come offline for maintenance as it was due to come down for a bowl replacement. When I say a pump set, this was a twenty-four-inch Kelly and Lewis pump, complete with its drive motor and speed controller, all of which required routine maintenance of some kind. At that time, the production manager, Harry Meyers, was pushing the plant's output to an absolute maximum and kept telling me the pump was performing very, very well, and there was no need to take it offline. This is what Harry said every time I said it needed to come off line. Our standard rule was that everything was noted weekly until the deadline, and then it became a daily request to take the pump off line. This particular pump, in the hydrate section, lasted ten days over the deadline. Then at around 02.00 hours on a Sunday morning, she blew. There were no standby pumps to bring online, as Harry had them all going flat out. The result was a major emergency shutdown, putting the entire plant into recycle mode while we fixed the problem.

A few days before this emergency, and as a precaution, I had asked the maintenance crew to move a complete standby pump set into the area, and hot bolt every flange that would be required, hoping to reduce the downtime of a shutdown. Hot bolting was a term for going around every flange, undoing each bolt one at a time, applying *Never-seez*, then doing it up again while the pump was still on line. When it came time to do a change-out, there would not be any hard to undo bolts. The result of the emergency was a two-and-a-half hour shut down before the plant could be ramped back up to capacity. The clean-up crews spent the rest of the day cleaning up all the hydrate on the floor of the pump area.

Harry came up to me later in the morning, when everything had quieted down a little, and said to me, "John, if ever, you recommend that something is required for maintenance, and I overrule that, as I have done here, remind me of this day. It cost the company just short of a half a million dollars last night, and that is not good".

The Gove Alumina Plant was also a training ground for plant engineers. The 50% shareholder in Nabalco was Alusuisse. Alusuisse, or Swiss Aluminium, was also setting up a refinery in Venezuela, and so we had about four or five engineers from Venezuela in Gove as trainees. We got to know these guys through the men's softball competition. Back in Venezuela they played baseball, of course, but we played softball on a baseball diamond, so this was near enough. These guys all spoke English very well and also played softball very well.

We entered a team into the competition, calling ourselves *The Misfits*. None of us belonged to any of the different sporting clubs around town, so we made our own. We made up a team comprising Venezuela - 4 players, New Zealand - 3 players, Canada - 1 player, Australia - 1 player, and Malta - 1 player. I can't remember the rest, which is a pity because they were probably the ones who did all the work. One of these guys was Ramon Tirado, who was also a very good swimmer. There was Eddie Romero, noted for giving the ball a kiss before delivery whenever he took one in the outfield, and another was Jose Rivas, or "Little Jose". This guy might have been short in stature, but was he fast!! (Even with the girls). Then there was Eduardo, who gave me a *Fleetwood Mac* album when they left to go back to Venezuela. We all had many good times. I played catcher and really enjoyed this position. I used to practice, taking the kids trampoline and turning it on its side. This gave me a good target, and the ball would bounce off it back to where I was. I practiced in a crouch position. My aim was to deliver a ball from home plate to second base and take anybody trying to steal second base out. Eddie would be on second base. He had a good pair of hands, and the magic kiss. Ramon would play first base and was very good in this position. Little Jose would be the shortstop, as he could cover the ground.

Ramon Tirado   Jose Rivas   Eddie Romero

Our pitcher was a big Maori guy named Hina Pirene. He could pitch underarm at 106kph, and I had to catch this. I did, and we made a good combination. Phil, my brother-in-law was also playing with us as he used to play competition in Wellington before coming to Gove. Phil was our back-up pitcher. We won most of our competition games, and if we didn't, it meant we were having too much fun. We had developed a clever strategy. If you could hit the ball into the outfield, it was almost a safe home run, as the opposition were always reluctant to go out there. The water buffalo grazed out there, and nobody trusted them. After the game it was always back to our place for a BBQ and a cold drink, with a swim thrown in. I'm sure the team used to come back after the game just to see Lyn in her bikini. I don't blame them.

I haven't mentioned how the kids were doing as yet. Marc was in his last year of Primary School and doing OK. Tracy would always struggle with the academic side of her schooling, but the social part gave her no problems. She was like a magnet, attracting kids from everywhere. I think she became an education in herself. She was the only child in a wheelchair, and the fact was, if she was not there, all of those kids at the school would never have seen such a thing in their school life. Tracy became known as the Pied Piper. The twins, well they were the twins, into everything that was physical. In sport, they excelled in it all, and if the competition was a bit weak, they would challenge each other.

Our first camping trip was out to Dalywoi Bay, just north of Cape Arnhem, on the north-western tip of the Gulf of Carpentaria. We went with some friends named Larry and Dawn Vlarhoff. We borrowed a trailer, loaded it up and one Saturday morning away we went. We got to the bay, picked our spot and set up camp. It was a good spot, with a bit of shelter but the sandflies and mosquitos just about carried us away.

4x4 and trailer

Next morning, I was up early and off down to the bay for some fishing. After about an hour, and yet to have a bite, I was greeted by four Aboriginal guys, carrying their spears and woomeras, walking along the inlet and heading to the mouth of the river. I kept on fishing. I think Lyn brought me down a cup of coffee (she felt sorry for me). Just before lunch, and still no bites. By this time I could not work out whether it was me, the bait, the fish, or the place.

Then I noticed the four Aboriginal guys coming back, but this time as well as their spears they were carrying fish; fish so big the tails were dragging on the ground as they walked. I gave up the fishing and watched these guys as they walked in from the water to a spot not that far from our camp.

They laid the fish down and raked some sticks up with their hands, pulled out a lighter and lit a fire. They wandered around collecting wood. Soon they had a fire that I was very jealous of. I was a bit peeved with the lighter though. They should have rubbed some sticks together or something. Very soon they had a great bed of embers, and they just dragged the fish onto the bed.

By this time the boys had seen what was going on and walked up to the guys. They were talking and clowning around.

The boys and their spears

I wandered up to one guy and asked how accurate he was with his spear. He laughed and said "Accurate enough." I asked if he could show me. Now he became a little more serious and accepted the challenge. He looked toward the river and saw a coke can, at the water's edge about 50 metres away.

"See that?" He said. I nodded. He raised his spear, and nestled it into his woomera. By this time, the others had noticed what was happening and were watching.

He drew his arm back and, with what seemed just a flick of his arm, the spear was on its way. It landed right beside the coke can. He looked at me, and I nodded, and said.

"Very good my friend. Very good". All the Aboriginal guys laughed and started clowning around with kids again. Soon their lunch was cooked, and they went to eat. I called the boys, and we went back to our camp. One of the boys asked if they could try some fish, I said "No, because you have not been invited".

We had many camping trips after that, going to the Latram River, which was a good spot. The Giddy River had some good holes for swimming, but too many crocodiles.

Around mid-1977, we sold the Nissan. I noticed few rust spots appearing because of the salty air. That's the price of living close to the sea. I gave it a good clean and polish, concentrating on the spots I found. It didn't take long to sell. But then we had to find some other mode of transport. I did the usual thing and canvased all those who were leaving the site. I picked up an old Chrysler Valiant wagon for the right price. It suited us for just going around town and stuff. This was also the end to our camping.

Around the same time, I decided to purchase a yacht. Sailing was something I had never done, but it always intrigued me that they could get so much speed out of some of these big yachts.

The Triton 24

I found a 24ft Triton. It had a deep keel, therefore was on a mooring out in front of the Gove Yacht Club. I paid $13,250 for the yacht and all that was in it. The charts, safety gear, wet weather gear, the lot; all came in the package.

The owner was a guy by the name of David Harvey. He was a New Zealander. He had set the yacht up so he could sail the Pacific. David had to return to NZ and needed to sell the yacht.

The day came when it was time for me to learn how to sail. I asked my next-door neighbour Dave Lambert, a yacht owner, if he could come with me and give a few pointers. We rowed out to the yacht, and Dave said he would sit in the cockpit with a beer. If I needed an answer, he would supply it. That was OK, as the best way to learn is do it yourself. So, I got the sails on, attached the sheet ropes, hoisted the main and headsail and tied them off. We were ready to go, so I went forward and dropped off the mooring. As the breeze pushed us backwards, I pushed the tiller over and we swung around side on to the breeze. I quickly sheeted on the mainsail and off we went. I then sheeted on the headsail, and we were flying. I had done it.

We had a lot of fun in the yacht. I would ferry the kids out in the dingy. They thought that was a lot of fun. We got to the yacht, and they would clamber aboard; all except Tracy. I would lift her into my arms, then climb aboard with her. She had her place at the back in the cockpit, and would control everything from there. The kids would fish off the back of the yacht, and I think they all caught a fish, even Tracy, mainly small sharks.

On a Sunday, Lyn and I entered the races organised by the Yacht Club. Everybody got quite serious about the whole thing. I had Lyn do the steering around the course, and I handled all the sails. I remember, in one race, we were pointing high into the wind. I was trying to get an advantage over another yacht and Lyn was right into it as well, in fact she had a hand on the tiller and her feet on the side of the cockpit.

The day came when we had a good downwind leg, so I chanced hoisting the spinnaker. I had rehearsed it many times in my mind, thinking about all the things that could go wrong and the best way to resolve those problems. Hoisting it for the first time went off without a problem. (I can't say the same thing for some other hoistings later on.) With the spinnaker up and the main and headsail full of wind, we felt like we were flying! We weren't really. They designed the Triton for oceans not for inshore racing.

Once, we went camping over on the Granites, a group of granite rocks in the middle of Melville Bay. They had sandy beaches and plenty of trees, so away we went with another family, the Thomas'. We filled John's small yacht with firewood and tied it to the back of the Triton.

When we got to the Granites, I anchored in a sheltered bay. It was getting dark at this stage, so the first job was to get John's yacht to the shore. He, Marc and I clambered on and paddled it to the shore. We left Marc on shore, armed with a lantern so that we had something to aim for when taking the girls and kids in. Marc said later that he was scared stiff, standing there by himself, as he kept thinking something was coming up behind him. We were not thinking too well when we left him without first checking the place out properly.

We got everybody ashore and carried all our gear up to higher ground. It gave Marc the chance to do his scout thing and make a fire. John and I put up a couple of our biggest tarps as a lean-tos, one for each family. The girls looked after the dinner. This was a good spot, and we spent most of the next day swimming in the little bay. Throughout the night, I would get up and shine my torch out to make sure that the yacht was still there at anchor and not out in the middle of the Gulf of Carpentaria. There weren't many spots to sail to and camp around the bay or, for that matter, even outside into the Gulf.

I sold, or should I say traded, or more accurately swapped, the Triton and car with a guy named Hans Dieppe in return for a Trailer Sailer and Toyota FJ40 4x4 plus cash. Apparently, he had wanted to get hold of that boat for a long time. I had not even sailed the Trailer Sailer, when a guy named Les Boyd came up to me and wanted a chat. I knew Les. He worked for the Non-Destructive Testing Department, (NTD for short), and with me in the planning department. We had to talk so that any equipment they needed to test was available. Anyway, Les wanted to talk about the Trailer Sailer I had acquired from Hans. He asked if I really wanted the yacht, or I had done the deal just to sell the Triton? I said "Yes." I wanted to sell the Triton and "Yes." I didn't really have a need for the trailer boat as there would always be a problem taking Tracy out in a boat thats stability was questionable.

Les told me that he had a need for a trailer boat so that he could take the family out on the bay, and no longer had a need for his 14ft *Windrush Cat*. He suggested that we just do a complete swap. I said "Sounds good."

On the first day I took the little Cat' out for a sail, I had a ball. It had a small headsail, and that made it easier to point up into the wind and to turn. I went back and forth across the bay, just outside where the other boats were moored. I had a hull up out of the water all the way across. Man, what an adrenaline rush! When I finally put it on the trailer and into the compound, I was absolutely buggered, but felt so good. Later on, Marc came with me, and we had a bit of fun, mainly for his memory banks.

The Windrush Cat

Terry Larsen, the local swimming coach and a supervisor in the hydrate section at the plant, invited me to sail to Truant Island with him and another young chap who was about 18 years old. Terry had a trailer-sailer. I think it was a "Cole 23". We would be away for a few days, as Truant was About 57 kms north east of Gove, out into the Gulf.

We headed off early one morning, heading for Cape Wilberforce, a few hours sailing away. Terry said he was going below to catch a little shuteye. The young guy said that was a good idea, and that left me at the helm. All was good, every now and again I would shine the torch on the compass to check direction. After a couple of hours, it was still pitch black, I felt this tug on the tiller, I thought we had hit something but not long after there was another one, and another. It then became a steady pull. It got stronger until I had my feet on the other side of the cockpit. By this time, we were going quite quickly, and I thought I would have to let the sails out, rather than go over. At that point Terry came up from down below, to find the wind blowing very strongly. It had started to rain heavily. I rounded up into the wind, pointing as high as I could, but keeping some air in the sails. After a while, the squall passed, and things settled down a little.

We reset our course for the Cape. We arrived close to mid-day but did not go ashore, resetting our course for Truant. We arrived late afternoon after making good time thanks to a stiff breeze. We sailed around the top and down the Eastern side before dropping the anchor in a bay on the southern side. We did a quick trip ashore, to have a look at the remnants of a "Moresby Bar". This is what the Navy used when they landed to have a drink. We didn't find any full cans, so we headed back to the yacht.

On the way back we saw a shadow in the water. It was longer than the dingy we were in, so we rowed a little quicker. It was by far the largest shark I had ever seen. We opened a beer, relaxed and watched the sunset before getting some dinner. The wind had died away, and the night was very comfortable. I slept in the cockpit, under the stars. You have not seen the night sky until you see it in the Northern Territory, and it is even better if you are many kilometres from the mainland.

Next morning, we went ashore again and walked down the beach. Here we came across a fresh buffalo dung pad; hard to believe, when considering the next closest land was 11 km away. We went inland a little, but the going was a little hard, so went back to the beach. We thought we would get back on board and sail around the island to see if there was anything else of interest. We did this, and we noted some good-looking sandy beaches for future trips. We decided there was not a lot more to see and so set sail for home. It was an uneventful trip home, and with a good breeze, we made good time, arriving just on sunset.

Lyn and I decided to go on a cruise. She saw one advertised in a magazine, sailing from Sydney on board the "Felix Dravinski" a Russian cruise ship operated by CTC lines. Lyn booked the trip to find that instead of going to the Fiji Hideaway Resort, they were now going to the Regent of Fiji (since renamed). CTC Travel apologised, but explained there was now a big function on and they had booked the whole Hideaway Resort out. So that was that, or so we thought.

June 1978, we billeted the kids out, Tracy to Maria's next door, but I can't remember where the boys went, probably with Risè. We flew to Sydney and boarded the ship. They then escorted us to first class, with the explanation that they had upgraded us. We said thank you very much. On the table in our room, we found an invitation to dine with the Captain. In a couple of days' time. We thought this was all very good.

The cruise went up to Fiji, calling into Suva for a look around, then on up to Levuka, a small Fijian island. There we went out to a village and tasted the Kava.

Lyn and I ashore in Levuka

Then it was on to Western Samoa, and another look around. We liked Samoa.

We went on a tour from Apia to the other side of the island. We saw the house of Robert Louis Stevenson, now a museum, and Mt Vaea, where he is buried.

We went back to Aggie Grey's for a beer, then returned on board.

Our cruise ship at Pago Pago taken from the cable car

The ship headed overnight to American Samoa. The boat docked at Pago Pago harbour, and we had a few hours to look around. We found our way up to the cable gondola and went for a ride. The ride goes from one side of the harbour to the other and then back again. (Unfortunately an American Navy P3 Orion aircraft hit the cable in April 1980, and destroyed it all.) From there we found a taxi and asked the driver to show us the island. We did not think much of Pago Pago, it seemed to be very dirty, compared to Apia.

Our freebie of dining with the captain was very entertaining. I was actually seated next to the Man; he was at the head of the table, of course. The captain could not speak very much English, but the first engineer who was opposite me, did a lot of translating.

The captain had a strange custom. He would not drink alone, and he only drank vodka, which he liked very much. The first time I noticed he would not drink alone was when he held his glass in front of him waiting for someone to join him. The chief engineer also raised his glass. Being a good guest, I did the same, not fully understanding what was going on, but I can learn quickly when I have to. They both proceeded to down their glasses, so I followed suit, and we all nodded our heads to each other.

I thought this was all very easy until I learned that the Skipper liked his vodka. After the fourth vodka he leaned over to me, and in very broken English said, "John, the First Engineer, he will have one more drink with us. He will go very red in the face, then he will ask to be excused from the table".

I was a bit taken aback with this, but sure enough, that is what happened. I think the meal was very good, and I know I felt very good.

We cruised back to Nadi in Fiji and booked into the Regent of Fiji, where we were to stay for seven nights. When we walked into our room, there was a huge bowl of fruit on the table, with a note wishing us a very happy and enjoyable stay. We found it a little strange that none of the other people in our group on the cruise had this bowl of fruit. They were now wondering who we were, with all this special treatment. We could only put it down to the complaint Lyn made when she rang CTC.

Early in 1979, we took a three-week holiday, with the Thomas', back to N.Z. We left Marc and Tracy with our neighbours Dave and Maria Lambert. Maria was really looking forward to having to look after Tracy, and having Marc would be good for all concerned. We took the twins with us down to Lyn's Mum & Dad in Katunga, Victoria. They would stay there, and get up to mischief.

We hired a motor-home for the trip. Lyn and I picked this up just north of Auckland. We drove back down to Auckland Airport, picked up Marie and John, who were flying in from Brisbane, and were on our way.

The Thomas', us and the motor home

After losing Dad, Mum had remarried a nice chap by the name of Hugh Saxon. Mum sold the pub. I believe someone took advantage of her situation, because she didn't get what she should have out of it. Anyhow, she was happy again with Hugh, and they were living in Pukekohe just south of Auckland. That was our first stop for a couple of nights. It was good to see my Mum again. She hadn't seen her kids for a while as Risè was now also up in Gove. Risè and Phil had moved up to Gove with their two children Angela and Martin. Phil scored a job at Nabalco in the electrical department and was responsible for recalibrating all control valves, flow meters etc. His contract was for a minimum of two years. Hilton would never drive to Auckland. It may as well have been on the other side of the planet for him. We spent a good day with Mum, showing Marie and John around the place, then it was off to New Plymouth to meet some old friends, Paul and Margret Wadsworth, who we first met when Marc was born. We were both members of Round Table.

The next day it was down to Wellington. We stopped off at Brother Hilton's place on the way, to see how he was going. He gave Lyn a big piece of eye fillet steak, and said, "You will enjoy that if you don't bugger it up in the cooking."

Hilton at that stage was working as a production foreman for Hutton's Smallgoods in Eltham. Everything that Hilton worked at was in Eltham. He bought a house there before he got married, and he is still there to this day. We said goodbye to him and Leone, then headed for Wellington to see Tony and Diane Eagleton. We rang Brent and Lynette before we got to Wellington. They were now married and living in Upper Hutt, and they came out to Diane's for the evening. It was good getting together, as all of them were around during our courtship.

Next day it was down to the Inter-island Ferry, for the trip to Picton. From there we went through the Marlborough Wine region then over to Blenheim and up to and over, the alps to the west coast of the South Island. We did the big round trip of the South Island, before arriving back at Picton, for another crossing to Wellington. This time we went up through the Hutt Valley and over the Rimutaka Ranges, then up to Napier. After a good look around, we drove over to Lake Taupo in the middle of the Island. We stayed a couple of days in Taupo, one day driving south around the lake shore to Turangi, a nice little spot. We then drove up to Pukekohe, to catch up with Mum for the last time for a few years. Next day, we handed in the motor home, and went off to the airport from where John & Marie were going to Brisbane, and Lyn and I were heading for Melbourne.

We had timed our arrival in Melbourne so we could wait around and pick up Marc and Tracy. Maria had put them on the plane in Gove that morning. It was a big journey for the two of them, one nine years old, and the other only eight and in a wheelchair. As Marc said, he was just along for the ride, as Tracy was charming everybody on board. Their plane arrived, and as the passengers started disembarking.

Lyn and I were looking for a hostess to explain what Tracy needed, when here they were, coming off the aircraft. Tracy being carried by a well-dressed businessman. Marc was right beside them and a hostess was following with Tracy's chair. The chap gave us his card, and said,

"You have two wonderful children. Congratulations, especially this one." As he handed Tracy to me, I thanked him very much for looking out for the two of them. We then headed up to Lyn's parents, for another couple of days, before taking the tribe home to Gove.

In April 1979 we had a letter from Brent to say that he, Lynette and the kids, Cory and Clair, were now living in Rabaul, on New Britain Island, New Guinea. He was working for a motor dealer in the parts department. We replied straight away, asking if they wanted some visitors. The answer was yes, and we were on our way.

Tracy just floating around and loving it

We packed up and flew to Cairns and spent a couple of nights. We froze it was so cold. Then we flew on to Port Moresby for a night, then Rabaul. We had three wonderful weeks there, swimming every day. Tracy really enjoyed it. She could just lie in the water and float so easily.

All the kids got on really well and had a good time. Brent took us to some WWII sites. One of these was down on the shore. There was a big cave. Inside was where landing craft parked nose to tail as far as you could see into the cave. Soon you realised the cave was man made. Another trip was up into the jungle and into more caves. We were walking through one cave when we came to a brick wall. Rumour has it they could not get the enemy out, so they left them there. We looked into one cave and a stairway ran up at about a 45-degree angle, to an anti-aircraft battery. Brent said, "Come on, I'll show you where it is".

We walked out of the cave, and along another path. It went up and up until we finally got to it. It was an anti-aircraft battery, sitting there looking like it was still operational. We went behind the battery to see a door hanging off its hinges, but looking behind it you could see down the stairs to where we had been in the tunnel. It was a good holiday, and the kids enjoyed it.

All the kids on an old anti-aircraft gun

Around the middle of 1979, Terry Larsen asked me if I would like to take over as a swimming coach for the school kids. He explained what the job entailed and how he did the job. The purpose of the training was to prepare for a monthly competition and the school sports at the end of the year. I said I would think about it and talk to the boss. I did, and agreed to take the job on. However, I told him things might be done a little differently, and some might not agree with my methods. So I started being a swim coach, after work. We started around 16.30hrs and went for an hour. I really enjoyed coaching the kids. They were all very receptive to ideas and different ways of doing things.

I would sit them all down together and we would talk about the correct stroke for freestyle; how the arms should work on both the power and return stroke, that on the return stroke the finger-tips should brush over the water as this helps keep the shoulders level and how they should not reach too far ahead. Reaching too far ahead made the body wave from side to side. All these things slowed you down in the water. I taught them that it was important to keep the shoulders flat to the surface. By stroking too deep, they tended to drop their shoulder. We would talk about the correct kick, and which was the best kick. We had some lively debates at some of these sessions, and that was good. I wanted them to question.

Soon, swim times were coming down, and the kids were happy doing what they were doing. I asked Ramon if he would come and give the kids some pointers on the butterfly. (Ramon represented his university at an intervarsity completion in the USA, but he would never tell me how he went.) It wasn't long before I had all these girls wanting to swim butterfly, just so they could be close to Ramon. I daresay a lot of their mothers would have liked to come as well. He was not a bad-looking chap.

The kids kept getting better all the time. In 1980 they invited us to swim in Darwin, in the Inaugural State Championships. The kids thought this was pretty cool until I told them they would have to raise the money for their airfares, etc. We decided to have a swim-a-thon. The kids would sell laps, i.e. 10 cents per lap and if they swam 10 laps that was a dollar from each sponsor they could get.

On a Saturday morning it was on. We had volunteer lap counters helping out. Other groups got involved and sold cold drinks, and parents cheered on their kids and everybody else's. It was a great day. The kid that made the most money was Tracy Barraclough. She had sponsors from everywhere! She said she could only swim one lap, so her sponsors were going to give her all sorts of amounts just for her to do her one lap.

Tracy's swim came late in the day, at the end of all the other swimming. She insisted on diving in "Like all the other kids." I sat her at the end of the pool. She had her floaties on and was ready for action. I got in the water, and I said to her, "I will be here, all the way, the next thing you need to touch is the other end." So in she went and started swimming her overarm, then changed to dog-paddle. It took her some time, but as she neared the other end the crowd that had assembled was unbelievable! They were all cheering and yelling. I will never forget it. (Another of those moments in one's life that makes it all worthwhile).

When I lifted her out of the pool, she had a smile that would not go away. She was so happy, I thought she might burst. I was overwhelmed when I looked at her card to see who she had as sponsors. They were from all over town; from the plant, and into upper management, and places I would not have thought of. As it turned out, she let someone take her card and get extra names. It is true that she touched so many people.

We held a swim-off to see which kids were to be the representatives of Gove. However, the kids made one stipulation, and that was that both Ramon and I would have to swim, or no Darwin. As it turned out, Ramon could compete, but immediately after the competition, he would have to get the plane back to Venezuela. It was a great weekend, the kids had a great time and did very well in competition.

Ramon and I had entered the 50 metres freestyle. I had my swim, and found that it was easier for a thirty-five-year-old to coach the kids and tell them what to do, than do it himself.

Before Ramon's swim, he asked me, "This freestyle, over here is it *free* style?" I said "Yes, it is."

The 50 metres freestyle was an event where all had a go, including budding Commonwealth Games reps. As it turned out, Ramon had a couple in his heat. When he stepped onto the blocks, I thought "This will be different."

Sure enough, the gun went off and in they went! The others came up and started swimming. Ramon was still underwater. When he came up, he was swimming butterfly. Not only was he swimming butterfly, he had not taken a breath of air. Ramon touched the end of the pool and had his first breath of air to find that he was in first place. After the race and all the excitement had settled down, he came over to say goodbye. He would have to go back to our room and get his gear, then off to the airport. He also asked me to scratch him from the finals of the 50 metres.

What a weekend! And what an experience. Something to remember forever. All the kids were on cloud nine. I milked Ramon's effort to the max when we got back to Gove. At the first training session, I explained why he swam without taking a breath. It is simply faster to swim if you don't have to take a breath all the time. Why butterfly? Because that was his best stroke, and after all it was *free* style.

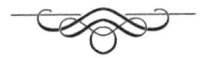

Chapter 8 - Bigger Adventures

Every Easter, the combined unions on site put on a picnic for the whole town. The company chipped in a bit on the side for a few things. This was a free weekend of everything for everybody. It started with a big parade. The townsfolk made mobile vehicles that had to have over two wheels. They had to be steerable and have brakes. A team of pushers supplied the power. Each year, the theme would be different. One year, the theme was cheese, like the dairy kind. Well, the different types of vehicles were amusing. It was a race of about two kilometres, finishing in the middle of town.

BBQs cooked food from 10.00 in the morning until ten at night. The beer was free for the same period of time. Those who had too much fell over where they were and slept it off. The great things were the running races for the kids and all the other kinds of sporting activities. Once, we were watching the kids running races, and Tracy said to me, "Dad I would like to compete. You could push me and the chair." I went over and asked the organisers if we could go in the race for her age group. The answer was a very strong "Yes!" I wheeled Tracy over to the start line and got into the correct group for the race. When I said the picnic was for the whole town, that included Yirrkala, an Aboriginal town out in the bush a bit. Anyway, the marshalling group got smaller and smaller, until it was our turn. Of course, Tracy was getting plenty of support and encouragement from her fellow competitors until they realised that I would push her. The race started. Tracy could not stop laughing, and it lasted the whole race. I was going as fast as I could. All the young girls around me were yelling "Come on, Tracy, faster!" The young Aboriginal girls were way out in front, and they too were laughing as hard as they could.

Trying to beat the kids.

At the finish, I think there were about six or seven girls in front of us but that didn't matter. Girls were coming up to Tracy and congratulating her. One girl said, "I will look after her, Mr Barraclough, and bring her over to you later." So I let her go, and the smile on her face was something you could never forget. Of course, I was ribbed something shocking because I could not even run faster than a bunch of ten-year-old girls.

The Beer Can Regatta was also a great day for all. It was much the same as one held in Darwin each year. They rowed some, and some tried to use the wind. There were even a few with outboard motors on them, one or two of which wound up on the bottom, as the beer-can boat broke apart.

The Latram River was a small river in the dry season, only three metres across and one metre deep, with a sandy bottom, which meant that it was ideal for the kids to swim in and for the parents to lie in or sit in a chair in the water and read a book. One time we went out with the Thomas', and of course we had to do it all correctly. This meant crystal glasses for the bubbly and wine, candelabra in the middle of the table, a tablecloth, and napkins, the lot, and to top it off a nice roast dinner waiting to be served.

The swimming hole down from the camp on the Latram.

The first trip out to the river was interesting, in so much as the Toyota we now owned had a little rust in her, so every time we hit a bump in the track the kids were showered with flakes of rust. Of course, there were complaints from all, but Tracy still thought it was great fun. I had a good look at the problem and decided the roof would not fall or bounce off, so I left it as it was and put up with the complaints.

Another time, we thought we would clean up some tree trunks that were littering a nice big swimming hole. We backed John's 4x4 down to the water's edge, got the rope and tied it on, then drove off.

As I was guiding the log around a pandanus tree, the log hit it. The next thing I remember was being stung by 27,000 paper wasps. (No, I did not count them, but there was a bloody lot). I took off and ran straight past the 4x4 yelling, "Shut the window!" After I had covered about 50 metres, I started to think that the way I was going was wrong, and that help was about 20 kms away in town. I did a big U-turn, still at the run. The Big U-turn was to avoid meeting the wasps head-on going back. I kept running as fast as I could.

Very soon I could see that I would hit the river. I yelled, "Everyone get out of the water!" I hit the riverbank and left the ground. The next stop was as deep as I could go under the water. I stayed down there as long as I could, but then had to surface and face the wasps, or drown. I chose the former. As it turned out, all the wasps had gone. They must have been angry little buggers, as they had pulled skin off my back and my buttocks through my swimmers. We didn't ever finish cleaning the river.

Gove was good for Lyn, because earlier she had found a job with the Accounts department at Nabalco and really enjoyed this. It was good that she could get back into the workforce. Her job was in accounts payable but three times a week they required her to go out into the plant to collect all the time sheets that Supervisors filled out. She looked forward to that part of her job. She would pull on her overalls, safety boots, hardhat and glasses, grab the keys to the Mini Moke, and away she would go.

Later she left this job to start a business with two other girls, Michelle McCombe and Lyn Lawson. (Michelle had been the secretary to the Superintendent of the Planning Department, Mike Caton, when I first started in Planning.) It all came about when the three girls were talking one day about the lack of good affordable clothing, suitable for our climate. One girl said that her sister could purchase garments at the right price and of the latest fashions. So, the girls started asking, "What if this? And what if to that?" The next thing, they were talking to the manager of the Walkabout Hotel about permanently renting a room. They talked about registering the name of their little partnership. They called it "*Gove Young Fashions*". The girls all had the same ideas about what it needed, and how to go about setting up and operating this little business. So, it was done and dusted. "*Gove Young Fashions*" was up and running.

They started up with a bang and put on a fashion Parade. They looked around for some very attractive young girls in town to see if they wanted to take part. The Walkabout Hotel came to the party and let them use the pool area. It had a big lounge.

The girls did some good advertising before the event so that when the afternoon came the place was packed. When the mannequins came out, most of the crowd did not recognise them, yet they were the girls from next door. The parade was a great success, and opening day was even greater. I remember sitting on the floor of their shop and counting the day's takings. The shop went from strength to strength, and the girls had a lot of fun along the way.

The Barra and Michelle counting the first day's takings.

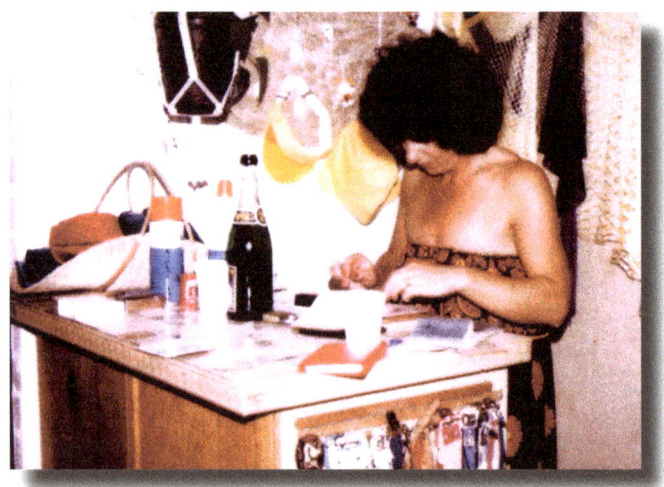

Lyn at *Gove Young Fashions* the end of day one.

Lyn played badminton to keep a little fitter. A few of the other residents got together and set the whole thing up. They played in the school assembly area, which was open-sided to let the cooler evening breezes through. There were a few very good players in town. One in particular was a Malaysian chap by the name of Whar Lam. He and Lyn had some very good matches, neither of them willing to lose. Some players went over to Cairns to play in a Queensland Tournament. They didn't win too much, but they all had a great time.

Around June 1981, the union movement withdrew their labour from the plant. This was quite disruptive for a 24/7 process facility. The company asked staff members to run the plant. This included all office staff, male and female. This meant that, as well as doing a lot of our normal work, we were also running the plant. We went onto a roster of 12 hours on and 12 hours off.

It amused me that, in fact, production went up while staff were running the plant. Why this was, I don't know. We were wringing 1.4 million tons from a plant that had an original design capacity of only one million. The company paid us our normal salaries, but then paid a generous bonus on top of the salary. They were good times, and we made the most of it. The export wharf was usually a no-go area for most employees, but we convinced Security to open the gates so we could go fishing after shift change at 23.00 hrs. We would fish until the early hours of the morning, then go home with a load of fish for breakfast.

There was a lot of friction in the town between staff and workers, many of whom were living side by side. Once a week, as I mentioned earlier, there was the men's softball competition, played on the town oval. The workers made up most of the teams and a few staff, like myself, also liked to play. This caused a lot of tension at first, until I explained that work was work and play was play. The company made the rules, and we all obeyed, but the company was not involved in sports. The strike lasted three months, and the only losers were the guys on strike.

In early October 1981, I tendered my resignation from Nabalco. We had decided that this good thing called Gove had to end. For Lyn and me it was great, and we could have stayed on for much longer, but for the children it was a different story.

As good as it was up there, it also had its disadvantages. It was very protected and sheltered from real life and all the problems associated with it. One day, the kids would have to face the real world of work and operate in it.

Marc was due to start high school the next year, the twins would start primary school. As for Tracy, she would have a special school to attend. Another problem was that, living in a rented company house, we could change nothing and we needed to change some things. There were already problems with the bathroom. We needed to change it so that Tracy could to do more for herself.

It had been a wonderful four and a half years for me and my career. I had moved into the management side of business and enjoyed the challenge. I realised that it really didn't matter what you were doing, as long as there was a challenge in it, and the bigger the challenge the more I seemed to enjoy it. Lyn had a great time. After the first six months things settled down and the place was good to her, with no real hassles to contend with, and we were very fortunate that Tracy had kept in good health the whole time we were up north.

Some time ago, we had decided that when we left, we would ship our vehicles to Darwin on the barge, then fly out ourselves, pick up our vehicles and drive down the centre to Victoria. I say we, because we had decided to travel with John and Marie Thomas. We were good friends with the Thomas' and the two families had seen a lot of each other in Gove.

A month or so before leaving, I purchased a Nissan E20 van from Nabalco and made it ready for the trip. I replaced the side panels with sliding glass windows purchased from down south. I was lucky that when my sister and family left Gove, after the two years of their contract, they left with me a big sea chest they had brought over from New Zealand. I modified this and made it our kitchen. I placed it right at the back of the van, allowing room for other stuff. I put an extra seat in for the twins. I had a system to which we could fasten Tracy's wheel chair, wheels in place. I put a roof rack on it right up at the front. So we could wheel the Tracy's chair up into the van, I modified the ramps I had made. They only needed a small change.

John and Marie towed a heavy-duty box trailer loaded with all their stuff. All of our furniture and stuff in the houses was to be packed up by the company into containers and shipped out to a destination 'to be advised.'

We planned to use our two-man tents on the way down. If they were good enough for camping, they were good enough for the trip. Lyn and I had one and the boys the other, Tracy slept in the van on a bed that we made up for her each night.

A week before departure, we took the vehicles out to be loaded onto the barge. In November, we had our farewell party down at the Walkabout Hotel. The next morning, it was out to the airport for the flight to Darwin. Many of our close friends came out to see us on our way - or to make sure we got on the plane. For the girls it was a wet farewell (plenty of tears). We arrived in Darwin and took a taxi to the barge depot, picked up the vehicles, and then it was off to the nearest supermarket to get supplies and some dry ice for the Eskies. Soon we were out of the traffic and onto the road heading for Berry Springs and the first night on another adventure.

We planned the trip south to take us about a month. This would take us to Lyn's Mum & Dad's, now living in Katunga, north of Shepparton, in time for Christmas. After Christmas, we would drive over to Perth in the van. I had an interview lined up with the personnel department at Wagerup. The Wagerup plant was very similar to Gove. As I said before, we spent the first night at Berry Springs, which are thermal pools, and so had some long soaks in them.

The next day it was on to Jabiru. We did not stay there. We called into the ranger station and saw a chap there, who advised us to go to Rainbow Springs, just down the road, and hang a left. We did all that and found the road into the springs. It was getting near sunset, and we drove past all of these lagoons. The birdlife was incredible! We found the springs okay. I told the boys not to go down to the water, as it was getting late and there were a lot of crocs in this part of the world. (A big croc took a chap 6 months after we were there.)

We set up camp. This place was magic. The kids weren't taken by a lizard, so all was good. In the morning, we checked the place out and the bird life on all the lagoons. We stayed two nights at Rainbow Springs..

Before we left Kakadu National Park, we visited *UDP Falls*. Short for Uranium Development Project, or as it known now *Gunlom Waterfall*. When we arrived, I told the kids, especially Marc, to stay on the bank. "Yes, Dad." With that, the kids took off, heading for water. I should have known something was not right, as there was not a lot of yelling and screaming, as there normally would be. Anyhow, thinking no more about it, I got Tracy out of the van, then we parents went down to the water's edge. I looked around. No kids!

I yelled out to Marc and got a reply from the other side of the waterhole. All the kids were over there. The waterhole was about 50 metres across, and they had all made it across. They were spread out up the cliff face, with Marc being about 10 metres off the water.

I thought to myself, "That it was a good effort by all of them." But said nothing. I just called that they had better get back to this side and to make it quick. "OK!" They yelled back and dived in from where they were. Marc said later that I did not say which bank.

We parked the van and 4x4 in a good spot and set up for a good early night. Unbeknown to us at the time, the spot we had chosen was also the spot where AAPT or Billy King Tours usually camped. That night they were out of luck. They had to camp in another area, one shaped like a circular dish. They built their fire in the middle and erected all the tents around it. What made it worse for them was that in the middle of the night it rained again, and it didn't just rain, *it rained*! The end result being that it filled up the dished area and flooded everything there. Before sunrise, they had left UDP.

The next day was bright and sunny, but before we could do anything, we needed to shift camp ourselves as it was a bit wet underfoot. We moved the vehicles without a problem. We didn't have a problem with the tents either. We had one kid on each corner of a tent, and two adults on the main ropes. Everyone lifted on the count of three and away we went. When we got to the top of a slight rise, it was down tent, put the pegs back in and go get another tent.

When all of that was done, we went for our walk up the waterfall track to the top of the falls and had a swim in the water holes above the main falls. Marie remained back at camp to look after Tracy and read a book. On our way back to camp it rained again. We got wet all over again, and that was all good. It was the Territory, after all.

We moved on to Katherine the following day, and that night it rained. It rained as it had in Gove, where it seemed the sky just opened up. It was just as well that, before leaving Gove, I got full sheets of plastic to go under each mattress. I told the boys to make sure they pulled the edges up when they got into bed. The rain ran down the hill in sheets and went straight though the tents but the kids remained dry and asleep.

The next day, we explored Katherine Gorge, taking the boat ride up the gorge. I even had a swim at the boat ramp. I think the freshwater crocs were more afraid of me than I was of them.

From Katherine, it was on down the road to Mataranka; more swimming in the springs. We headed, the next day, for Alice Springs. We stayed a few days in the Alice and visited the museum and a few other highlights of the place.

We travelled on to Stanley Chasm, getting there nice and early, unloaded and found the track up to the gorge. I followed the others, making my own time as I was pushing the wheelchair, and the going wasn't like a paved road. Tracy chatted the whole way up, but as soon as we got to the gorge she fell silent, just looking at the size of everything.

Tracy at Stanley Chasm

It was here that a woman approached Lyn. She was in tears. Lyn asked if she was all right? She said she was, but she was just so overcome at seeing Tracy up there in the gorge and in a wheelchair. She did not think that was possible. She told us she was from the UK, part of a tour group.

When it was time to go, I realised the chair had a flat tyre. There was no choice but to carry Tracy. I picked her up and said "My little girl, you must put your arms around my neck and hold on tight." "Oh, yes." She said, and grabbed me so hard it just about strangled me.

I gave her a squeeze and off we went at a trot. At this stage of her life, Tracy weighed in at about 36 kilos, and I had about 1.5 kilometres to go. John said, "I'm coming with you." He picked up the wheelchair, put it on his shoulder, and followed. When we got to the car park, my arms and hands felt they would drag on the ground. It was also a big effort from Tracy, and I could see she was exhausted, but she did not let go, or even ease up in her grip on me. All three of us collapsed and waited for the others.

The next day, it was out to *Ormiston Gorge National Park*. It is further west along the MacDonnell Ranges. What a magical place this is! We spent the night there and took some very good photos. It had a great water hole for swimming, with a sandy bottom, and was perfect for Tracy just to sit in it and enjoy the cool. We went for a walk up the gorge, and found that it opened up into a big pound. The gorge was the natural drain from it.

That evening, it was drinks time. We had this every night and would all sit around, and talk about the day that had been, the good points and not so good ones. We thought it was strange when a guy came up to our camp that night, and started talking about different things, then touched on the subject of UDP Falls. He had heard that somebody had camped in Billy King's spot, and they were rained out and had to leave. We said, we had just been there but didn't see any signs about reserving a camp spot. The chap said, "There is no sign, but everybody knows it is my spot." Then we told him we were the ones who camped there, and that maybe he should put up a sign. The guy said with a laugh, "Yeah, I know it was you guys, and I hope you enjoyed your stay." We said we had enjoyed it and promised not to camp in his spot again.

The next day, John told me he wanted to go a little further on down the road, turn left, and go down the Finke River Track, which was the riverbed. Driving the van counted us out, so I told him we would head back toward The Alice, and take a right-hand turn and head for Hermannsburg Mission and meet them there. Neither of us had to wait very long for each other, so we replaced the food essentials and even got some dry ice, but things were quite expensive. Our next stop was to be *Palm Valley,* which is in the Finke Gorge National Park. John followed us for this trip, which was just as well.

To get to the valley meant driving down the Finke riverbed. All was good for quite a while but then down we went in the sand. It was time for everybody to get out and push, except Tracy. I told her she was the team leader, and she was responsible for motivation, which meant a lot of yelling encouragement.

I think I said the wrong thing, because she made a lot of noise. The good pushers did a great job, and we were soon clear. So, "All aboard!" and off we went. This happened twice more. After getting out the third time, I said that it was time for a cuppa. John said he would go on in the 4x4, to see what the track was like.

Having a cuppa after getting bogged.

The billy boiled, and we made tea. All of this with the temperature sitting on 42C. John arrived back about 15 minutes later, so we had another cup of tea. He gave a report on the track and said that he turned around after the depth of the river reached over the mudguards of the Toyota, which basically meant that our van had no hope of getting through. Therefore, we decided that it was on to Ayers Rock, now known as Uluru. I turned the van around and got bogged again. "Everybody out!" I turned to Tracy and told her that this was the last time we would be stuck. We got out of that one, loaded up with kids again and off we went. I went through the soft spots a little faster, almost floating through them, with Tracy laughing all the way. We fuelled up at Hermannsburg Mission, then it was on to the Rock.

We reached the camping ground just on dusk and had to set up. We had a system, and everyone had a job, even Tracy. In 20 minutes we had the camp set up; all tents up, beds made, kids showered and in PJ's, dinner on the stove and just about ready. We made drinks for all, and it was time to sit and recall the day.

We had some visitors while we were sitting around. We could see them creeping around the campground looking for food. Dingoes. We then realised that this was where Azaria Chamberlain had been taken only three weeks before. A little spooky, but we made the kids aware of the dingoes, reminded them to be sure to close their tents properly, and told them to yell out if they heard anything.

After an uneventful night, we did a circumnavigation of the Rock by car, after which we said we would do the Rock itself. Lyn volunteered to look after Tracy. Tracy was not happy because she wanted to come as well. It took a bit of doing, but she finally agreed to stay with her Mum. What a climb! And what a view! It had rained about three weeks before, and the countryside had this green tinge to it for as far as the eye could see. It was spectacular. Another night in the park and early next morning it was off south again.

From the turn off on to the Stuart Highway, the South Road as it was known, the surface was just dirt. It would be another 1,350 kms before we could hope to feel bitumen again. We found the road very corrugated from side to side, and sometimes it was 25 metres wide. At times, we were down to 15 to 20kph because it was so rough. I tried to speed up and do what the 4x4's did, i.e. go over the top of the corrugations, but in a vehicle that wasn't designed for rough roads, it was hopeless.

Mount Willoughby was the place to refuel both van and people. They had cabins for hire, so we thought we would treat ourselves to a bit of luxury. We asked if we could have a look at the cabins. After the first one, we all decided our tents were better. We went just outside the front gates of the place and set up our own little camp on the side of the road.

The next day it was off to Port Augusta, with a slight detour to have a look at a place called Woomera. This all went well until we got to the south side of Woomera and John got a puncture in the inside rear tyre. He looked around, almost not knowing what to do. With the temperature sitting on 38C, it was not a place to hang around. I stepped in and said "Give me that wheel brace and I'll do the job. Just pass me the tools I require." In under ten minutes, it was all done, and we were ready to go once again. One of the boys asked "What's that Dad?". I turned around to see a major dust storm coming our way. I said to John "Best we get out of here, and get set up for the night in Port Augusta, if we can."

We got to Port and set up, always looking to the sky, but it was diminishing. Then Marc and Lea informed us that there was to be a birthday celebration that night, for Marie. Marc took me to one side and told me they needed to bake a cake. It was all ready to go, but just needed an oven or something. We went over to the amenities block, and he found what he was after. So, after dinner that night, we had a treat for Marie's birthday. It was a damper cake, complete with candles and all. They cut it up and offered it around. It was good, and I went back for seconds. Marc and Lea had been planning this event for some time. Now we knew why they were always changing seats in the vehicles. It was so they could plan a little more.

After dinner, the twins and Peter went missing. We could not find them anywhere, until we looked outside the park, and here they were, all three of them, down the street buying ice creams. The park we were staying at was right on the Stuart Highway and it is always as busy as. They had crossed the highway. I don't know how. Anyway we dished out a little discipline in such a way as I didn't think they would do it again.

The journey had to continue, as we were running out of time. The next day it was off to Peterborough, then on to Morgan and stayed the night in Renmark. The next day it was on to Mildura and through to Robinvale, where we spent the night. Next morning, as we were about to leave, Marie asked Marc to take off his jumper as it was too warm to have one on. He was very reluctant to do this, but in the end he did, to display to us all that he still had his PJ top on. I guess this is what happens when you sleep in and have to dress in a hurry. From Robinvale, it was on to Swan Hill, and we stopped at Echuca for the night. This was to be our last night together, as in the morning Marie and John were heading down to Morwell, in Gippsland, and we were going to Katunga, just north of Numurkah. In the morning we said our goodbyes and went our own ways.

We arrived at Lyn's parents' place to find that her dad was in hospital after having a heart attack. Her mum had tried to contact us, but these were the days before mobile phones. We had a very quiet Christmas that year. After the Christmas break, I rang Wagerup, to find out when I needed to be there for the interview, and was told it should be before the end of January. That gave us a leaving date no later than the 16th January. However, we did not want to go if Dad was not out of hospital.

Dad came home on the 9th January and still looked a very sick man. Early in the morning of the 16th January, we headed off for WA. We got to Waikerie that evening. Lyn said she would call home and see how Dad was. She came back to the van crying. Her dad had passed away on the afternoon of the 16th. Her mum had been trying to contact us and had rung the police for help. We had to go back. The next morning, after not much sleep, we headed off back to Victoria. When things settled down, we had some time to think on what we would do. I rang Wagerup, explained our circumstances, and said that I might call them in the future. Lyn's Mum and youngest sister Debbie would have to leave the farm, as they had already sold it. Mum and Dad had planned to move into Shepparton, had purchased a block of land, and signed a contract with Jennings to build their new home.

Lyn and I talked a lot about our own options and future. We decided that, in the short term, we would buy a house in Shepparton for all of us, then Mum and Debbie would have somewhere to stay. We started looking. In the even shorter term, we all moved into the Shepparton Caravan Park, still in our two-man tents and Tracy in the back of the van. Mum had a chat with Jennings Homes and found she could cancel the existing contract to build the home, but in return would build the new house that she wanted. She found a block of land and purchased it, and Jennings started straight away. We had found a house in Varcoe Street, not that far from where Mum would be, and so we bought it. It was on a short contract, and we were all able to move into it and out of the caravan park. I got a job in Mooroopna, which is just over the Goulburn River from Shepparton. The job was with a company called E.D. Parsons. They designed and manufactured fruit and vegetable grading equipment. I was a foreman in their machine shop, starting in February 1982. This was not the sort of job I was after, but it was only a short-term thing, I hoped.

Then, in April, Tracy became ill and needed hospital attention. The doctors wanted some scans taken. Tracy had an allergic reaction to the drug they used in the scan process.

Tracy died on 20th April 1982, aged 11 years, and so began one of the saddest times of our lives. She was such an inspirational little girl. With all of her problems, she always had a smile. She had a laugh that was contagious and was loved by all with whom she came in contact. This little girl had a life that was so full. She had done so many things, been to so many places a lot of other people would never get to, or get to see even a part of them, in their lifetime.

There were tributes for her from New Zealand, Geelong, her friends at the special school at Shannon Park in Geelong, and from Nhulunbuy town; from the school, the swimming club, all her friends, and from the management and staff of Nabalco Pty Ltd. Tracy is now resting in the Shepparton Cemetery beside her Pa, who died 3 months before her.

Pa & Tracy at rest

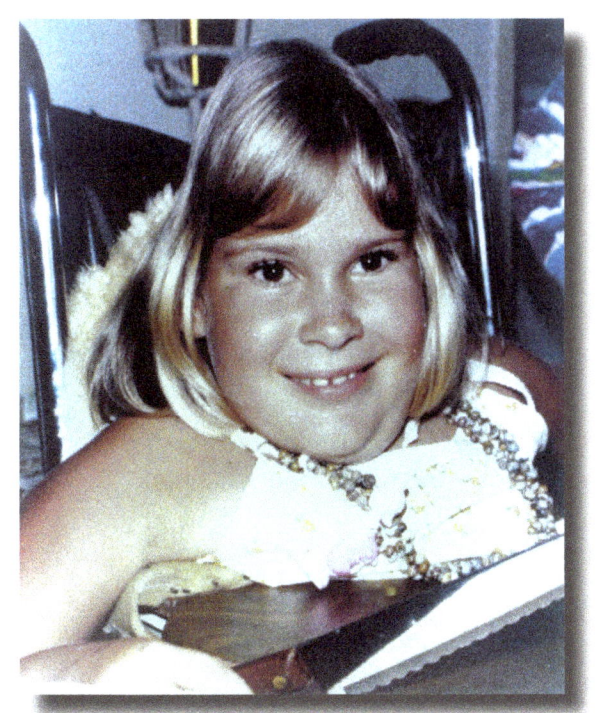

What a Girl!

Work at Parsons was interesting but not challenging. They were well behind in production, but I soon brought it up to where it should have been. I became friendly with one guy in the design and drawing office. His name was John Sache. After a while, we discovered we had a mutual interest in model boats.

I had been quite active in model boating on our first trip to Australia, when a guy I was working with at Silcraft industries, Peter Hunter, said that his old man played with model boats. Peter Hunter was a chap I got on well with. We had similar interests, in cars mainly. Peter used to work on the engines to make them go faster. Another guy who worked at Silcraft was Rob Darnell. Rob brought a black HR Holden, it was an ex-taxi, so we knew it as the Tijuana Taxi. Peter did a bit of work on this for Rob, and the thing went fairly quickly. They invited me out for the day with them to the Calder Dragstrip. Where they were running the Taxi. Rob was driving, and the thing surprised everybody by returning a time of 13.1 sec for the quarter mile. Rob Darnell went on to produce one of the best, (and noted around the world to be so), replicas of the Shelby AC Cobra. (Sold as a Robnell). It was hard to pick the replica from the original.

I got in touch with Peter's dad. His name was Murray. Murray made nice boats, and they were very quick. I bought a hull from Murray and started to build a boat, but returning to NZ stopped that for a while. Another guy I got to know in Geelong was Rod Smith. He worked at NSK Bearings when I was there.

We went out on Sunday mornings and had some fun. We went to a big lake up behind us in Highton. I would take Marc along and sit him in his high chair (without the legs) beside the shore and he could watch all the racing. Rod had some very quick boats and was always trying to make them go faster. This need to go faster was one of the main reasons I started to manufacture tuned pipes.

Tuned pipes were actually a reverse cone megaphone. A megaphone acts as an extractor. The reverse cone on the end sends a shock wave back up the pipe. This crams the unburnt gas the extractor has pulled though the combustion chamber back into it, thus charging it with extra unburnt gas and raising the compression ratio at the same time. When tuned, it would act as a supercharger though the exhaust port of a single cylinder two-stroke engine. I bought a TIG welding machine and rolled some 1.5mm zero temper aluminium into cones, then welded them up. Being able to custom make the pipes and tune them into our motors gave Rod and me an advantage.

Anyway, back to model boating. One day, John Sache mentioned that he had always had a desire to build a scale model ship and asked if I had ever thought of building one. I said, not really but I admired the workmanship in models I had seen in museums and displays here and there.

He told me that he intended to import a model in kit form from Italy. If I wanted to, we could share the freight. He gave me a catalogue booklet and said, "Pick one." I didn't need a lot of time, as I had always thought *HMS Victory* had a very notable history and was still preserved in Portsmouth harbour. John had chosen *Sovereign of the Seas*, noted for tipping over when she fired her first broadside. It cost us $750.00 to get them in and the rest was up to us. John had his model finished in about three years. He made a very good job of it. I'll give updates on mine as we go along.

Coming up to June 1983, I was getting a little restless. I found the job was not challenging enough, and so I thought I might try my hand at dairy farming. By this time, I had given away any thoughts of going to the west. Our commitment to being there for Lyn's Mum and Debbie ruled out that move.

Farming was something I had not done before, but I had been around cows a few times at Mum and Dad's farm. Lyn and I talked it over and decided it was worth doing for the boys.

Marc was going to Shepparton High School, and the school was starting to have a few problems with drugs and stuff. The twins were going to Guthrie Street Primary School and were starting to become influenced by city kids, so we agreed that we would do it. I looked around and found a little farm out on the other side of Tatura, an area called Harston. It was a 108-acre farm, milking 96 cows, and rearing the young stock, but the heifers were agisted out. It was a walk-in-walk-out sale, and they wanted $250,000.00.

Looking at the property, it was a bit ordinary, but had potential. The farmer who was selling had done little around the farm for quite a long time. We decided to give it a go, so off to the bank. It just so happened that the bank manager, Brian Shaw, was the same guy we had as our bank manager in Nhulunbuy. We got the loan to buy the property, based on the budget forecasting I had done using the payout figures from the dairy company. Before we moved onto the farm, the dairy companies had readjusted the price of payout for a kilogram of butterfat down by almost half. This put us against the wall before we had even started.

Chapter 9 - The Challenges

In early July 1983, I resigned from E.D. Parsons. On the 27th July 1983, we moved onto the farm and became dairy farmers. The cows were coming up to calving, so it was a matter of getting the milking shed ready for the upcoming season. When the time arrived, there were a few self-taught lessons in calving, having to pull a calf from its mother and all that sort of thing. The local vet in Tatura was a great guy, and very helpful. I explained to him I was new at the game, and he said he knew that. The word was around town.

The cows seemed to know when it was time for milking, as they would all start heading for the shed at around 16.00 hrs. The milking went smoothly most of the time. I say *most*. There were one of two hiccups from time to time.

Colostrum is the first milk from the cow after calving. Nature designed it to be the first milk that a calf receives after birth. It cannot be sent to market, so was milked into a bucket and fed to the new calves, which is where it was supposed to go anyway. Milking the colostrum into a bucket was a bit of a pain. I said to myself, "This won't happen next year".

I made that statement a lot in that first year. I made it again about feeding the calves. Lyn did this and did it very well, but the system needed to be better.

The tanker came for the first load of milk. As it left, I said to Lyn "That means we might get paid next month."

The next big challenge was herd testing, done during the milking. It is a good means of knowing what the individual cows are doing production wise. The first testing went off great, as did all the others.

Soon it was time to mate the cows. Mating is a matter of observation. When a cow stands and lets another cow mount her from the rear, it is a very good indicator the cow standing is in season. However, you are not observing all day, so one must apply tail paint. This a strip of special paint applied to her tailbone. When the paint is rubbed off, the cow could be in season. Then it is a matter of calling the Artificial Insemination (AI) Technician. When you have decided on the bulls you are going to use on the herd, you order the semen you require from the technician. The selection of bulls is based on the herd testing figures. It is a waste of money to use a good, expensive bull over a cow that is not producing well, or does not have good genetics.

These things are happening at the same time and always at the beginning of the season. It is a great introduction for someone who has not done it before!

A week or so after moving in, Mother Nature exerted her power and gave us 30 frosts, one after the other. It was so cold that the water pipes in the dairy froze. I had to go around with some hot water to thaw them out. It was so cold the cows did not want to get up and come to the shed. They would remain lying down where they were warm. Then it was a matter of kick-starting a couple, the rest would then get the idea. When a cow gets up on her feet in the morning, one of the first things she has to do is to relieve herself. This leaves a nice steamy hot pad of "you know what". I found that I could wriggle my gumboots into this and almost straight away I would have nice warm feet. As the cows emptied the paddock, I would look for another pad, a little closer to the gate.

This farming game certainly teaches one to be very well organised. When things settled down a little, I rang the agricultural department and asked if I could have a visit from an on-farm consultant. The guy duly turned up, and we went for a walk up the farm. I explained to him what I wanted to do with the paddocks and asked what would be the best way of going about it.

My idea was that I wanted to split the production paddocks up into roughly thirty evenly sized paddocks. This would give me one paddock for a day and night, dividing it with an electric fence, and when the cows came off the paddock, it would be topped (cut all the uneaten grass with the slasher,) then left for thirty days before the cows would go in again. He said it was a great idea, and he knew of a couple of farmers doing much the same thing. He then said, "Let's see how we can do this." After a couple of hours we did it well in theory, but I still had a lot of fencing work to do.

As things settled down, I had time to think about irrigation. I didn't know how to do it, as I had never done this before, so I did it in the same way as I had learned to sail, 'open the gates and see what happens'. This I did, and I had water everywhere. But I learned how fast the water flowed across each paddock, and how long it took to water it completely. With a bit of planning, it all got better and better.

The summer months were the quiet months, if you ever have any of those. I started thinking about the things I said would not happen next year. The three major projects were to be milking the colostrum, feeding the calves and feeding the cows in the bale.

We handled the colostrum by installing another milk line. As a fresh cow came into the shed, she could walk into any bale and all I had to do was take the milk line off and reconnect it to the third line that took the colostrum out to the milk room.

There we collected it in 200 litre plastic barrels. At the end of the evening milking, and after the milk had been taken for the new calves, I would add natural yoghurt to the barrel and give it a big stir. This would sit overnight. In the morning, after another big stir, I could take the yoghurt to the older calves. The product they were drinking had the same consistency as thawed ice cream. The new calves got 2 litres of pure colostrum night and morning for seven days, then they had 4 litres per day of the culture, fed in the morning.

The third project was to feed the herd in the cow bale. The reason was simple. The cows spent about one and a half hours walking to and from milking, including the time standing in the yard waiting. This was time they were not eating in the paddock and not making milk. I went to our dairy company, who were into feeding systems, and got some ideas. Then I went home and designed my own system for a fraction of the cost. I built and installed it towards the end of the first season, but did not use it until the start of the second season. I had a silo installed and connected the feed system to it. The system worked well and production went up enough to cover all costs and more in the first six months.

The guy who owned the farm before us was a bit on the lazy side, and all the farm rubbish went into a pit he had dug. There were bits of machinery, parts of machinery, even a litter of stray cats.

Horse

One of the kittens came out one day when the boys were down there. It was tiny and riddled with fleas. You can guess the rest. The kitten became part of the family, but not before it went through a major de-fleaing program. The boys took on the problem of naming this little creature, and they came up with *Horse*. Of course I asked where that came from, and the answer was from the comic book *Footrot Flats*. That left me with the problem of what to do with the rest of the kittens. Good neighbours of ours, by the name of Frank & Judy Lahm lent me a 410 small-bore shotgun and then there were none.

I cleaned all the rubbish out of the pit and took it to the tip. Then, with a bit of plumbing, turned the rubbish pit into an effluent pond that treated all the effluent from the dairy. With the pond being higher than the surrounding area, when it was full it would flow into the old bull paddock as fertilizer.

I had finally found the challenge that I was after. Of course, there was more than one, with herd management, pasture management, irrigation management and financial management. My sister Risè sent me this poem one day, but didn't say where it came from or if she had written it herself.

The Farmer

When he became a dairy farmer
He was full of hope and joy
For he'd wanted to be a farmer
Since he was a boy
But dairy farming was something
He knew nothing about
But he was keen to learn and listen
And was sure he'd work it out
He was born and raised in the city
Lived in an urban scene
And disillusioned with city life
He wanted some air that was clean
The neighbours gave some good advice
To this novice from the city
They tried to advise him what to do
And some looked on him with pity
He found out where milk came from
And how to get it out
He had to work from dawn to dusk
Of that there was no doubt
He found that there were springers
The forward and backward kind
But thinking of cows jumping forward and back

It nearly blew his mind
He learnt to carry milk cans
And cart them to the road
The carrier watched and grinned
To see him struggle with the load
He learnt what signs to look for
When a cow is ready to mate
And that the cows will always know
When a latch is left off a gate
And if the electric fence is off
They seem to know somehow
And eat another 3 day's feed
All in one swift blow
He's learnt to despair when the rain won't come
And the feed just withers and dies
But he's known the thrill of a new-born calf
Facing the world with blinking brown eyes
He tried his hand at showing cows
And handled it with finesse
In judging ring and milking comps
He was pleased with his success.

One of our neighbours was the Fleming family. Their son, Richie, was around our age. He did the milking on the home farm, and during the day did contract work for other farmers in the district.

We were talking one day, and he said he was going to night school, and was learning to weld. His goal was to have the ability to build some equipment, instead of having to buy it all. After a while I told him of some stuff I had done. It did not take long for him to ask if I could design an 8-foot laser grader for him to build. I said I did not have a drawing board anymore, but I could do the basics for him. This I did, and some time later Richie had himself a laser grader to tow behind his 4X4, 135hp, Massey Ferguson tractor.

He said it worked well, and he was soon doing contract work with it. A while later when he had a slack moment, he did two top paddocks for me, and said it was payment for my part.

I remember in 1985 the family had gone into Shepparton one evening after milking. I can't remember what it was for. On the way home we were coming along the Tatura Road and I saw this light in the sky, I knew what it was straightaway, but said nothing until I found a place to pull over and park on the side of the road.

I told the boys to get out and watch the display, and remember it, because they were watching the Aurora Australis, which is a phenomenon caused by solar winds and earth's magnetic field.

I had never seen it this far from the South Pole. It is usually only seen from the very southern parts of the mainland, Tasmania and New Zealand. It was playing in mainly red colours, with just a little green here and there. I have never asked the boys if they remembered that night, but I am sure they do.

Time for an update on the model of HMS Victory.

Before I left town and headed for the farm, I had the first of the spruce planking on, and sanded it to the correct shape, which was fairly critical around the bow area and the stern where it went up into the aft cabins.

Spruce planking

With all of that complete and looking good, it was time to cut out for the gun ports and install the brass surrounds. As Victory was a 103 gun ship of the line, this took a fair amount of time. With all of that done, it was time to plank it over with mahogany. However, I got all of this complete before heading to the farm.

Mahogany planking and deck

Frank and Judy Lahm, who share-farmed a dairy property behind us, had a party. It was a good party and I think I might have had a little too much of a good thing, because the next morning I was not a very healthy boy, and still had to milk the cows. I got the cows done and had breakfast, but still felt off. On the advice of my boss (Lyn) I went and saw the doctor. He said I had a stomach ulcer, but it wasn't a bad one, and he gave me some tablets. He also asked if I smoked. I replied, "A little." "Give it up right away it's bad for you!" Was his reply. When I think back to when I had my last cigarette, it was at the party, at 04.30am on the 29th April 1986. I have not had another since.

Our friends who travelled down from Gove with us, John and Marie Thomas, used to come and visit. Every time they came, John would say that he was jealous of us and what we had. Around March 1986, John asked if there was a way that they could come and work the farm with us. I said I would think about it.

I had met a guy by the name of Ray Carr. He sold farm equipment. Anyhow one day we were talking, and he said he did not know what to do as he had just lost his father, and they would have to sell the family farm and herd; everything. I started thinking about this and wondered if there was a way that it all might work. I rang John, and told him that if he wanted to come farming, this was the only way I could see it happening.

The idea was that John's capital contribution into the partnership would buy the herd of cows that Ray had at *Myola Park* (the family farm). Lyn and I would move into *Myola Park* and share farm the property, while he and Marie would move into the home farm, *Tra-lee Park*, where we currently were. John and Marie had given the little farm the name of *Tra-lee Park* in memory of our Tracy Lee. They had a sign made up and put it at the front gate. So, from then on it was *Tra-lee Park*.

John liked the idea, so I said "Think about it". I then rang Ray and put the scenario to him. He said he would think about it as well. The next day Ray rang with a few questions, one being to allow the farmhand, Ron, who had been employed by Ray's father, to stay. He lived in a caravan at the back of the garage, which was out of the way. I said I didn't have a problem with that. He added that his mother who was living at *Myola Park* would now move into Tatura and was in fact already looking for a house. There were a few other minor things that both parties needed to consider, but apart from those, it was all go. He then asked when we would move in, and I said a week or so, before the first of the cows were due to calve. He told me the first were due in mid-August. I said well let's look at the 31st July 1986. And so it was that we were on the move once again.

We had a the local solicitor draw up a partnership agreement between John, Marie, Lyn, and I. This covered us all in case something went wrong. The partnership would farm 600 acres, milking 250 cows. Financially, we would run the farms as one entity, and we would draw wages from that. On the labour side, we would each run our own farms. I would give John a hand with the breeding program in the first year. After that, it was up to him. I would also help him with the haymaking, as making the small bales was far more labour intensive. I guess that I was lucky. The equipment already at *Myola Park* included very good hay equipment, including a round baler and a round bale feed-out machine.

Calving down a herd of 150 cows was not a lot different to doing it at *Tra-lee Park*. I had a major problem though, and that was I was having a lot of very large calves. I was having to pull almost all of them. Sometimes I needed the vet for the problems were more than I could handle. It did not take long to work out what had happened. When Ray had lost his Dad, he also lost the management of the farm. The farm-hand did his best, and thought he was doing the right thing, but he overfed the herd in the last month of pregnancy, resulting in the large calves.

The herd had been herd-tested, and so I had the records to look at decide on the bulls I would use. There were some very good cows in the herd, but also a few hangers on, and they would be the ones that would go to market first. It also gave me an advantage in that I could mate those great cows to a very good bull using AI. It also gave me the knowledge of which ones not to waste good money on and mate them with an easy calving beef bull. This was one of the benefits of herd-testing.

I had installed a feeding system in the milking shed some time ago, but hadn't been used for some time, so one of our first jobs was to get it working again. We did this, and it worked well.

One weekend, we visited Lyn's brother Graham. He had a sheep property up in the Strathbogie Ranges. He had bred a dog I thought I needed at *Myola Park*. Our farm was over four times the size of the little farm, or should I say *Tra-lee Park*. Anyhow, this dog was only a young pup. Its mother was a pedigree Border Collie, and the father a Kelpie. The pup had turned out black and white. Her face was very symmetrically black and white. The first time we met, I had a feeling that this little dog was very smart. She would just sit and observe, rather than run around like a headless chook. I liked that.

We took her home that afternoon. I had already fixed up the dog kennel. The dog kennel had a big run area attached, which was ideal. That night at dinner I had to lay down the law.

The dog, now to be known as Jess, would not be a household pet. She was a working dog, and would be locked in her kennel, only to come out for work, and this would be the case for twelve months. I did not have to train this little dog, (just as well because I didn't know how to). She seemed to know or sense what she had to do, but would always look at me for confirmation. After the first twelve months, we allowed her down to the house. The kids tried to spoil her, but she never forgot her job, or what she had to do. She was a great dog.

Meet Jess, a worker and companion

One day we had a stray cat come in the front gate. One of the boys saw her walking down the driveway, not sneaking down the side but right down the middle as if she owned the place. She was very friendly and very pregnant. The bottom line, the other female of the family said she had to stay, and duly named her *Mrs Puss*. The kittens were born, and Lyn got rid of most of them around the area.

Mrs Puss did not enjoy going inside much, probably because of Horse, and so I set up a part of the outside laundry for her, and this she much preferred. Jess and Mrs Puss became great mates and would lie together in the sun. Little did they know it was a friendship that would last another twelve years.

The next calving year was the complete opposite from the first year. I had no calving problems at all, and the cows got into full production very quickly. When they don't have a setback to start the year, everything is much better. The twins, Geoff and Tony, helped me with the milking as they had done down at *Tra-lee Park*, and were a big help. During calving time, they would help Lyn with the feeding of the calves. It was also good that they never forgot the golden rule when going around the farm. If you go through a gate that is shut - shut it after you. If you go through a gate that is open - leave it open. Marc only followed those rules when things were desperate, and that was not very often.

We joined a lot of the herd to an easier calving Angus beef bull. We had decided, with John and Marie, that we would keep all bull calves, and the heifer calves not earmarked for herd replacement would go to market. So that second year Lyn, with some help from the boys, reared over 100 calves. We had a good system sorted out by this stage, with the yoghurt mix we were feeding them working really well, and we had very few health problems.

At the beginning of December 1987, we did a very early milking and headed off down to Melbourne and Kooyong Stadium to see a live concert by Stevie Wonder. I had been a fan of his since our days in Gove, when we all used to dance outside on the stretched out tarp that was our dance floor. It was a fantastic concert and we all really enjoyed it. In late 1979, I had purchased the digitally recorded album of his journey through *The Secret life of Plants*. On this album, he played every instrument, did all the mixing and dubbing and produced it; the lot. It was truly a work of only Stevie Wonder. I would lie on the floor with my head between the stereo speakers and listen to the thunderstorms coming through the rain forest. It was so real.

Late in 1988, I was getting terrible headaches that were coming from my neck, the old injury raising its ugly head once again. In retrospect, I was trying to protect my neck all the time, and the muscles down my neck and up into the back of my head would spasm. This caused the aches. In the end, I saw a good physio who worked on pressure points to fix the problem. She showed me the point on my shoulder blade, that if massaged, would also relieve the headache. Sounds silly, but it worked.

She also showed me exercises I could do to stretch the muscles in my neck when I needed to. This worked fine from then on.

Marc had left home to go to Footscray. He was working in the electronic industry. Thinking about the big picture, and our children getting older, I thought there could be a better way for the four of Marie and John, Lyn and I to enjoy our way of life. What I came up with was as follows. If we sold the herd and the replacement stock from *Myola Park*, we could buy the 9-acre block of land opposite *Tra-lee Park* that was on the market. We could then also build a small A.V. Jennings home on it. We would move into that, and I would take over the pasture and the irrigation management. John & Marie would look after the herd only. This happened in July 1989. We moved into the *"Little House on the Sand Hill"*. John's brother-in-law Dick had purchased a block of land, I think it was 26 acres, just up the road from *Tra-lee Park*. He had purchased it as an investment block. Dick told John to use it. The block was not irrigated, but had a small dam. This meant that I could grow a lot of feed in the winter and spring, and bale it for later.

We had bought a new tractor for *Tra-lee Park*. It was an Iseki, 70 hp, two-wheel drive. The old one, that was on the farm when we moved in, had given up the ghost. The trouble was that we really needed a front-end loader. So it was a sketch-and-build thing again. I had a look at a few others around the place and got some ideas. What I turned out was a good front-end loader that worked well. The only thing it lacked was a professional paint job.

Another guy from up the road, a mate of Richie's, came to see me one day. He said he needed a round bale feed out machine, one that would feed out both sides. All the commercial ones only fed out on one side, and if you put the bale on the wrong way around you had to tip it out and try again. To make things a little more difficult, he did not want to modify the one he was using but to have a completely new one. This was a little more than I had bargained for, and wondered why I couldn't keep my mouth shut, or say no. Anyhow I built it and it actually worked very well, even if I do say so myself. However, I did not paint it, just left it painted in primer, and said he could do the rest. Well, what do you expect for nothing?

Geoff and Tony were attending high school at Mooroopna High. They caught the bus each day in front of the house. Their studies were going well, but the social side of their life was much better, (taking after their mother, I think). On the sport side of things, they were very, very good. They had been highly competitive at primary school. I remember talking to Joe Chant, the principle of Harston Primary School, where the boys had attended earlier. He said that he had to play the boys in opposing teams.

If they were in the same team, that team could not be beaten, and that applied to any sport. But when playing in opposite teams, they almost destroyed each other. Mooroopna was quite a bit bigger, and there were more students with more talent.

After the first year, Geoff gave up competing against his brother and took up music. We bought him (or he bought, I'm not sure which), a Boozy & Hawk clarinet. He practised on this at every opportunity. He studied to read music, and play from a music sheet, and further to being able to compose a few pieces. In his third year, we went to a music concert at school put on by the students. Geoff and David Marven, (a friendship that would continue through school and to this day), were playing their clarinets. The music was very good, and the students played well. Then came an item on the agenda that really surprised us, for it was a version of *Green Sleeves* arranged by Geoffrey Barraclough who was also playing lead clarinet. We knew nothing about this piece of music he had written, and it blew us away. The performance was very, very good, and received a great round of applause when they finished.

Lyn's mum had a birthday. Some of her other daughters came up, and we had a birthday party for her in the park beside the Shepparton lake. It was a great day, and for this Geoffrey had arranged that he and David, along with their music teacher from school, would provide the music for the afternoon on their clarinets. Needless to say, there were a lot more than just our group listening to the very good performance.

Mum's birthday entertainment
The Teacher   Geoffrey   and David

Tony stayed with athletics and enjoyed all track and field. He told me at one time that he didn't know which event to concentrate on. I replied that he was very much like me, and that he would probably be well above average in all fields of athletics, but not excel in any one. He said, "Where does that leave me? I want to win." I told him that what he needed to do was to concentrate on the decathlon. He thought about this for a while, and said, "You're right, Bossman." (The boys nick-name for me).

Tony went on to win the High School Athletic Championships, competed in the Victorian High School Championships, and won the decathlon. He then went on to the Australian All Schools Championships in Tasmania and got himself a third place in the decathlon. They then invited him to go in a team to America to compete and attend the *Mt Sac Relays*. Tony later told me about the highlight of the trip. I was waiting for him to say he met this girl, but he didn't.

When they were at training one day, a guy came up to him and they started chatting, for quite some time, about athletics and training, etc. When they shook hands and parted, he realised he was saying goodbye to the great Carl Lewis. Tony said that was a day he would never forget.

At that stage he was competing at a high level in the decathlon events; running 100 metres in 10.8sec, high jumping to 1.98 metres, shot putting to 14.5 metres, pole vaulting to 4.20 metres, throwing the javelin 64 metres and the discus to 52.0 metres, running the 110 metre hurdles in 15.75sec, long jumping to 6.75 metres, running 400 metres in 50.5 sec, and 1500 metres in 5min 12 sec and achieving around 6000 points, all at the age of 15 years.

In January 1988, Marc notched up 18 years on the planet, and decided that he would like to vote in the next elections. But he had a problem, he was a Kiwi. So, I told him, "If you would like to become an Australian Citizen, so that you can vote, I'll do it with you." So, we did this, and it all happened at the Tatura Council Chambers. We could now both vote, but I kept my NZ. passport because I could be a dual citizen. This also made me a Kiwausse.

The Family Barraclough
Geoff, The Barra, Tony, Lyn, Marc

Chapter 10 - Bigger Challenges

Another update on HMS Victory is about due, but I'm afraid there is nothing much to report. I did a few little things and tidied up. I cut out the material for the decks and fitted them in. I built the main structure for the stern cabins and also started on the work around the upper bow.

In June 1989, we decided that we needed a little more income, so we dissolved the partnership, and I got a job while Marie & John stayed on *Tra-lee Park*. Lyn and I retained the AV Jennings house we had built on the sand hill. I found a job in Shepparton doing something, I'm not sure what, but I kept on looking. In early August, I found an advertisement for a Workshop Foreman with Bonlac Foods in their Metal Fabrication Department. After interviews, I started on the 27th August 1990. The Manager of Metal Fab was a chap by the name of Murray Parker. He knew me from our model boating days, back when Lyn & I were living in Geelong. We both used to go to Springwood Lake to run our boats at some races.

The job at Bonlac was good, and things were going along well. We were flat out building the feeding systems, and other little projects that Murray would come up with. Coming up to Christmas, I suggested to Murray that by using some scrap material from the feeding systems, we could make a few simple products, like hose holders for the garden, and we could sell these at the Bonlac stores around the state. He said we didn't have enough labour to do that sort of thing. I suggested I had three sons at home who would be doing nothing on a Saturday morning, and I would teach them. So it was that the boys were working and earning a bit of pocket money and learning everything from welding to spray painting.

Another day, Murray and I were talking about something, and he said that he had this vision of building rotary milking platforms as a service to shareholders, like the feeding systems. I said, "Well, why don't you do it?" His response was, "I would not know where to start." "You start at the beginning, and that is to have a drawing." I replied.

A couple of days later he called me into the office. I was shocked to see a full-size drafting board, with paper, and all the equipment needed. He asked if that was all I needed to design and draw a rotary milking platform, I said "Yes, that's all I need." He said, "Good! So you can start now?"

The project started a little slowly. I was having trouble designing the base of the platform and getting the correct angle for support wheels to be machined. I overcame all that, and by June I had completed three separate designs of platforms, one to milk 50 cows and for another 70 cows. The third one was a little different, being for 120 cows. This was for a very large herd that would be split into two and would enter the rotary on opposite sides, because a cow takes approximately 7 minutes to milk, and the platform would take about 14 minutes per cycle. All the platforms had speed controllers so the platforms could be sped up a little when the cows had less milk. They looked all right.

It was then that I dropped the bombshell on Murray that I would be leaving to go north to build a house, and I would head off about the end of August.

I called in to see Murray 18 months later to see how things were going. He had a big smile on his face when he told me they were up to number 20 in platform sales; I could not believe that there was such a demand.

Lyn told me all the time that it was too cold in Victoria and she wanted to go to Queensland. So, in mid-June 1990, we packed up the car and went to Queensland. I think we stayed with the Bibers (my boss in Gove). It was they who suggested that we have a look at Munruben Woods, a new housing estate south of them. The next day we had a look and bought a block that was 5000sqm. I told Lyn at the time that I would not mind building the house myself for that block. We talked a bit more about that, and by the time we got home, it was decided. I would go to night classes and do a Building Inspectors' Certificate course, which I did.

During the building inspectors' course, I met a young girl (by young I meant in her mid-twenties, to me that was young). Her name was Lisa Martin, and she was a trainee draftsperson. She was doing the course for more experience. I told her why I was doing the course. She thought that was great and asked if she could do the drawings for me at no cost. I said that would be terrific, but had not really thought about the design at this stage.

I told Lyn when I got home, and she thought that would be a good idea, too. So, we put our heads together and came up with something that was a little different. It was an enormous house by our standards, but we thought we would see what Lisa would do with it. I gave the sketches to Lisa the next day. She smiled. She liked what she saw. Over the next week or so Lisa came up with variations on the original, but we always seemed to go back to the beginning, and when we moved north, that is basically what we built.

The block had a natural roundabout through the gum trees, so we built the house behind this to make use of it. It all worked out well. Later, when the house was finished and garden and front lawn established, I took a photo and sent it down to Lisa so she could see that it happened.

Marc had his 21st birthday on the 12th January 1991. My Mum flew over from NZ, and Lyn's Mum came out from Shepparton. We invited a lot of people from everywhere. We decided that we needed a hangi to feed them all. When I do a hangi, I like to use banana leaves to seal the top before putting the dirt on, but being Victoria there are no bananas, so I had to find something else. Good old cabbage leaves came to the rescue. I thought that there might be an odour from them, but they were ok. It was a good day.

Marc's 21st birthday, with his two Grandmothers

I still enjoyed listening to music, something I did not do too much of when I was farming, mainly as there was not time, or I was too tired. I had bought a pair of good speakers. They were English *Kef*, and they made a big difference over the ones I had originally bought in Darwin, way back when. Now with a bit more time I would lie on the floor of an evening in front of the speakers and listen to all my LPs, (that I still have).

Early in 1991, I told Lyn that I would not mind going to see *The Phantom of the Opera*. It was playing at the Princess Theatre in Melbourne. We tossed this around for a week or so, and then decided we would do it and take the boys with us. So late one afternoon we headed for Melbourne and the show. And what a show! Anthony Warlow and Marina Prior were the two stars. I knew a little of the story, but this show was a whole lot more than I expected. It was one of those events that will always be in the memory banks. After the show, it was back in the car for the two-hour drive home, reliving the opera we had just seen.

On 14th August 1991, I left Victoria to go north and build a home. I had bought a Ford van, as I had thoughts of setting up a business selling and installing feeding systems in Queensland. As it turned out, it was handy to take all my tools, my tent, and everything I needed to build the house.

Back in June, before I left Tatura, Lisa had given me the final drawings of the house. It all looked good. I found a company in Brisbane, Solid Building, to do the detailed drawings for me, and David Shaw, a Civil Engineer, to do the soil testing. With all of this complete, I only needed the Building Permit before I could start. I went down to the Beaudesert Shire Council and got the permit for building and also the permit for the Bio-Cycle waste system for the house.

The only problem was that I was not permitted to live on site during construction. I was planning to pitch the tent up in the back corner of the property, and put up a 6m by 3m shed to store all my stuff and make a bathroom as well. I told my neighbour about my problem, and he said "That's easy, pitch the tent on my property and just go back and forth through the fence!" I thanked him and pitched the tent and got the shed.

I took a couple of days off while waiting for a guy with a Drott (small bulldozer) and went up to Noosa to see Brent and Lynette. They had come back from Rabaul and were now in Noosa with their own retail business. It was good to catch up, and when I mentioned the house project, he offered to give me a hand for $25.00 an hour. I took him up on the offer and said I would be in touch.

The guy with the Drott arrived and levelled the building site. He did a little landscaping as well. I had met another guy who lived in the estate and he was a bricklayer, very handy, so I also hired his services. I asked him if he could give me a hand to lay-out the building site. The plumber arrived, and the trenching was done, and the pipes laid. The concreter arrived early in the morning, a few days later, and by that evening I had a slab down, all 318sqm of it.

Marc was getting married at the beginning of November, so that was a break, with a trip down to Victoria. I left on a Friday night and just kept driving till I got to Tatura, where Lyn was renting a house. Marc and Monica were getting married at the Mitchelton Winery, near Nagambie. I had a bit of a run-in with her father, who had been drinking straight vodka for most of the reception. But enough said. A couple of days later I was off north again. Within two days, the framing arrived. I had found a company that was doing pre-fab house framing. I got them to do the walls and roof, and this saved a lot of time. I gave Brent a ring. He arrived, and we were into it.

The house was a boomerang shape, but through the centre of the house where the angled parts came together was a raised cathedral ceiling, supported by eight 300mm diameter columns. On top of the columns sat laminated Tasmanian oak beams, 300mm by 65mm. It was 9 metres from front to back, which meant that Brent and I had a lot of hard work as we had to lift each of the beams into place by hand.

After we supported everything, it was time to set the four end rafters in place on the beams, coming together against the ridge board, which also had to be lifted in by hand. We cheated a little by doing a layout on the slab floor, so that the rafters were all cut at the correct angle.

Under construction

Once we had the prefabbed roof trusses up and in place with the purlins, I called a guy I met in the early days when I had just started the job. He was a roofing contractor and said he could do the roof for me. He came out and started laying the Colorbond roofing. He did a good job. I say that because the roof never leaked. It was white, to reflect as much heat as possible.

I constructed the outside of the house in brick with plasterboard inside. It was a big house, with 4 bedrooms, a family room, rumpus room, kitchen, dining room, meals area, lounge, study, bar and wine storage, all coming to about 261m2 plus another 57m2 for the double garage and workshop. Under the cathedral ceiling was a raised timber floor. This meant bolting and gluing the joists onto the slab floor, then running the plane over them so they were flat. The tongue-and-groove hardwood was then fixed to them. After the floor was sanded and polished, it looked really good.

Brent had finished up, as we had finished most of the timberwork and I needed the bed for Lyn. I hired plastering contractors to do the plastering, and they did a good job as well. That left me with the painting. It took me one week, which was good going. When Lyn arrived just before Christmas of 1991, we had the house to lock-up stage.

Geoff came up with Lyn, as school was finished. Tony stayed down in Shepparton as he had a job, making a couple of bucks, although I think the real reason was an attraction to a girl.

Lyn had an eventful trip up to Queensland. She not only had Geoff with her, but a female friend of his who wanted a lift, together with Jess and Mrs Puss, and there was a trailer as well. Mrs Puss gave her some problems, even though Lyn gave her plenty of pills to knock her out. Jess just looked on and sort of said to herself, "What's all the fuss about". In the end, Mrs Puss went out to it. Jess just sort of said, "Can we get on with the trip now? I'm enjoying this." It took Mrs Puss a week to get back to normal.

Around the middle of January, Lyn said we needed to get jobs, as we were running out of money. I said I had a job, I was enjoying, and it was not quite finished. She said it was near enough, and I could finish it in my spare time.

Lyn also went out and got a job. She was lucky as the job was close to where we were living. She was picking mushrooms for a company called Queensland Mushrooms. It wasn't much of a job, but it was a bit more income. She wasn't there long before they offered her another job as a Training Officer. Her task was to train all the new pickers in the correct way to pick and pack the mushrooms. This job she enjoyed, as it was much more challenging. The company had a high turnover of pickers, and this meant she always had plenty of work.

Lyn applied for a job for me and arranged for the interview. I went for this, and got the job with Tool Supplies as a counter sales person, selling hand and power tools. I started my job in February 1992.

I was one of three guys selling tools, and after the Branch Manager resigned in June 1992, I got his job. It meant a lot more responsibility, but I now had the use of a ute with a canopy on the back (very handy). The company had a branch in Rocklea, in which I worked. The head office was at Zillmere, with another branch in Townsville. They had the Queensland agency for Stahlwille tools. These were German made and noted as being the recommended tools by aircraft manufacturers. I took notice of this, as quite a few of the customers were from the Air Force base out at Amberley.

I told one of these chaps that if they wanted a few tools, to get together and phone through an order and I would deliver them and save them a trip into town. My first trip out to Amberley was a bit of a learning curve, but it all worked well. Word got around of what was happening and the orders grew. I was making a trip out there every fortnight or so.

One time I was talking to the chaps, and I heard the roar of a jet engine, but it sounded different. I said, "What the heck is that?" It was an engine on the test bed, they said. "Would you like to have a look?" "You bet!" I replied. From the outside, all you could see was a big concrete pipe standing vertically on top of an elbow that came out of a concrete building. Inside the concrete building they introduced me to the chap who was conducting the tests. He showed me around and explained what it was all about. We went into another room and I could see a large jet engine ready for further testing. It was hanging from the roof on three load cells. These were to measure the output power from the engine at different throttle settings. Many cables were connected to the engine, and these ran back into the room where we were standing. I noticed that the fuel pipe feeding the engine was about 65mm in diameter. I asked if it was big enough and was told, "Just." I was looking at all of this through a glass window and was told it was 350mm thick, and the concrete walls were about the same thickness.

They handed me a pair of earmuffs and told me to put them on as the testing was about to start again. The engine on test was a Pratt and Whitney from an F111. I watched from a distance of about 5 metres and was in awe of this thing. The power was incredible; you could feel it, see it, and hear it. I asked how many rpms it would do and was told 13,500 at full throttle, but the auxiliary drive to the oil pump gearbox spun at 110,000 rpm.

The exhaust from the engine was pointing towards the big concrete elbow on the outside wall. Around the periphery was a mass of water sprays cooling the exhaust gas a little before it disappeared up the big concrete pipe. It reminded me of the Wairakei geothermal area in NZ.

The flame coming from the engine was white hot, and the cone was about 500 in diameter and about 1500 long, very impressive. The chap running the test said, "Feel this." He opened the throttle to full AB (after burning). The noise doubled instantly and you could see the thing straining on the load cells. The cone of flame out of the exhaust was now about 750mm in diameter and 3000mm long, more impressive!

I asked what would happen to the engine now the tests were complete? The chap told me that, once they analysed all the data, and if all was in order, it would be installed into an airframe. The other engine would have some hours on it already. The aircraft would then do a full test flight, putting the reconditioned engine through more testing. This testing usually took place off shore out in the Tasman Sea, where at the conclusion of the test the pilot would open the throttles and take the aircraft through the sound barrier, then beat the sound back to shore.

There was another time the chaps showed me the swing-wing of an F111. There was not a lot to see, as it was all fuel tank. One of the guys had to crawl inside it to check for leaks and stuff. The pivot pin and bush for the swing-wing set up was very interesting. The pin was about 150mm in diameter, and the fit between it and the bush was as loose as, I guess it was about 5mm. I asked about this and they gave me the logical answer. When the aircraft is at operating temperature, around -50 Deg C, everything is perfect. I had some very interesting trips out to Amberley, and enjoyed talking to the chaps out there about different aircraft and stuff.

I stuck it out at Tool Supplies until June 1993, when one of my customers told me they were looking for another worker at the place where he worked. I started with Lusty EMS. Graham Lusty used to build semi-trailers down in Swan Hill Victoria. This was until a certain politician said we are having 'the recession we had to have,' or words to that effect. That event sent Graham bankrupt. He left Victoria and came to Queensland and worked with his brother John, who was also in the trailer game but made different types of trailers.

Bob McDonald operated a business in Rocklea called Equipment and Machinery Sales, or EMS. John Lusty's factory was next door to EMS and Graham and Bob got talking and agreed that Graham could help by overhauling some equipment for Bob. It was then they started manufacturing equipment such as crusher and sizing screens for the mining and gravel industries. Graham and Bob decided to set up a partnership called *Lusty EMS*.

I came on the scene just after Graham had agreed to build a tyre-shredding machine for a Reiner Wensel. Crown Engineering did most of the major work and machining. Crown were into machining a lot of equipment and specialising in gear cutting. Ray Sutching, a good guy who I was later to work with a lot, owned Crown Engineering. I was doing mainly fitting work with a bit of welding thrown in.

We outgrew the workshop we had at the back of Bob's place, so we moved to another workshop over in Salisbury. Graham started building semi-trailers again, but this time concentrated on aluminium bodied tipper-trailers. This was all good, but not long after that he moved again to Rocklea. We had the site set up well with a machine shop, fab shop, and assembly area. We had a separate office block in the front, with enough room for Bob to move his office over and a chap who did some work for him drawing mining equipment.

In June 1994, I was machining some bearing housings for a crushing screen, working to sketches on a bit of paper. I was told there were no drawings. I had bought a computer drawing package very cheaply. It wasn't a good one but I made up some drawings of the bearing housings. They were not very good but gave them a bit more formality than a sketch on paper. I took the drawings to work and hung them up behind my workbench with all the sketches. To cut a long story short, the next day Robert Cheslin, the draftsman chap who worked for Bob, came up to me and asked about the drawings I had done. We talked for a while, then he asked if I would like to work for him in the drawing office. He said he would train me to use AutoCAD software. I said yes, I would, but asked him to let me think about it. I went to Graham and explained what had happened, and he said, "Go for it, if that is what you would like to do."

Which was why, in June 1994, I started with PROCAD as a Contract Draftsman. Here I was, going on fifty years old and learning AutoCAD. The work in which I was involved was detail drafting, using both 2D and 3D on various projects. It included layouts and detail of complete crushing plants, modular children's playgrounds in 3D and some work on the early tyre shredders. One job in particular was very interesting, and that was using a digitizing board to trace aerial photographs and convert them into an AutoCAD file. I could then change this to whatever was required. The photographs I was digitizing was a series of shots of the Brisbane River, from the mouth up to Ipswich, a length of 53 kilometres. I had to include all the wharfs and private jetties, and all the sandbars in the river. This job was for the Brisbane City Council, so they could better manage the river.

Years later, along came Google Maps.

Anthony and Geoffrey had their 21st Birthday on the 8th March 1994. We had the celebration at 8 Arlington Court. I dug a hole and made another hangi pit. The boys brought their girlfriends. Tony was living with a German girl, but it did not last too long. Geoff brought a girl he had met by the name of Michelle Oostenbroek. Everybody had a good time. The hangi was very successful once again.

Michelle and Geoff

Geoff and Michelle had been seeing each other for a while, and decided to move in together, hoping to save some money to buy a house. Later in 1994, on the 4th September, Michelle had her 21st Birthday. It was held at the house they were renting over in Belmont, a suburb of Brisbane. They also wanted a hangi out the back. That was ok. The backyard was very big. He obtained permission from the renting agent, as long as he filled the hole in after. It was a good hangi, and it fed a lot of people.

Our house was an ongoing project. The house itself was finished, but then came the gardens and landscaping. Out the back we had a lot of room. The house was positioned in the middle of the block, and the block was 5000 m2, which gave us a lot of room front and back. At the back, the ground sloped up behind the garage and workshop. A retaining wall fixed that. I put a garden above it, just to give Lyn something to do.

Behind the meal area, which was built on the raised timber floor, were timber-framed windows looking out to the back, so we had something to look at, I paved a big area that became an open courtyard. The retaining wall continued around the courtyard, to a set of steps that took you up onto another level.

This area looked a little vacant, so we installed a 27-foot-long fibre glass swimming pool to fill in the spot. Beside the pool, I put in a heated spa. I paved all around the spa and pool. This was a major job, as the pool was made up of curves, for strength I guess. Beyond the back of the pool was more garden, just as a backdrop to the pool, and then lawn to the back fence.

Down to the right, the rest of the block was left natural with native trees and shrubs. It was an area we later found great, as a lot of native birds, and reptiles used it as their home as well.

The back of the house from behind the pool

One day, I had a phone call at work from Lyn, saying she had a major problem in the form of a goanna that liked the swimming pool. She asked, "How do I get rid of it?" I said, "See if you can get the long handled pool leaf scoop under it and lift it out."

She went to try this, and the thing just flattened itself on the bottom of the pool. Anyhow, in the end, she managed to get the leaf scoop under it and lifted it out. When it hit the ground it took off, straight across the back lawn and up the fly-wire door of the laundry. At that point Lyn said, "Bugger you!" and went inside and waited for it to leave of its own accord, which it did.

There was a bit of lawn behind the other side of the house with more garden behind that. Out the front, I created a roundabout for vehicle traffic with the entry going straight to the garage, but also continuing around and back out to the front. We built a dry creek bed through the middle of the roundabout, covering the bottom with stones and a few rocks here and there.

There was no front fence, just more garden beside the driveway. We left most of the front as a natural garden with trees and shrubs. Lyn planted some ground cover and stuff to fill in a bit. Up nearer the house I put in a lawn with a low garden in front of the house, and a low hedge along each side of round timber slabs as stepping pads to the front porch.

As you stepped in through the two big timber doors, you were on the raised timber floor, with a brick wall in front of you. It went back at 45 degrees on both sides, and continued along the raised floor, so that in behind that wall was a large kitchen.

The kitchen

Further on from that was the meals area, looking out through the timber-framed windows to the paved area outside.

The dining-lounge area

Off to the left-hand side was the lounge with the dining room back from that, beside the meals area. Further to the left was the study and master bedroom, which had a big corner spa bath with a shower over. We liked this idea of the shower over a corner spa, and we used it in two more houses.

Off to the right-hand side was the rumpus room, with the family room behind it, and the bar and wine store in the far corner. Further to the right were three bedrooms, the bathroom and the laundry.

Having built a wine storage room at the back of the bar, I had to get some wine to put in it. First, I had to build some wine racks. I made these from some good Aussie hardwood and gave it an oiled finish. I had joined the Westpac Wine Club (later to become Cellarmasters) back in 1986 and bought some good wines but they were for drinking and not for storage, so I had to change what I ordered to some more wine that I could store. This was all good, but I found the storage was not cool enough, so I could not store the wine for as long as I had hoped.

It was a big house, by our standard anyway, and we enjoyed living in it.

The front of the house

Chapter 11 - Different Challenges

Another update on *HMS Victory*; I continued with finishing off the bow structure, then concentrated on the stern detail. Things were a bit easier now as I could leave the model on the bench with a cover over it. I would put it away after every time I worked on it. Radio control and power models were starting to take up my time.

Once I had a workshop, it was a bit easier to make stuff. I bought a lathe and drill press, so I could now make all the bits I needed to make the boats go faster.

I caught up with Rod Smith, who I worked with at NSK in Geelong. He had also moved up to the Brisbane area and was still playing with boats. He had set up a retail business selling model boat parts, which he imported from overseas. This, of course, gave me a better outlet for the tuned pipes that I was making.

The last boat I built had a 22c Zenoah engine in a boat that was a metre long. I incorporated a lot of new and innovative things with this boat. I was pleased with the results when it went through the time traps and clocked a speed of 74kph. I was happy with that and I don't think I ran it again. I was becoming very busy with work and having to go overseas and stuff. I just never seemed to have the time.

In February 1995, unbeknown to me, Reiner Wensel was talking with Graham, and mentioned that he was looking for somebody who could take on the job of managing the overall building and installation of the tyre shredders, and travel to install shredders overseas. Graham had said, "You need a good Project Manager, and the guy you want is over there." He was pointing to me. So, Reiner came and saw me the next day, and put it to me. I said, "My answer is yes, but let me confirm tomorrow after I talk to Lyn." I talked with Lyn and the next day accepted the offer from Reiner. It was a bit difficult, as Procad was doing all the drawing for Reiner, but of course I would now do it all. But that's the way it goes.

At Crown Engineering,
the shop foreman, Ray & myself.

I started with Link Pty Ltd in Feb 1995. I enjoyed the work with Reiner's Company, coordinating and planning the work around different manufacturers who were producing components for the shredders.

Crown Engineering carried out most of the heavy work, with a few smaller companies helping with conveyors and bagging towers when needed.

I haven't yet mentioned the third member of the Link team, Don Gough. I was the fourth, as Reiner and his Australian wife, Mary, were one and two. Don was different. He was not into a lot of things but was brilliant. He was about my age, lived by himself next to the Link office, and hardly ever went out. He was invited to be a member of MENSA. Io qualify for MENSA you need an IQ score of 132 or more. Don did all the hard work. If I needed some calculations done, Don was the man. He did all the electrical designs and drawings, as he had taught himself AutoCAD.

In June 1995, I turned 50. My little Lyn organised a bit of a get together with the kids and a few friends. I was a quite a low-key event celebrating something that I did not really want. However, she organised a balloon ride over Brisbane city. It was an early morning start, and after the trip it was back for a chicken and champagne breakfast. I did not know any of this, of course, and when the phone rang at 03.00 am, I was quite startled and even more so when the bloke at the other end asked to speak to Lyn. They had cancelled the flight because of unfavourable winds and would ring us in a few days when things were better.

We got the call a few days later and so at 04.30 in the morning we were off to West End in Brisbane. I took some photos of Nettie holding on to the balloon as it was being inflated and I thought to myself, "If that thing wanted to go, she couldn't stop it." I had visions of her hanging onto the thing and floating away into the distance. All of that rubbish didn't happen, and we soon got into the basket and were quietly drifting toward Brisbane.

Up, up and away!

I noted that before we left the ground, the operators sent up some black balloons so they could see the pattern of the winds up above. It intrigued me to see the balloon head off to the west as that was the breeze we were feeling, then the balloon would change direction and go another way. Then I realised that's how they went, in the direction they wanted, and it was simply a matter of changing altitude. We lifted off from West End and drifted up toward the city.

When we reached the river by Roma Street, we found a change in wind direction that took us along the river and over South Bank and on down the river a bit more. It was a great trip, just drifting along and watching all the cars running around like ants, except ants got somewhere, but the cars never seemed to get anywhere. We kept going, past the 'Gabba and came down for a very good landing in the Coorparoo Sports Ground. The support crew arrived, and they packed things up quickly. The passengers piled into a minivan and we were off for some bubbly and chook to finish up a good morning.

On 10th November 1995, Lyn turned 50. She didn't like it, but there was very little she could do about it. I decided that I would give her a bit of a surprise by taking her to Vanuatu for the weekend. As we both had jobs, we couldn't be away too long. I didn't tell her anything about it until the last minute. And I mean *last minute*. I mentioned that we were going out and would be staying overnight, so we would need a small overnight bag. I headed in towards Brisbane and took the airport turnoff. Now she was really confused. She said "Are we going to pick up Risè and Phil?" I said "Maybe."

I parked the car and went into the check-in area, saying we had time to look at the shops. She was engrossed with something in a shop, so I said I would just check up on the flights. I went up to the check-in counter and handed over the tickets and passports. The chap said, "Where is your wife?" I explained what was going on. He could see from the date in the passport that it was her birthday. I pointed her out, "That's her, there in that store." He said, "Good on you. Have a good time". I went back to Lyn and followed her around the store for a bit longer. Eventually I said, "We had better go and check on the plane. We will have to go through here to go downstairs." Of course, this brought us to emigration, where I handed over passports, etc. Now she was totally confused. As we were walking down to board the aircraft, she said, "There is no Risè, is there?" "I never said there was." I replied. She didn't say anything else until the plane was in the air, then she turned to me and said "Thank you." We had a great weekend.

Geoffrey and Michelle moved out of their flat and came to live with us. They wanted to save more money. They had set themselves a goal of owning their own home before they got married. This they achieved.

Geoff and Michelle married in the Wellington Point Church on the 2nd December 1995. Geoff had his old school mate David Marven as his best man and brother Marc as groomsman.

The morning was not pleasant. It was raining. I don't know why, but I was standing in front of the garage when a strange car pulled in. It was my sister Risè, and her daughter Angelia. They had decided at the last minute to come over from New Zealand and did not even have time to ring. The reception was held in Webstead House. It was a good day, and everything went off as planned.

One weekend in 1996, we went to a travel expo, trying to pick up a bargain, I did just that, but I did not tell Lyn the whole story. She was looking at something, I can't remember what, and I went to another stall and started asking a few questions. I liked the answers I got, so I explained that my wife was over there, and it would be a surprise, and could I ring them the next day and finalize it all? The next day I rang them and booked the whole thing. I told Lyn I had booked a six-night package holiday to the Solomon Islands for her birthday.

In November 1996, we headed off to the Solomon Islands, landed at Honiara Airport, or as it was then known, Henderson Field. We arrived at our motel and relaxed. The next day we walked to the markets. I hired a car, a little Mazda 2, and we drove down the island to some war museums and cemeteries. The Americans lost a lot of men and equipment in this battlefield of the war. We had a look at the town museum and purchased two carvings there.

Around mid-morning on the next day, I said that we needed to pack and go, as our flight left at midday. Lyn asked, "What do you mean?" "I couldn't say." I replied. At midday we were called to our aircraft, a twin-engined Islander, Lyn wasn't sure about this. We got on board with another couple and a single guy. Our pilot was a young girl, I mean in her mid-twenties.

Once in the air, we set a course for the bottom of Guadalcanal Island, landing on a grass runway. The terminal was a tin shed. We were asked to carry our bags to the end of the runway and onto the beach where we would be met. Sure enough a chap was there. He said everything was fine, our transport would be along very soon.

We waited for about 15 minutes, and along came a canoe with an outboard motor on it. This thing wasn't small because we all fitted in, together with all our baggage. Soon we were motoring along passing lots of islands, some small and some not so small. We finally arrived at our destination. The canoe ran up the beach and we all got out. We were on the Island of Tavanipupu. It was a five-star resort, with accommodation in native huts. The amenities were tops.

We spent three nights in this paradise. I did some snorkelling off the bottom of the island. The fish colours were amazing. You could swim out over the reef to deeper water, and then there was nothing, the bottom disappeared into the abyss. It was a great holiday, and a great birthday present for the little girl.

1996 was also time to move on from Munruben Woods. We thought we would go and live on the north side of the river, because it seemed to rain a bit more. We went north a few times and looked around for a house to buy. If we could not find one, we would design our own and have it built.

We found the suburb of Bellmere, west of Caboolture, and liked Riverside Circuit, but there was nothing to buy except a block of land that had a big slope down to the bank of a creek that fed the Caboolture River. We thought of ideas of how a house might fit on a block like this and came up with some rather good ideas, which still needed some work.

We bought the block, 45 Riverside Circuit, and went to find a builder. We chose Queensland Family Homes. They were working in the same estate. We showed him our ideas for a house. He liked them and told us he would look at the block, take some levels and see what he could come up with. Meanwhile, we put the house at Munruben on the market with a chap we knew, Peter Bocock. He was another person from across the ditch. The house sold much quicker than what we thought it would, so we were out on the renting market. We found a house on a corner in Grey Gums Court, at Regent's Park. Meanwhile, Chris Taylor, the guy who owed Queensland Family Homes, had some ideas he wanted to run past us, so we arranged a meeting. We liked the ideas, but suggested a couple of other things that made it a little different to other homes.

What we would build was a garage on a slab. It also had a good workshop on the right-hand side. The entry was to the left of the garage, and beyond that was a family room and two bedrooms with a bathroom between. From the entry you went 1200mm down steps, through a glassed walkway, to another level with a timbered floor. To the left was the laundry, behind sliding doors, and opposite that the TV room. Further on to the left was the galley kitchen with a long, island bench. This had cupboards at the back, along with the oven, hot water service and linen cupboard and drying cupboard. The kitchen was part of a big open area looking out into large trees down on the river bank. This open area was the dining and lounge. The master bedroom entrance was beyond the kitchen. It was all timber floored, with a scissor truss ceiling above and a deck all the way around its perimeter.

Front of the house

The lower section of the house was built on stilts, because of the slope of the block, but this became a further advantage when we got Chris to flatten the area under this part on the house. It gave us 90-square metres of entertainment area, which we later had concreted then tape and tiled.

From the side

Chris made a start on the house, and all was going well. Lyn and I decided that we needed to be a little closer to the action, so we rented another house, up at Hillcrest Gardens, west of Morayfield.

Chris was getting close to finishing the house when he went bankrupt. This was not good. I approached him and offered to pay for all material required to finish the house if he supplied the labour. He agreed to this, and we got the house finished, and passed the final building certificate.

We decided that we needed a pool, but space was very limited. I approached a pool company. They came out and looked at the site, and between us we decided that we could fit in a kidney-shaped pool. After an excavator had been in to dig it out, away they went. We also thought the back wall would be dirt, and that wouldn't be good.

We got a guy to come and build a fake boulder wall around that side of the pool. It incorporated a waterfall using the return water from the filter, which spilled over from a little pond and into the pool. Opposite the wall, the pool was at the edge of the entertainment area. It all worked well.

Rock work by the pool

One weekend morning, not long after moving in, we woke early to a very loud roaring sound. It seemed to come from down towards the river. I got out of bed, pulled on some pants and went out onto the deck, to be greeted by a very large, and very low, hot-air balloon. The roaring was from the gas burners. All the passengers in it started waving, so I returned the gesture and called Lyn. There were two balloons. They were coming from south of the river and were still trying to gain altitude. For a while, they were a common thing at the weekends.

Lyn decided that she would get a job in Caboolture, as it was not workable to travel across to the other side of Brisbane to Queensland Mushrooms. She was lucky enough to get a job in the new shopping centre that was about to open in Morayfield. Her job was with Katie's, as a salesperson. She did this for just over a year until another shop in the centre, Chap's Menswear, poached her. They made her two IC. This was a good move. She liked this position and enjoyed working in menswear. I started getting some new clothes. She brought home a great sports coat. It was as comfortable as. It was made of wool and sported leather patches on the elbows. This jacket was very handy, and I wore it on all my trips overseas. Another jacket came my way because she couldn't resist it. The price had been heavily discounted and I think she got a staff discount as well. It was manufactured from Alpaca wool and silk. The jacket was black and gold, although it was very subtle, and was a colour that could be worn with anything. It was very light, but also very warm in winter. It was also a great jacket, and I still enjoy wearing it as often as I can.

Some time later, Butterfly Silver poached Lyn from Chaps to work part time. She liked the idea of part time, so away she went. She stayed with Butterfly Silver for about 18 months, which got her to retirement age. Then she found she could not even get a part pension, as I was earning too much.

Lyn's E180

In November 1997, we purchased our first Mercedes Benz. We traded in the Mitsubishi Lancer that we had since new for a 1995 model 180E Mercedes. It wasn't a world beater in performance, but Lyn loved it and felt very comfortable in it.

My first flight for Link was to the USA in May 1998. A shredder we had sold to Gilkie Enterprises, a company in Corcoran south of Fresno, was having problems, and from the description of the fault it required the removal of one of the bearing housings. After going through all the drawings (PROCAD had done these), I found that Robert had made allowance for thermal linear expansion of the rotor, but it was being taken in the wrong place. This meant we had to remove the housing and modify it.

I flew to Sydney, then to Los Angeles, and changed planes there to get to Fresno, where I was met and driven to Corcoran. I completed the necessary work, entailing removal of the bearing housing, having the local machine shop machine the bearing diameter a couple of thousands of an inch bigger, then reassembling it all and testing it, after which the machine was running as it should.

I enjoyed the company of Gilkie's staff. The boss, Mathew Gilkie, and his family were very kind and hospitable people. After I had completed the work on the shredder and it was back in production once again, Mathew's brother came up to me and said that they would like to show their appreciation for the work I had done. He invited me to dinner, along with the maintenance foreman from the workshop. We went into Fresno to a restaurant Mathew went to quite often. The chef had worked for Richard Nixon at the White House until there was a change in leadership. The first thing to do was get a good bottle of wine, so it was off down to the cellar to choose our own.

This was some cellar, complete with cobwebs, dust and the lot. I was amazed at the selection of Australian wine that was there. However, our host selected a wine that he said was appropriate, and I certainly did not argue. Sitting at the table, having this nice (sorry, a bloke cannot use that word), this top class wine, my host asked if I had ever had escargot. I said no. I had not, but I would try anything. Therefore, I had one of the best entrees ever, and a very good thick fillet steak followed that. It was a night that I would not forget.

Another time, Mathew invited me back to his place for dinner. I met his wife, a very charming lady who apparently used to read the news for the local TV channel. Mathew suggested we go to the saloon while waiting the call for dinner. Saloon was the correct word, as the entry was through a pair of swinging, half-height doors. The room was set up as an out west, frontier bar from back in the 1800s. Behind the bar was a model train sitting on its tracks. It was one of those engines with the big fat funnel and was also from the 1800s. After admiring the model for a while, Mathew said it was time to go and select some wine to drink now and some for dinner. We moved to the back of the saloon and went through a door, and before me was a cellar such as I had never seen. It must have had around thirty dozen bottles of wine, from all over the world, with another section for ports and another for liqueurs. The next thing I see is the train coming out through another set of swing doors covering a hole in the wall. It came to a stop in the middle of the cellar.

Mathew indicated that I should choose a wine to drink before dinner. Having done that, we placed the wine on one of the carriages. Mathew did the same, but selected three for four. We loaded all onto the train, which slowly started moving off to disappear through another pair of doors covering a different hole in the wall. We went back to the bar, and there was the train, parked behind the bar once again, waiting for us to relieve it of its load. It was a great night and will also be remembered.

They drove me back to Fresno the next day, and I caught a plane to San Francisco then on to Louisville in Kentucky. Reiner was there at a Tyre and Rubber expo, displaying the products we were manufacturing.

There was another exhibiter at this expo and he was also selling tyre shredders, but this guy was from China. The product that he was selling was almost identical in the way it processed the tyre to our shredders. Reiner was not happy about it, and went over to this chap and shirt-fronted him. Reiner was a good-sized bloke, and I guess this intimidated the little Chinaman. Reiner told him that his product was in violation of a world patent that he owned. Reiner then suggested that the Chinaman should not be selling his products at that expo and if he saw him there tomorrow Reiner would get the law on to him. Tomorrow came, and no Chinaman, so that was good

The exhibition lasted two more days, and on the last night in town we went out to a nightclub. Mathew and another chap had come over from Corcoran, and we all went together. The name of this, I recall, was "PJ's." What this meant. I have no idea, but the girls looked very good, and they were not in pyjamas.

Reiner was staying on in Louisville to tie up some loose ends or something, so I returned home by myself, via Chicago, San Francisco, Sydney, and on to Brisbane. I remember the trip from Chicago to San Francisco was my first flight on a Boeing 777, and I was very impressed. Back to Brisbane and back to tyre recycling.

I made another trip to the US. This time it was to San Francisco, to do some work on a shredder that Reiner had sold some time before. This machine needed some upgrading, and the delivery system needed sorting out. It would take about a month to get everything the way it should have been.The trip had a bit of urgency, and Reiner could not get any cattle class tickets with United, so he booked Business Class with JAL. In addition, I was leaving in four days.

The trip was via Narita airport in Japan, stay over-night, then fly out to the USA the next evening. I got to the airport hotel and booked in, then looked around a bit, and talked to a travel desk about what to do the next morning. I was told that Narita township was within walking distance and had lovely botanical gardens that were worth a look. Next morning, I checked out and left my case with the reception desk, and away I went, following a map they had given me. I had a good look around, bought some lunch, and started heading back to the airport about 14.00 hours. I checked my baggage in, and was on my way to San Francisco to arrive about 07.00.

I stayed a hotel in the city and drove out to the plant in Alameda each day. They still drive on the wrong side of the road over there, and that can be a bit of fun. My accommodation was a hotel and downstairs was a very good Japanese restaurant. I managed to get through every main dish on the menu, and some for a second take, in the time I was there.

One weekend, I went for a drive out through Stockton and into the Sierra Nevada Ranges and wound up in Yosemite National Park. I had a good look around, then back to town. Another weekend, it was down to Fresno, and from there it was up into the Sequoia National Park, and Kings Canyon National Park. What a great drive that was. It would have been a lot better if Lyn could have been there with me.

Another weekend, I went down the coast to Monterey, stopping along the highway for a breakfast of pancakes and fresh strawberries. After arriving at Monterey, I drove around looking at the sites and then took a walk out along the Coast Guard Pier. From there it was off down the coast a little further to Pebble Beach, home of the famous Concours d'Elegance. It was now time to head back to San Francisco, but I went through San Jose for a change of scenery.

I got myself another bladder infection about ten days before going home. Larry Barnblat, Reiner's agent in the US, got a prescription from his doctor for some medication so I could get some relief. It took the edge off the problem, but would never fix it up. I hung out until it was time to go home, and while talking to Lyn one night asked her to make an appointment with our doctor, Jim Devane, another fella from across the ditch.

The flight home was the only one I ever took without having a drink of alcohol. I had water instead. It was also the only trip responsible for me losing a birthday. I left the US on the 10th June and arrived home on the 12th June. My birthday was on the 11th. Bugger!

Next day, I went off to the doctor. He explained that the bladder has a very low blood flow and therefore a short two-week burst of antibiotics never gets rid of the infection. He recommended that I go onto a lower dose for about three months, and that should fix it. It did, and I was a happy camper once again.

Tyre shredders work by tearing the rubber from the steel beading of the tyre. The beading is that part of the tyre that seals it against the steel rim of the wheel. The bead has a lot of high tensile steel wire running around its circumference. It is much easier to shred the tyre with the bead removed.

SH 1500 and in-feed conveyor.

The blocks that did the tearing were cast in white iron, chilled and then ground to size. The shaft that held the blocks rotated at 320rpm and was 500mm in diameter and driven by a 250kw motor.

The tyres were fed down from the top of the machine and into the feed chute, which controlled the feed of the tyre into the rotor. The product that came out was about 25mm square and was mixed with bits of the steel beading. The rubber came out of the bottom of the machine on a vibrating table.

Mounted over this was a belt magnet that removed all the loose steel and sent it to the waste bin. The rubber was conveyed to a fibre separating table, which removed most of the fibre that came out of the shredder. The product then went to a rotary screen that sized the rubber and sent it into bulk storage bags.

Reiner was working on selling a shredder to a company in Spain, which would be a complete plant. I was working full time on the design and drawings for it. Reiner sold the plant, and so it was manufactured. They shipped the duly completed plant off to Spain. Lyn and I thought about the upcoming trip and thought we might have a holiday at the end of the job.

I put this to Reiner, and he was in agreement, saying "Go for it!" Lyn booked some time-share for a two-week stay at La Manga, on the Mediterranean coast.

Early in January, son Tony had joined the company to help us with some testing work, and was packing gear for Spain.

On 9th Feb 1999, Don and I headed for Madrid. We got to Murcia, where the plant was being installed. The installation was going well, everything was falling into place, as it had on the test assembly back in Brisbane. Don and I were into the Spanish way of working and actually enjoyed it, but we both admitted that we didn't seem to get much done in a day.

The routine was to arrive at work at nine, coffee at ten to eleven, lunch was down to the pub, a few drinks with a hot lunch, back to work at two, knock off at five; a very full on day.

SH 3000 discharge end

Don and I were talking over a coffee one day and I mentioned that the shredder needed a redesign, keeping the same principle but improving the feed system and the discharge, making the unit more compact. The fibre-separating table could be two storey, with another table on top of the current one, which would allow a second pass of the material after the granulation process. While I had his ear, I kept going and suggested that four granulators could be mounted vertically on a table with a 250kw motor mounted underneath, driving the granulators with timing belts. He liked that idea and said that we should talk it all over with Reiner when we got home. I knew Don would think further on the ideas, and when we got home, there would be other design changes as well.

Tony turned up in Murcia a couple of weeks later, having driven to Spain from Germany, where Reiner had organised to borrow his father's car. Tony had picked up the car and driven to Spain. Now we had some wheels. When he arrived, he commented on our accommodation, calling it the "No Pulse Place". He was correct to a point, but that was OK.

We got the installation done; well nearly done. It was time for my holiday. Don and Tony did the finishing touches. Tony was to stay on for a couple of months to help with the training of staff and operation of the plant.

Lyn arrived after travelling from Australia on her own. We then went over to La Manga and found our accommodation. On our first night, Lyn had some extreme stomach pains, and as our room did not have a telephone, I had to go to a public phone. I was trying to get a doctor or an ambulance, but I did not speak Spanish. After trying everything, including the resort manager and the timeshare people, I still had no joy. I went back to our room to find she was a little better. We managed to get through the night.

Next day, she felt much better, and we thought we would walk down the road to Porto De Tomas. It was about five km away. There was a marina that had some beautiful boats tied up. We walked up and down looking at them all. It was time for lunch, so we went to a restaurant that served the best spaghetti I had ever had, with a great bottle of red. What could be better? Then came the walk home, but we made it.

We spent the first week of our holiday right at the northern end of La Manga, and moved into town for the second week. We took some public transport into Murcia and hired a car so we could look around the place.

Reiner and Don came over for lunch one day. They were heading back to Australia the next day and leaving Tony behind. Next day we went down to Cartagena for a drive and found an old seaport the Spanish Armada had used way back when. It was great to look around this place.

One night, we locked ourselves out of our third-floor accommodation; well I did. We went out onto the balcony to have some drinks, and I shut the door behind me without checking the lock. It worked. We could not get back in.

After much cursing, I managed to lift the door off the latch and get it open. Soon, we were on our way home. Tony stayed on and met a girl through the guys who owned the recycle business. Her name was Beatriz Rodrigues. Not long after Tony got back to Australia, Beatriz arrived. They both got a flat, and that was that. Within a short time, Beatriz got a job, which is not that difficult if you are an Electrical Engineer.

Things kept going the same. Reiner had an enquiry for a shredder with double the car tyre capacity and the ability to handle truck tyres. The truck tyres were a different story again, as the rubber was much harder and the profile of the tyre much thicker. Another challenge.

Reiner, Don and I talked for a while about the concept of building a machine with an output per hour of 1500kg by doubling the rotor width and fitting two drive motors. It was to be designated the SH 3000. So, I got into it, and things started working out very well. The new machine had two variable speed drive motors on the feed system. Don sorted out the electrics.

For the discharge, I designed a primary screening system on the discharge-vibrating table to give three different size products from the shredder. (I put this concept into the SH 1500 later on) Two 250kw motors, one on each side of the machine, handled the drive, each driving a 1200mm diameter pulley on the rotor, with the pulleys also being the flywheels. (This was the same as the SH3000 but two times over).

Crown Engineering built the first SH3000. We assembled it in a spare shed behind their workshop. It all went together very well, We had learned many little tricks along the way and this made things a lot easier. We assembled the whole machine before the first test run. We had this great big machine that stood 3.5m high, 2.0m wide and 8.0m long, including the feed conveyor and discharge screen and conveyor, all painted a (can't say nice, cause I'm a bloke) light green, and it was now just waiting for someone to push the button.

Along came Reiner and Ray, and a lot of guys from the workshop who'd had an input into the final product. Reiner had the privilege of pushing the button, and it started with this deep lowdown hum, getting louder as it gained rpm. The soft start phase finished, and the electrics switched into full power. All we could hear was a sweet hum from this great green monster. Everyone clapped and three cheers went up for everybody involved. It was a good feeling.

Reiner then started each of the other drives until all were running. I thought the only thing missing is tyres. Reiner fixed that. He went to the boot of his car and pulled out a couple of car tyres and threw them onto the input conveyor.

We all watched as they progressed up the conveyor until the first one tipped into the feed hopper. A few seconds later came this loud rattling sound as the tyre was being torn apart. Again, we all watched as the pieces of rubber came along the discharge conveyor. After the magnet conveyor that removed most of the steel, the product started across the primary screen where a percentage dropped through. It all continued until there was no product, only piles of steel and rubber, with some fibre hanging off them, and this was set out in three little pyramids.

I had not noticed Reiner go over to the wall behind his car and roll a truck tyre over to the input conveyor. He looked in my direction, caught my eye, and said in a very loud voice, "Shall I?" I replied, "You are the boss." With that, he let the tyre fall onto the feed conveyor and it started progressing to the top. Don had hold of the temporary control panel, and hit the speed controller for the feed system, slowing it down to a minimum rate. He said, "I can always go up." This very loud rattling sound started again, but a whole lot louder, as our brand-new shredder devoured the great big truck tyre.

The product started coming out on the conveyor, but in a much greater volume than before. It all continued along the conveyor until there was none. I breathed a great big sigh of relief and just stared at the product on the floor. I bent down and picked some of it up and looked at it closely. It was as it should have been. A hand tapped me on the shoulder. I stood up, and it was Reiner with his hand out. I took his hand in mine, as he said, "Well done. That is a great effort". Behind Reiner was Ray Sutching, the owner of Crown Engineering, and he said, "It is a pleasure and a privilege to work with you, and to be involved in the products you design." I was pretty chuffed with what he had said, and it has stayed with me ever since.

Those were the sort of words that make someone go on to do more. And that is what I did. I would wake up in the early hours of the morning having the solution to a problem with the design I was working on. I learned that if I then wrote it down, or even drew the idea, I could go back to sleep thinking of something else. (By that I mean another design problem I had.).

The one design that would take up most of my time was the GR 400. It was a granulating machine using product from the fibre separator, and intended to reduce the product to a size of #30 grit, which is almost a powder; something between sugar and caster sugar. I was using the design that had been in my head from the meeting I'd had with Don in Spain. This was a machine that had four granulators on a heavy table, standing vertical, all driven by a single 250kw motor, mounted under the table, and driving each granulator through timing belts. The granulator feed was in the top of each machine and used gravity to do the feeding, with the blades spinning at 310 rpm. The product was discharged from the bottom of the machine and into a tube conveyor. This product, although very fine, also more fibre with it, and so was delivered to another fibre separating machine before going to the bagging tower, where it would be graded and delivered to the appropriate bulk bag.

The problem I had, discovered by Tony in some testing he had been doing, was that the temperature generated during the reduction of the rubber was extreme and the drive shaft of the granulator suffered from linear thermal expansion. It was enough to make the blades of the machine touch each other.

Water cooling of the spindle seemed to be the cost-effective answer to the problem. I changed the drawings to include the water-cooling system, and while I was about it, redrew the body of the granulator itself to water cooling. I then thought if I made the base of the machine in cast aluminium, the waterways could be cast in and I could do it the way I wanted it, instead of being dictated to by machining constraints.

So it was off to see a guy who used to live up the street from us. His name was Brian Foyster, and he was a pattern maker, just the bloke to tell me if I could or could not do what I wanted. Brian said all was good, but he would make the pattern a little different to the design I had. It would be a little dearer for the pattern, but the casting cost would be much less.

I went back to the office and saw Reiner. He liked the idea, but said to hold off a bit as he didn't have any positive sales right now, but when we did, that is the way we should go. I modified all the drawings to the cast base, put the granulator aside and started on something that I had been playing with before the granulator. They put Tony off at this stage, as there were no sales on the books and therefore not a lot for him to do.

My next job was the PS6000 Primary Shredder. This piece of machinery was intended to take truck tyres that have had the bead wire removed. Its operation would consist of two heavy shafts rotating in opposite directions, with big white iron blades mounted on them. Staggered around the shaft in a helical pattern, when it rotated they gave a feed along the shaft. With the tyre being fed in between the two shafts, the action of the blades would cut the tyre into pieces about 150mm square, and carry them to the non-drive end and the discharge. The pieces would then be conveyed to a bagging station, or directly onto the main shredder input conveyor.

The first part of the design was a gearbox that would take 62kw of power at 960rpm and deliver it to two parallel counter-rotating output shafts revolving at 6rpm. I also designed a pressurised lubricating system into it, running off a separate lube pump, accessible from the outside of the box, that supplied all the bearings and gears. It was a big gearbox, and it was a big challenge. It all came together, but I must admit I went out to Crown Engineering to talk to the guys about the gears required.

Crown machined replacement gearing for a lot of mining equipment and also rebuilt large gearboxes. I did not know a lot about gears and calculating the pitch circles, etc. I knew about involute curves and things, but that was all. So, when I had the final design of the gearbox fitted in the shredder, I took it around to Crown for the approval of the box design in the operating position.

The only thing they said, and with a lot of enthusiasm, was "When can we start?" I said, "Not yet. Reiner has to sell one first."

Chapter 12 - The Biggest Challenges.

Another update on *HMS Victory*. With the bow and stern finished, apart from the painting detail, it was time to start the planking on the decks. This was a time-consuming task, but I got there. After that, it was time to finish the gun ports, install the chain-plates, make up the walkways around the coamings, install the fire bucket rack and finish the belfry. In other words, do all the little things that needed doing. I was working towards having most things completed by the end of 2005 so it would be ready for the masts.

Victory ready for masts.

Marc had a birthday on the 12th January 2000. Our son had reached the age of 30 years. Makes one feel ancient, doesn't it? To celebrate the event, we had a party. We used the entertainment area under the house. Tony was into a bit of artwork, so I commissioned him to paint a mural on the wall around the pool pump and filter enclosure.

Wisteria flower decorations   The pool came in very handy

He painted hanging wisteria flowers, which looked very good. It was a work I still have not paid for. Marc's girlfriend, Samantha Drury, came along, together with a lot of his friends from the city. A few wound up in the pool, which was great. Lyn had made him a birthday cake, and as usual, it was very good. So nothing remained.

Time was moving along. It was coming up to Lyn's 55th birthday in early November. What was I going to do this time? After much pondering, I rang my sister Risè in Auckland, and asked if she had a spare bed for us for the Friday night. The plan was to fly her out of the country and go out to dinner in Auckland, then come home again the next morning. However, the flights did not work that way and I could not get a return flight until the Monday. That is the way it was. I did not tell her until the last minute that we were going anywhere, let alone where to, or for how long.

On 15th December 2000, we started moving into our new home. We had purchased a block just down the road from where we were living at number forty five. The new house was at 31 Riverside Circuit. It was in the last stage of the development, which was the best stage. We'd had our eye on a block up on top of a rise in the road. I went to the Sales Office to put a deposit on the block we wanted, only to find someone had already purchased it. Therefore, we bought the one next door, and actually it was a better block. It gave us a longer back boundary fence, beyond which was the Caboolture River. Now started the job of designing another home. We had already been talking about the next one for quite some time, and a had done a lot of the basic design work. We had to find a builder, so we went over to Bribie Island. The Pacific Harbour development was happening there. We were looking at some display homes (always looking for ideas), when this guy came up and started talking about building a house,

His name was John Tasker. He was the salesman for Mike Ingamells, the builder. We talked for a while, and we said that our block was over in Bellmere. He said, "That's OK." He would come and have a look, so we arranged a time. John Tasker came and saw the block and the slope it had. We explained the ideas we had for the house and how it would fit on the block. He took all of this away and told us he would be in touch. A couple of weeks later, he rang up and said he had something for us to look at, and could we come over to Bribie to see him? We did this, and he showed us a preliminary drawing of our new home. It looked all right. He had been back to the block and taken some measurements of heights and the slope across the block.

What he was able to do was to put all three-floor levels under a simple roof, thus giving one common gutter height all around the house. This meant that in the master bedroom we had eleven-foot ceilings, with the upstairs home theatre and office creating a mezzanine above the lounge room. It also meant that the two main living areas would be on slabs, and this we liked.

As you came in the front door, you would face two sets of stairs. The stairs on the right-hand side would go down to the living areas and master bedroom. At the bottom of the stairs, on the left-hand side, would be the cellar. It was under the stairs but would go back a further metre. The stairs on the left would go up to the theatre and office. Further to left on the same level as the entrance would be two bedrooms and a bathroom, with a toilet at the end of a short hallway.

Lyn and I suggested some other changes, more in keeping with our original sketches. This was all agreed to, and John said he would go and work out a price and come back to us before going to the drafting stage. All of this took place around June 2000. This meant we now had to sell our home at number forty five.

We gave it a bit of a spruce up and put it on the market. The agent came around to have a look at the property and to give us a valuation. After looking around, she told me she had no idea of what value to put on the house, because the property was so different. So I told her at what figure she would list the property, and not a penny less, as they say. That was the amount that we would receive, with no bartering involved.

John Tasker came back to us with a price for building the house at number thirty one. We thought it reasonable, and so the process started. We sold number forty five without too much of a problem, (I underpriced the house again, but that's all right because I'm only a Bloke). Once again, we were having to rent. We found a house not far away, in Bishop Lane, and this is where we stayed until we could move in.

The landscaping, would be a major task because of the slope on the block, the areas we wanted blocked up for a flattish area and those that we would leave as they were. "If I were to give you a drawing showing the landscape design, would you be able to do that at the same time?" I asked John Tasker. His answer was yes, and that's the way it was. Well, pretty close to it. There was still a bit of shovel work, but that was OK.

With the basics already done we got stuck into the retaining walls both on the front and side, where the Japanese garden would go, and the steps from the front lawn down to the patio that would be off the dining room. There were more steps from the other side of the patio down to the back fence.

Lyn and I sort of had a deal. I would do all the landscaping and she would do all the plant design and layout, followed by the planting. It all came together well, although it would always be in the category of work in progress.

One Saturday morning, when the house was finished and the landscaping started, John Tasker came around and brought two guys with him. He introduced them as Peter Klesnil and Kerry Beggs. John told me he had brought them over from Bribie Island to look at our place. I said, "You look, and I'll make coffee." That was the start of a friendship with both of them that still continues today. Peter and his wife Draha, (short for something in the Czech language) come to Australia every year at the beginning of November, and stay until the beginning of May. Then they go back to their other home in Richmond, Hampshire, in the UK. Kerry and Marlane built their home on Bribie, out near the Pacific Harbour Golf & Country Club.

While Lyn was at work one Saturday morning, two guys and a woman came to the front door, and introduced themselves as judges for the HIA Housing Awards. They told me they had looked around the front of the house, etc. and liked what they saw. They asked who had landscaped the block? I replied, "Us and Company." They looked at me and said they had not heard of that company. I said, "No, it means that my wife and I did the landscaping." They commented that it was well done, then asked if they might look inside. I said "You are welcome." In they walked, but did not go any further. They stood in the entrance and looked.

They looked down to the living area, and the Italian leather lounge that was sitting on the polished parquetry floor,(it had just been delivered), then up to the theatre on the mezzanine above the dining and living area. To the left were the two bedrooms and a bathroom. To the right opened the door to the garage. Two of them went back outside again, and looked at the front of the house once more. They said, "How is all that in there? From the outside it looks like a single-story house." With that, they slowly walked through the house, stopping now and then to comment on something or to ask a question.

They went downstairs (1200mm), opened the door immediately to their left, and found a wine storage area underneath and behind the stairs that had a stud height of 3.3 metres, and said, "How is that?" Opposite the cellar they looked at the TV room with another 3.3 metre ceiling height and an outlook over a Japanese style garden with a peaceful trickling water feature. After they reached the living area, they looked to their right, into the master bedroom, also with a 3.3 metre ceiling height, and saw a queen bed above which was a 2 metre by 1 metre cut out in the wall, which allowed light and ventilation from a high sliding window in the outside wall beyond. Behind the wall was the walk-in robe and dressing room.

To the left was the ensuite, with a shower over the corner bath, and a full-mirrored wall behind and above the two washing bowls. The ensuite had a view out of the window to the Caboolture River below.

After walking all around the downstairs area and out onto the deck, they moved back up the stairs, turned and went up towards the home theatre. Having reached the top of the stairs, they found the office on the left, with overhead cupboards, and a room divider containing a display cabinet for *HMS Victory*.

On the other side of that was the theatre, with a pull-down screen and projector. I had a Denon receiver for full 5:1 surround sound, supplied by five Kef speakers, plus my two trusty C40 Kefs that I had purchased back in 1987 for $950.00. They were hooked up to the Technics system I had purchased when in Gove. The room divider unit also had a pullout shelf for my Technics turntable. It all worked very well.

When they had finished their tour, and were up at the front door again, the spokesperson asked, "Is it correct that Mike Ingamells built this house?" I said that it *was* correct. They then asked, "Who designed the house?" I said, "My wife and I drew the original concept design of the house and gave it to John Tasker. He made it work under the one gutter line." They just nodded their heads and said I would probably hear from them.

Around June or July 2001, we received an invitation in the mail to attend the HIA Housing Awards in Noosa, to be held the following month. We booked some accommodation, deciding to make it a long weekend. We had a table at the presentations with John Tasker, Mike Ingamells, and their wives, plus a few others I can't remember.

As the evening progressed, we all relaxed a bit and were beginning to enjoy it all. Then they announced, "The winner of the custom-built homes from $150,000 to $200,000, for the year 2001, is Mike Ingamells." As Mike was going up to collect the prize, they started showing a slide show. It was of our home.

The easiest way to describe what happened next is simply to say, "We all went nuts"!

When things settled down a little, Mike and John came up to Lyn and I and said, "Thank you for giving us your home to build, and if you ever plan on doing it again, contact us".

31 Riverside Circuit

The lounge

The dining area

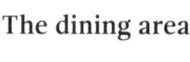

The back deck

This home was nick-named by Risè as "The Barra Resort."

On the 5th May 2001, Marc and Sam tied the knot. They held the wedding at "Hawkins Garden Nursery". It was a great day. They held their reception in a restaurant called "Dukes" owned by a bloke they knew. In fact, it was near to where they were flatting at the time. It was a great spot, and the afternoon went off well.

Michelle & Geoff, Lyn & I, Marc & Sam, Tony & Bea.

Towards the end of 2001, Reiner took another trip over to Europe to do some selling of products. We learned that he was seeing an old girlfriend. I could see the writing on the wall. Things would change within the company.

I went to see Graham Lusty to ask how things were going with him. We had a good long chat about things that were happening around the traps, and he mentioned that if push came to shove, he required a Compliance Manager to set up workplace health and safety in the company, and compliance to regulations for all the trailers they were producing. Reiner took another trip to Europe in January 2002, and on returning, told his wife, Mary, that he was going to Europe to live.

I started back with Lusty EMS in February 2002, as Compliance Manager. They gave me a Toyota ute as part of my salary package. I would use it as a company work ute during the day, but I had use of it to go home, and at weekends. I went back to school again to get my accreditation in Workplace Health and Safety, achieving this at the end March 2002.

Implementing workplace health and safety was a challenging thing to do when I was starting from scratch. I considered the best way to go about it, giving myself 6 months to have it completed. I bounced this off Graham, and he was happy, so I was into it. At the same time, I started gathering all the info I needed to ensure and confirm that all our products conformed to Australian Design Rules.

With this under control, I started standardising the drawing office. There was a young draftsman already working there by the name of Michael Coffey. I bounced a few ideas off Michael on what I wanted to do as regarded drawing standards and creating uniform designs for most of the components we manufactured. He threw in a few ideas that made a lot of sense. Michael was using drawing software from Autodesk called Inventor. It drew in solid 3D, a whole lot different to the program I had been using at Link, which was AutoCAD. It drew both 2D and 3D in lines. Therefore, I was off on the standardisation thing, and maintaining the other things I had to do.

Lyn and I had thought for a while that we would like to go over to Japan and have a look around. We could catch up with Ted and Noriko while we were at it. So, in October 2003, we booked it all and got ready. It would cost us, all up, $10,000 for 10 days.

I had been to Narita Airport before, on one of my trips to the US with Link. (That trip had been for a rush job and Reiner could not get any economy tickets, so he booked business class to Tokyo, a night's stopover, and the next evening to San Francisco.) The Japanese built that airport for the 1964 Olympic Games. Ted was there to meet us and helped us out to the train that would take us to town. Ted and Noriko lived to the north of the city, in Saitama.

My friend Tatsuo (Ted)

We had a good look in and around the city centre. The gardens were all manicured and all the paths were constantly being swept and cleaned. The people were very friendly, and it amazed us to see bicycles standing in the parking racks with the basket on the back full of shopping. They were just left there until the owners returned. Imagine trying to do that back home! We caught up with Ted and Noriko and went out for dinner. We brought each other up to date on our families, and what had happened over the last thirty years.

We boarded the Bullet Train and headed for Osaka. We spent a couple of days looking around. Has this country got temples? They are everywhere. So, when we were all templed out, it was back to Tokyo, catch up with Ted again, then a couple of sightseeing trips out into the country. Time was now running out. We headed out to Narita again, and I showed Lyn all around the city. It was very impressive. I had enjoyed it when I did it by myself, but this time we had a bit more time. The next day, we flew back to Australia.

Brendan

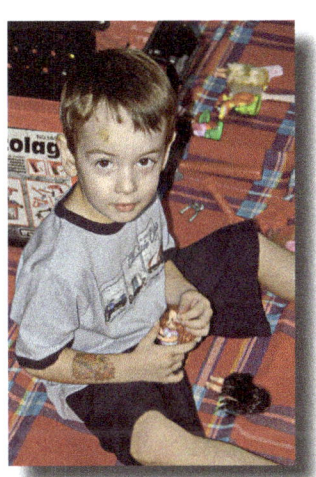

Our first Grandson arrived on the 11th July 2003, exactly 30 years to the day after my father had died in New Zealand. Brendan Stroud Barraclough was born to Geoffrey and Michelle, and all was well.

July 2003 came along, and some big changes were happening at work. Lusty EMS had been bought out by Maxitrans Australia. First, Graham asked me if I would like a change of title to Project Officer. This would mean taking on any projects that might come up to make things happen better and more efficiently. I said, "I would like that, and when is this going to happen?"

He replied, "Right now! Maxitrans have just bought a 7000 sq metre workshop and there is nothing in it. Your first job is to design, manufacture and install a production line for manufacturing standard aluminium bodied semi-trailers, and a production line for one-off special trailers. Maxitrans wanted to send up one of their engineers to do the job, but I told them I had the right person up here to do it and he will do it in 8 weeks, which is the date we move from here and go there."

I said, "Thank you very much, Graham".

When I look back, it was a massive job, but I got it done, and in the eight weeks. There was a complete spray-painting booth large enough to drive a truck and trailer through. The supplier delivered this. I had to design an overhead monorail system at both ends of the booth, and through it.

Then things settled down to a steady job. The production line for the one-off special trailers was fairly simple and only needed the overhead welder beams. These rotated around a central column, and carried the welder overhead to where it was required so that the leads were not on the floor. This was one of the biggest workplace health and safety issues, and so I was really doing it for myself. I designed these and had them manufactured by Graham's team back in the other workshop. I fitted three on the No 1 line, and one on the special line.

During the last few weeks of this project, I developed a hernia. I was walking around the workshop with my fingers down at my groin, pushing my stomach back in. I had that operated on when the job was finished.

I was then doing some desk based work, compiling the total inventory and the bills of material required from each trailer, and having these uploaded into the management system. This was called Manage 2K and was a system developed by Maxitrans. It worked very well.

On 16th Sept 2003, Marc and Sam move into their new home. They had been looking around for a long time, trying to find something that they could build and make some money. Half as a joke, we suggested that they he and Sam talk to the people who were selling in our estate, and see what they could get. They did and bought a block four doors up the road from us. Then it was finding a builder time, so we told them have a talk to John Tasker, which they did. It was a combination of Mike Ingamells having a bit of time between jobs and the house being smallish that let it all come together. They had the floors left as chipboard, and I sanded and applied the polyurethane. The block was very steep, but the house worked well on it, and it was only four doors up from us.

The 11th June 2005 was the start of a period that I will not forget. It started a long time ago when I said to my sons, "When I turn 60, we will all go and jump out of an aeroplane. It will be a voluntary thing, because the aeroplane will fly perfectly well. They call it Skydiving." Before the 11th, I reminded the boys that it was still on, and I had booked the day for a skydive, followed by breakfast for the participants, and it was on me. I knew that if the old man was paying, they would not pass it up. I did have a problem, however, in that the skydive people had a weight restriction of 100kg. I was the smallest of the four at 93kg, but the boys averaged 106kg. I explained to the skydiving company that it was a team thing, and it was all or nothing. They said OK.

So, on the morning of the 11th June at 10am, we all assembled at Suttons Beach, Redcliff, ready to throw our lives away. We checked in. I paid the money and we went to be kitted out in the gear we needed. Then we climbed into the bus and were on our way to the airport at Scarborough, where the plane was waiting. Many people would not have flown in this aircraft, as it had no door on the side, meaning we could all fall out. However, they assured me that this could not happen. They all accused me of trying to find a way of backing out. I said, "No way, I'm game if you are game, 'cause I'm a Bloke!" We all piled into the plane and were ready to go when I realised that I was the last one in, which really meant that I was to be the first one out. But that's all right, 'cause I'm a Bloke.

I remember that while the plane was climbing it seemed to take forever. We had this great view of Redcliff, Scarborough, over to Beachmere, and further out to Caboolture. As we turned out to Bribie Island with Morton Island in the distance I was enjoying all of this, because I was trying not to think of what our altitude was.

The orange light came on. We shuffled closer to the door until we were half out of the bloody thing, with nothing to hang onto. I looked at the boys, and pumped my eyebrows up and down, as if to say, "This is it - the end. See you at the bottom, or wherever." The green light went on, and then nothing. The bloke who was hanging on to me pushed us both out of the bloody door. Like, what do you want to do that for? Then you hear the roar of wind, as you are dropping towards the planet at 130kms an hour. You realise that the only things that will stop you making a big hole in that thing is the bloke on your back, and that bit of rag above you.

(I'm writing a lot of rubbish, because I actually could not wait for it to happen. When it did, it was fantastic.)

To fall through the air and be able to move around as we did was great. The chap on my back, who was another Kiwi, did this over Queenstown in the off season. He was very good. He had a Go-Pro strapped to his wrist and was taking a video of the whole thing, so I had to at least look brave. As we were coming down, he said "John, we will do something different. Be ready to lift your legs as high as you can." With that, he turned and headed out to sea. I thought, "Here we go, you've got a nutter on your back, Barra! What are you going to do about that?" With that, he turned and headed back for the beach. I noticed in the distance that Marc was already on the ground. (That's what happens with weight and gravity.) We dropped low, heading for the beach across the flat water, getting lower and lower. Then my back man said, "Lift your legs, John, as high as you can!" I did, and we went lower. I'm not sure if my wet pants was from salt water or some other kind, (I joke). We were flying across the water, and then I saw the beach and a wall of sand in front of us. At the last nano-second, my back man pulled on the cords controlling the rag above us and we lifted up and over the sand ridge, to drop vertically down on the beach in a standing position. It was very well done, and I experienced such a great feeling while it was happening. The rest of the boys dropped in, and we all did a lot of backslapping and hugging. I think from relief! It was for me, because I had been responsible for taking the males out of four families for a bit of fun, on an old man's whim.

The Skydivers after the jump.

When things settled down, and the photos had been taken, I told the girls that we would see them back at 31 Riverside for lunch. With that, I rounded up the boys, and we headed off for breakfast-come-brunch at the local pub. I could still taste the adrenaline, so I had to have a few beers just to try to get rid of it, but it persisted all afternoon. Before we headed home, we put on the tee-shirts the Skydive people had given us, and they all fitted. They also gave us a video of the flight, and with the choice of music we wanted on it. The most appropriate I could think of at the time was *Staying Alive* by the Bee Gees.

The party at No. 31 did not need us, for it was in full swing by the time we all got there. The place was full of family and friends. It was great. My little girl had made this really fancy birthday cake for me. She is good, that girl. Then she gives me this great big photo album that covers my whole life. As I said, she is good. I guess that is why I still love her.

On the 22nd April 2005 Emmily Rose Barraclough arrived. She was to be the first and only granddaughter.

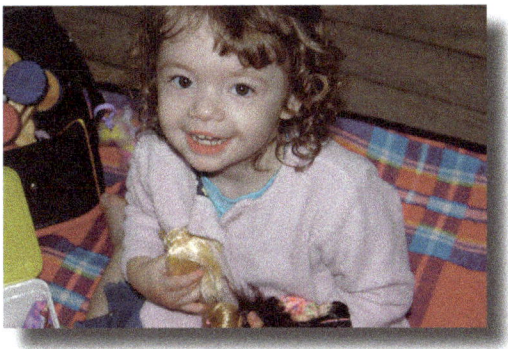

Emmily

Around September 2005, Marc and Sam had a birthday party for Lyn and I. My birthday had been, was gone and done, but the little girl's, (Lyn's) was still to come.

It was a surprise party. Everybody else knew about it but us; even my Mum who, at 87 years old, flew across from NZ and had a ball. There was the pretence that Tony and Beatriz were having a housewarming party down in the city, and we were to take Marc and Sam. That was all good. Unbeknown to us, a sneaky plan was in place. When we called to pick them up, they were not quite ready so of course we had to go inside to wait. All the lights were out until we were through the front door and onto the landing at the top of the stairs.

The lights went on and the whole of the dining and lounge area, down below, was full of people, all singing happy birthday.

What a surprise! My Mum was there. She had arrived two days before the party, and we did not know anything about it. John and Marie, our friends from the Gove days who had also had been our partners on the farm, were there along with Renè and Ursula Biber, my boss from Gove and our good friends ever since. In addition, there were the friends we had made in the street. Geoff and Tony topped it off. Geoff had shaved his beard off that morning. Then both boys went to Tony's hairdresser and got identical haircuts. For the party they wore tee-shirts that they had not had on since Gove, 25 years ago. Here were two guys, both over 100kg, in shirts they last wore when they were about 7 years old. As you can imagine, there were a few bulges out from very tight seams. It was a great night and certainly was a surprise.

The boys in their "T" shirts

To top it off, Marc and Sam gave us a night at a place called the Tamarind, a B&B up at Maleny beside the Obi Obi creek. On our night there, we went to the restaurant for a wonderful Thai dinner cooked by a chef who was a winner of the Jaguar Award. It was a wonderful night out. After a great sleep, our breakfast was delivered to our room in three trips, first came cereal and fruits, the second trip was bacon and eggs and to finish up, a big pile of pancakes.

Marc and Sam decided that they should do an extended trip overseas before settling down to parenthood. On the 31st October 2005, they headed off to south-eastern Europe. They had a good look around, then made their way up into Central Europe itself, to Germany, France and the UK. From there it was over to the US of A, landing in New York.

They explored that city, then moved on down to Cape Canaveral and did the big tour of the Kennedy Space Center. From there, it was across the country and up to Seattle. They visited the Boeing factory and other places. I am not sure if they went down and did San Francisco and Los Angeles, or if they went straight to South America. There they had a good look at Ecuador, Peru, and Chile. Finally they left Chile and headed for Auckland. From Auckland, it was down to Queenstown to do some para-gliding and a bit of hiking, then back up to Auckland to call on his Grandmother and Aunty Risè.

They met up with Cousin Martin and his wife Irini there, and of course a very young James. Then it was back to Australia, arriving on the 10th April 2006.

There was a big welcoming committee waiting for them at the Brisbane Airport. All of Sam's family had turned up to give them a big welcome home. When they got up to Riverside Circuit, there was another family who gave them the same sort of treatment.

Vic Hague lived with his wife, Mary, a few doors up the street from us when we were at No 31. Vic and Mary were from across the ditch, but had been in Australia a while. Vic had his own business as a painter and paperhanger, a trade he had learned in NZ. He was fortunate that his reputation was so good that he was never out of work, and therefore could choose what he worked on, and when. Mary was a good cook and had produced her own cookbook called "Mary's Muffins". It is 76 pages' worth of wonderful, and sometimes very different, muffins. She gave Lyn one of the books, and we have tried many of the recipes. Mary volunteered in the kitchen at Caboolture Meals on Wheels.

Vic was what you would call an endurance athlete. He and two other guys were the first ones to do the inaugural trip in sea kayaks down the west coast of the South Island of New Zealand and into Milford Sound from the seaward side. It made a lot of news back then, at home and overseas. I think people often do it nowadays.

Mary passed away from cancer in about 2004, and it hit Vic very hard. He sold the house and went to another suburb of Caboolture to live with his daughter for a short time, until he could sort things out.

He then decided he would take a trip to the UK, but Vic being Vic, he took his bicycle and cycled all the way around the UK. Having done that, he went over to Ireland and did the same thing. He returned via NZ, and went down to Nelson, his old hometown. He got a job with a company operating sea kayak tours, old friends from the past, in Tasman Bay. He was to start for the following season, so he had a bit of time up his sleeve.

When Vic returned to Australia, Marc and Sam were about to go on their big OE, and they asked Vic if he wanted to do some house-minding. He jumped at the opportunity, as it suited him. About 6 weeks before Marc and Sam were due home Vic came down and saw me to ask for a hand in getting his four-wheel drive down to the freighting Company, who would get it down to the boat. He was heading for NZ, and he would be off in a week.

The next morning Graham who lived next door to Marc and Sam's place could hear the TV playing very loud, as it had been the night before. Graham went over to see what was wrong, knocked on the door several times and got no answer, so he walked around the house and looked in the window. All the lights were on, and Vic was lying on the floor. Graham did not go inside, but came down to see me. It was about 6.30 in the morning and was very early for our doorbell to be going off. I went to the door, and it was Graham looking very upset. He told me what he had found. I asked him if he wanted the key to Marc's house to check it out, but he said that he would rather I do it. We went down to Marc's place. I unlocked the front door and went in, down the stairs and over to where Vic was lying, facedown. I went into the TV room and turned off the television. I looked at Vic lying beside the kitchen island bench. His glasses were beside him, but broken and twisted. I thought they had probably been in his hand as he reached for the bench. He often carried them like that. A coffee cup was shattered on the floor. Vic was dead, and it had happened before midnight. I believe Vic was dead before he hit the floor. I put my hand on the back of his shoulder. It was cold. Then I noticed that the top part of his back was all bruised. "That came after." I thought. I went back to Graham, and said, "There is very little we can do here, I will go home and ring the Police, and take it from there." The police came and inspected the scene. They rang for the morgue vehicle and gave me the number of a company that would clean up. Then came the task of informing Vic's daughter of what had happened. She took it pretty well. The autopsy showed that Vic had a very rare heart condition, one he would not have been aware of. It chose that night to raise its ugly head.

In December 2005, Andrew Wibberley, the Manager from Maxitrans in Victoria, and now manager of the Darra shop, came to me proposing that I be a contractor for projects. He told me that basically it was a name change, and things would remain the same even though I was now on contract, but I couldn't keep the car. (When Graham had finished up with Maxitrans, I had inherited his company car, a Holden Commodore which replaced the ute I had been driving.)

Andrew had said the first project would be to take the drawings of an American tri-axle trailer for which they had gained the manufacturing rights. This trailer would deliver hot mix bitumen into the paving machine while mobile. It did it with a conveyor under the load, and thus it was a controlled delivery. He said, "Redraw the trailer in metric, and then build a prototype from those drawings." I thought, "Bloody hell, what am I doing? Life was supposed to be easier than this."

When I first looked at the drawings, I thought, "How did the Yanks ever build these things from this?" There was so much information missing from the drawings. Anyhow, this was my job. I got stuck in and redrew the trailer completely. Luckily, I had some damned good tradesmen helping me build the thing. I redrew a few things as the job progressed along.

The big test day came, (the guys and I had already tested the thing before the official test). We knew a couple of guys from head office would be there, so we had to make sure it would work. Come the day, it did, and we all smiled. The design was so simple that it worked very well. It was good, and everybody was happy. I tied up all the loose ends and gave Andrew the package of drawings and said the electronic copies were in the system. He then said, "What are you going to do now". I replied, "I think I might see about getting my next project". He replied that I was smack on. He showed me a piece of extruded aluminium section, and said, "This will be the sides of a walking floor trailer that you will design, based on some parameters that will control the size, etc, create all the drawings required and all the jigging and facilities to make this an assembly line product."

I was a little taken-aback with the size of this job and said, "Andrew, I will need the assistance of an engineer on some of this stuff." He looked at me (a strange look) and said, "But you are an engineer, are you not?" I said, "No, I am not. I'm a Fitter and Turner". With that, he just looked at me. He must have been thinking of all the stuff I had done in the past. He then started laughing, and kept laughing, as he came around his desk and took my hand and shook it very hard. He then said, "Well, good on you! Anything you think you want an engineer to look at, you let me know."

This was also a challenging project. The new extrusion would make up the walls to the new trailer. It was a fairly basic walking floor trailer, using a Hendrickson tri-axle, air bag suspension with disc brakes, and all the goodies. However, the floor was based on an American imported system that would convey the cargo from the front to back of the trailer, using hydraulics and slats in the floor.

The chassis would need to have a coaming along the sides so the walls could drop into it. The sides had to be assembled on the flat and in a jig, with each piece of extrusion pressed into the previous one assembled, until the wall was the length of the trailer.

I decided this would best be done using oil-controlled air rams, forcing one section into the last one. The extrusion had a tapered lead-in that would click into place and make a wall as solid as if it were one solid sheet. At the completion of the wall length, a top coaming would be added, and "Huck Bolted" to the wall extrusions. On completion, it would be lifted by the coaming, using an overhead crane, and the whole assembly lowered onto the chassis and again "Huck Bolted" in place. The front of the trailer had a flat sheet with an extruded radius fitted at the corners. This made it "self-supporting", and so also supported the side panels.

Designing the assembly table was a bit of a challenge, having to incorporate all the different sized trailers that would be required, but I got there, with the help of my engineer - myself.

Around six months before this, I was driving to work one day, and had a pain in my chest, for no reason. I did not take a lot of notice at first, but as it got worse I pulled over and waited for it to go away, which it did. It was quite severe and worried me a little. Later at work I rang Lyn, and she said, "Why not stop off at the doctor's on your way home? I will ring now and make an appointment." I did that, but could not see my usual doctor, so saw another instead. After an ECG and a lot of other stuff, she said to me "John, I would like you to go to hospital, for further observation." I replied, "OK, I'll go straight home and get Lyn to take me in." To that she replied, "No, you cannot do that, I'm ringing the ambulance now to take you in." I replied that I had just driven from the other side of Brisbane to get to the doctor's, the hospital was only another 5 minutes away. "I'm sorry I can't let you do that," was the reply. In the ambulance on the way to Caboolture Hospital, I asked the paramedic what my problem was. He replied, "Your heart rate is very low, and we don't know why." I said, "It is always low, that's normal." Then he challenged me. "OK, John, what do you think your heart rate is right now?", "Right now it is probably sitting on 58". He said, "It is 59." "At least I won that round." I thought.

Sitting up in bed in the Emergency Department, wired for every sound there was, I was feeling a bit tired, so relaxed a bit more. Then all the alarms started going off, and nurses came from everywhere. They did something to the monitor, and then all went away again. I was just relaxing a bit more, and the alarms went off again. This time I was watching the monitor, and at 40 beats per minutes was when it went nuts.

The nurses came and asked if I was OK, "I'm fine." I replied. I relaxed again. This time I closed my eyes, and off the alarms went again. I opened my eyes and the monitor was showing 38 beats per minute. I closed them again and the same thing happened all over again. One nurse in particular was a wake-up to me, and came over and said, "John ,will you please keep your eyes open." A Bloke can't have any fun anymore.

That evening Lyn came to see me, together with Marc and Sam. We were chatting away about stuff, and about my problem, whatever it was. Just before they left, I told Marc of my little game with the nurses, and he told me that the whole time he had been sitting on the side of the bed, the monitor had been recording a constant 40 beats per minute.

I got out of there the next morning, with no explanation, no medication, nothing. Not even a "Don't do it again!"

Chapter 13 - The Best Challenges

Another update on *HMS Victory*. I did not do a great deal to the old girl. When I tried to get things ready by 2005, well that didn't happen. I was close, but I still had a bit of finishing and painting to do.

In 2010, I made up and fitted the masts. It took a bit of time to get the correct heel on the masts. They don't just stand straight up. The foremast is racked forward slightly where the other two are racked aft.

Victory with masts

Pete and Draha Kelsnil, whom we had met in the early days of 31 Riverside, and with whom we had struck up a friendship, took up the suggestion that they allow us to show them New Zealand. My thoughts were that we would hire a motor home and see the North Island. If everything went well, we could do the South Island the following year. They thought this was reasonable, so the planning started for March 2005. This is our Travel Journal for that trip.

> ***03rd March 2005*** *- We all flew to Auckland and went to my sister Risè's place. Next day it was into the city by train, for a look around, go up the Tower, and over the Bridge, and all of those things. Picked up the Motor home and got ready to go.*

> ***07th March 2005*** *– Headed out of town and got on the highway South heading for New Plymouth. First stop was Waitomo Caves. Went down into the glow-worm caves and did all the tourist type things. Then it was back into the machine and kept going south down through the Awakino valley, following the Awakino river. It was a good drive, then to New Plymouth, where we were booked in to Paul and Margret Wadesworth's home.*

08th March 2005 – Had a look around New Plymouth, to Brooklands Bowl, Pukekura Park, and the first house we had purchased on Airedale Street.

09th March 2005 - Early start, heading for Wellington, stopped at Virginia Lake, at Whanganui, for the usual pit stop activities, and a leg stretch. Then off to Wellington to catch up with Diane Eagelton, our friend whom Lyn used to flat with, when she first arrived from Australia. Had a great night reminiscing on old times. Next day it was off to have a look around Wellington, did all the spots including the Museum of New Zealand. Even went up to Mt Victoria, Lyn actually that it looked different in the daylight, as she had only seen it with the lights on.

10th March 2005 – It was off to the north, going out through the Hutt Valley and Upper Hutt. Over the Rimutuka Ranges, and into Masterton. Had a break with the normal things included. Then it was on the way to the Manawatu Gorge. When we got to the other end of the Gorge, I turned around and came back again. It was worth seeing, even though river was not in flood, because when it is, it's a site to see. We had lunch at the Vidal Winery (not bad the wine was ok but did not hit the spot). We kept on the heading that would take us to Napier for the night.

11th March 2005 – Went for a drive out to Cape Kidnappers and the Gannett Reserve. Did a slow trip back to Napier, going through Hastings for another look, after only passing through the day before. We then had a look at the art déco in Napier. This city is now becoming famous for it.

12th March 2005 – Time to pack up and head for Taupo, had a quick look at the lake before finding the park for the night.

13th March 2005 – Did some sightseeing around Taupo, up to the De Brett's Hotel and spa baths that Lyn and I used to go to, a long time ago, it had all changed a bit from back then. Also had a look at the Huka Falls and a ride in the Jet boat, all of it good stuff. Also went out to Orakei Korako Geothermal Valley.

14th March 2005 – We were now heading for the Blue Lake, and a look at the buried village, and did the Mai Ora Village. We had been shopping that morning, and Pete could not believe seeing New Zealand Green Lipped Mussels on sale for $2.99 kg. Therefore, Pete was cooking dinner that night. Mussels cooked in half a bottle of Sauvignon Blanc, as an entrée, followed by Blue Cod, and the trimmings as the main course. Not bloody bad for some campers.

15th March 2005 – Today, it was into Rotorua, to do the Wai-o-Tapu Geothermal area.

16th March 2005 – This morning it was the Hells Gate Geothermal, and by this time everybody'd had enough of geothermal. Therefore, it was off to Mt Maunganui, for a look around.

17th March 2005 - Back to Auckland and explored the Auckland Museum.

18th March 2005 – Today, it was off to the Bay of Islands and Paihia.

19th March 2005 – It was onto the "Cream Trip" Ferry, for a trip out around the bay of Islands, pulling into Russell. We went for a walk out to the "Signal Flagstaff", which was the place that Honi Heke kept chopping down the flagpoles down. It was then back on the ferry to Paihia.

20th March 2005 – We went out to Kerikeri, the Mission House, and the "Old Stone Store", the oldest building in New Zealand. We drove out to The Treaty House, the site of the signing of the Treaty of Waitangi in 1840. We also saw a well-preserved Maori Canoe, now used for ceremonies. They made this one from two Kauri tree trunks, spliced, to join them. Later we went to the Maori Pa named Kororipo Pa.

21st March 2005 – We were now heading for Auckland. We went the long way around, which was around the Oponony road, this took us to the great Kauri forests, and the God of the Forest "Tane Mahuta". We learned an interesting fact about how the Maori prepared the tree for a canoe. They would first select the tree, and then chop down all the trees, upwind of the selected tree; this would put the selected tree facing the full force of the prevailing wind. In doing this, it would strengthen and harden the fibres of the tree on that side. The opposite side, nothing happened. This would be the side that would be hollowed out, and the hardened side would become the bottom outside. All of this would take around 15 to 20 years. From here, it was on to the Kauri Museum. This would be one of the best I have ever seen. Then, on to Auckland to hand back the Motor Home, and grab a plane to Australia.

Some trivia on "Tane Mahuta".

Trunk Height -	17.5m.
Trunk Girth -	13.8m.
Total Height -	51.5m.
Trunk Volume -	244.5m3.

It was a very good trip and we all enjoyed it. However, Pete said that it was the first and last time they would use a motorhome.

The four of us and the motor home.

In Feb 2006, I needed transport. On most days, Lyn was using the little Benz. I had lost my company car, and I had an hour travel to get to work. One day on the way home I saw an old Benz in a car yard, I must admit I looked at the price more than I looked at the car. I mentioned it to Lyn that night, and got a favourable answer, I thought things are looking up. I must have done something right, as they say. I know I will get thumped for thinking it, let alone writing it, but that is what Blokes do, just make it hard for themselves.

Next day, I called in to see the guy who would get a commission for doing nothing. I found him and had a look at the car. I asked, "What is your lowest price?" He replied, "That's it, on the windscreen, $6,000." So I said, "You miserable bugger! I'll take it, and I will pick it up tomorrow night on the way home from work." I don't know how I got to work, and one of the guys gave me a lift back to the yard after work. So, I drove home in a 1986 model Mercedes Benz 300E. She had a 2998cc, fuel-injected, straight six engine, and just purred all the way home. It was like driving an armchair, big soft leather seats. Gee! This was better than the lounge chair at home. (Shouldn't say that either.) Now we had two Mercedes in the garage. What a false impression that would give!

March 2006 was the month planned for the South Island trip with Pete & Draha. We decided that this time we would hire a car, and the accommodation would be B&Bs, so we made our plans.

The trip unfolded as follows;

1st March 2006 - We all flew out of Brisbane, heading for Christchurch, arrived and picked up the car, and then it was off through the city and out to Akaroa. Akaroa is an old and quaint settlement with a long history back to the French, who settled here.

2nd March 2006 – A day to look around Akaroa, not that it needed a day, but it was good to acclimatise to New Zealand. Went out for dinner that night and had some very good Deep Sea Blue Cod. Man was that good!

3rd March 2006 – Heading for Nelson, on the way, a stop-off at the Bulla Gorge, and The Swing Bridge.

4th March 2006 – A day of sightseeing, we went back around Tasman Bay and headed for Tarkaka. Had a look at the Waikoropupu Springs, very impressive, the amount of water coming to the surface, is incredible. Then it was back to Nelson for the Night.

5th March 2006 – Heading for Blenheim, but did a sightseeing thing around Queen Charlotte Sound and into Picton, I think we had lunch here, and then off to Blenheim, still with time to do Matua's Shingle Peak Winery.

6th March 2006 – A day for looking around a bit more and head for Kaikoura. Stopped off on the way to see the salt harvesting at Lake Grassmere had a look at Clifford Bay on the way back.

7th March 2006 – Had a good look around Kaikoura. Plenty of seals on the beaches. They have whale-watching trips out of the bay. The water is very deep and it attracts the whales.

8th March 2006 – Another quick look around Kaikoura, before heading for Hamner Springs. Had a look around Hamner Springs. Not that impressed. I thought I might take a spa at this place, but no, it was not to happen. Not impressed with the spa either.

9th March 2006 – Early start, we are heading for the Franz Josef Glacier. Had a look at Hokitika on the way South.

10th March 2006 - Up on the glacier it was a good walk and climb. Got some good photos once up on top. Back down again, and a coffee and a bite before heading for Queenstown. Had a bit of time when we arrived so took a quick trip up to Coronet Peak. Chucked some snow around and said, "We've done that now it's too cold." Went back down, found the accommodation, and settled in for the night.

11th March 2006 – *Decided we would head for Arrowtown and Skippers this day, so headed up Coronet Peak again. But halfway up took the turn to the left at the turnoff to Skippers. It was a very scenic run with a lot of single lanes making it interesting.*

12th March 2006 – *Time to look at the Kawarau Bridge and the Bungy Jumping. It was back into town for a bite to eat, then over to the Skyline Gondola. All was well.*

13th March 2006 – *A slow and leisurely trip down to Te Anau for a look around, then on to Manipouri.*

14th March 2006 – *Up early and head for the lake and the trip across Lake Manipouri, to the Power station that is 600mts below the level of the lake. We all got onto the bus, and away we went around and around, down and down for 2kms, and there was the power station. Built in a big hole in the Southern Alps, it was carved out of granite. The water would fall 600 metres down to the turbines and then discharge out into Doubtful Sound, a fiord in the Southern Alps.*

After the big sightseeing thing at the power station it was then back on the bus to Doubtful Sound and a boat ride out onto the fiord. The day was overcast and it had been raining since yesterday. It did not do much for the photography, but the sight of all the waterfalls falling into the sound was incredible. There were some falls that poured their water over the edge of the Sound, only for it to be caught by the wind and whisked away, or others that just simply formed back into clouds and started another journey. It was a great trip and it went out to the Tasman Sea before turning and heading back. They took us back up to the lake on the road track, then onto the boat and home.

15th March 2006 – *Time to head back to Queenstown for a trip on the vintage steam ship across to Walter Peak Station on the other side of Lake Wakatipu. It was a good trip. They set the station up well.*

16th March 2006 – *Time for a trip down the Kawarau river valley. The Kawarau is the outlet of Lake Wakatipu. In places it runs through a solid granite cutting where they mined 11 tons of gold from the river back in the 1800s. Now there is nothing. After the river, it was on to Cromwell, to find a winery called Two Paddocks. We found it, and tasted the wine, and it was very good. It goes without saying that the Barra brought a couple of bottles home to Australia. The Kiwi actor Sam Neill owns Two Paddocks wines.*

17th March 2006 – *Back on the road heading for Christchurch, and the Airport, and home.*

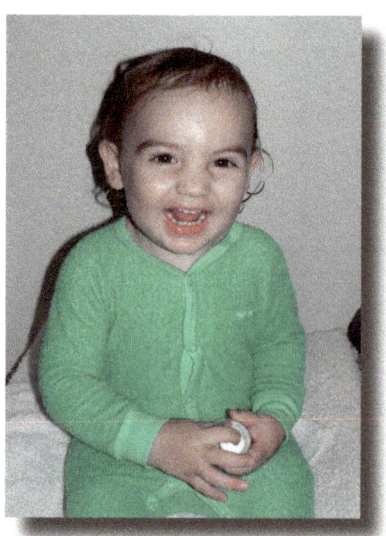

Rohan

On the 31st July 2007, Rohan John Barraclough decided that he needed to be breathing some air, so he did something about it. He had a good start with a birthweight of around 4.82 kg, or 10lbs 10oz I take my hat off to Sam, as it was a natural birth.

Around August 2007, son Tony mentioned that Sedgman, for whom he and Beatriz worked, were looking for a Design Manager for the Moatize Project. Tony was working as a contract draftsman, Beatriz (or Bea for short), had made a name for herself as being one of the best Commissioning Electrical Engineers around. Moatize is a town in Mozambique, Africa. It is just up the road from the town of Tete, which is on the Zambezi River.

I rang the personnel department at Sedgman and made an appointment with Steve Lloyd, the Engineering Delivery Manager. I could not meet the Project Manager, as he was on annual leave.

It was not that I did not like what I was doing at Maxitrans. It was just a bigger challenge to head a design team of Engineers in designing a coal processing plant capable of producing 4000 tons of coal per hour. At the time, this made it the largest single-site coal processing plant anywhere in the world.

I got dressed up in all my finery, (no, I didn't). It was a good interview, I thought, ticked all the boxes as they say. Steve was a great guy and we seemed to hit it off. I left the meeting on the understanding that I would be hearing from them one way or the other in the next few days.

Four days later, there was a letter with an offer of employment. I had the job, and with $30,000 more that I was currently earning. How could I refuse? I drafted a letter of resignation and did the final copy for Andrew. I went to see him the next morning and explained the situation. He was a little surprised, but wished me all the best.

I started with Sedgman on the 24th Sept 2007. The first couple of weeks in the new job were a bit slow, just meeting the people I would be working with. Trying to remember names was the hardest. I met the other department heads that I would be involved with, as well as the two people from "Vale", a Brazilian Company and our client, who were going to build the plant in Moatize. Their names were Edison Petter, a Mining Engineer, and Renato Souza, a Process Engineer. I also familiarised myself with what had already been done, thus getting my head around the contract between Sedgman and the client, which I found later to be invaluable. But it was mainly getting my head around the process. It was going to be a massive plant, with the main building alone being 200 metres long and 50 metres wide and 30 metres high.

Jim Hughes was the Project Manager, a shortish Scotsman. We got on well from the start. Jim was going to make my job a whole lot easier than it might have been. He informed me of the meeting schedules that were coming up, where I would get to meet all of those on the project.

It did not take me long to realise that this was going to be a big job. Completion date was to be on or before June 2009, with a budget of 21 million dollars. I was relieved when Jimmy said that it was his job to prepare the budget report.

In November, I moved into my office. It was next door to Jim's, and that was very handy. It was decided that we should go and look at the Dawson plant up near Maura, in Queensland. The plant for Mozambique was basically two times the size of the Dawson plant. Therefore, we hopped onto an aeroplane and went up there for the day. Not knowing too much about coal processing, it was good. Good to see the size of the place, as it was much bigger than I had thought.

Things went along smoothly and we got to Christmas. We had the usual Christmas party and all that. Sedgman was the first company I worked for that actually put on a Christmas party for its staff. When I say it was put on, I mean that all of us went to a restaurant and had a party, and the company picked up the tab. Well, not quite like that, but pretty close.

Around November 2007, I traded the old 300E in for an SLK230. I used to go past it, sitting in the car yard, every morning on the way to work. One morning I stopped for a better look.

It was a clean little 1999 model, with the Mercedes-invented folding hard roof. At the push of a button, this thing folded down into the boot. I thought this was another reason I should have it, and so it was. After getting only $2,500 as a trade on a $41,000 little car, I can't say that I was overjoyed.

Little did I know but I... correction, *we* were going to have a lot of fun in this little thing. I called it a "Go-Kart on Steroids". With a 2.3 litre supercharged engine in something that weighted nothing, it was a rocket. If it wasn't for the traction control system, one could get into all sorts of trouble.

Our SLK

Early in December 2007, we went to see the Lionel Richie concert at the Brisbane Entertainment Centre. This was a great concert. He literally had everybody dancing on the ceiling. Lionel Richie was another that we danced to in the Gove days, so it bought back a lot of memories.

In January 2008, Ross Brims, the Manager who was actually responsible for the job of drawing up of the contract, reminded Jim that written in the contract was the wish of the client to be informed, monthly, on the progress of the job. The client also wanted to be given forecasts of the completion of the various stages, and that these monthly forecasts were to take place in the client's offices in Maputo, Mozambique. They decided that Ross, Jim and myself would fly to Johannesburg, in Africa. Jim and I would then fly to Maputo the following day for the meeting, then fly back to Johannesburg, then return home.

At the beginning of February, off we went. Edison Petter had mentioned that he too would be at the meeting to make things a little easier. The first trip was a huge learning curve for us all. We flew to Sydney, stayed overnight, then next day, at 10.30, the flight to Johannesburg took off, arriving at 16.30 their time. It was a flight of about 14 hours. We went to our hotel, the *African Pride Melrose Arch*, in the suburb of Melrose. Midmorning on the next day, our limo would take us to the airport for the trip to Maputo. We would arrive in Maputo mid afternoon and would stay at the Avenida Hotel.

On the following morning the meeting started at 10.00, with a stop for lunch. It reconvened for the afternoon. At the close of the meeting we went back to our Hotel. We returned to the airport next morning and flew back to Johannesburg. By then it was Thursday evening. The flight to Sydney, Australia, left early Friday morning. We transferred to the Sydney Domestic Terminal and flew off to Brisbane.

As I said, this was the first trip. For the next trip, a month later, Jim and his wife came and spent Sunday night at our place, as he lived at Buderim and we were a little closer to the airport. We all had a good dinner and a few wines. Jim and I organised to have a cab waiting early the next morning. We picked up an early flight to Sydney to connect with the African leg, with enough time in the lounge to prepare for the departure.

The African itinerary was much the same as before, but when we got to Maputo, we went straight to the office of Vale and started the meeting. We closed the meeting at 17.00, to resume the next morning if required. The next morning, as soon as the meeting finished, it was off to the airport and back to Joburg. It was now Wednesday evening, which meant that we had all of Thursday for shopping or sight-seeing, before the Friday flight back to Australia.

On that second trip, I had my usual seat, number 17 in Business Class of the 747-400, (a great aircraft). I got to my seat and the hostess was there with a glass of the bubbly stuff, and said "Good morning, Mr Barraclough, would you like your usual glass of Glenlivet before lunch?" "Of course." I replied, "That would be great. Thank you very much". It really was the correct way to travel.

We arrived at the Oliva Tambo Airport in Johannesburg. and proceeded through emigration and customs. The Customs process was a stamping of the passport, baggage check virtually did not exist. Later I asked someone why this was, the answer was, "You cannot bring anything into Africa that is not already here."

We walked out into the arrivals lounge. It was full of people, but what caught our eye was a very big sign, held up by a very big man, saying "Mr Hughes". We went over to this chap and as it turned out, he was our driver. He said, "Your limo is waiting gentlemen, follow me." And that was that, every time we got to Joburg he would be there, and would drive us wherever we wanted to go.

We arrived at The Melrose Arch. As we walked into the foyer, the girls at the reception desk called out "Mr Hughes, Mr Barraclough, it's good to see you again! Your rooms are all ready for you".

As we were coming into land at Maputo, I could see black smoke rising from fires all over the place. I thought, "That's strange." We landed and got into the terminal, but no further. The terminal was in lockdown, as there were riots all over the city and it was not safe to leave. There were soldiers with AK-47 automatic rifles on their shoulder, standing guard all around the perimeter of the airport building. What else was there to do, but go to the bar and wait for something to happen?

We got talking to some locals who told us there were more flights due in around 19.00. Jim said, "Let's see if we can get on the return flight to Johannesburg." So off he went to the airline desk. He returned and said, "We are out of here at 21.00. We will get them to come to Johannesburg for the meeting." He asked, but they would not come to Joburg. Next morning, it was back to Maputo where it was all quiet. The riot had been over the price of fuel.

The Thursday sight-seeing was good. We took a trip out to the Lion Park, and I had the opportunity of patting a white lion cub. It was just like an overgrown pussycat.

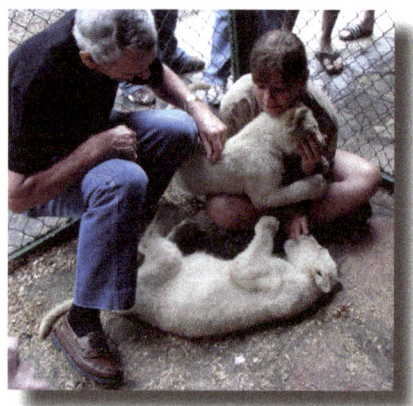

Patting a white lion cub.

On another trip we went to Mandela Square at the Stanton shopping centre, to do some shopping. I bought my little girl, some diamonds from Brown's Jewellers just to keep on the right side. Jimmy did the same and bought a bracelet for Cheryl, the trouble was Jimmy did not see the two extra zeros on the price tag, and wound up paying thousands instead of hundreds

The trip in July 2008 was a memorable one, as, when we left Sydney airport, the captain came on the cabin speakers to talk about our trip. He said that we would be travelling south down the east coast of Australia and would turn right over Hobart, heading for South Africa at around 52 degrees south. When I heard this, I thought, "We have not done this before, because this would put us over the ice shelf." When the hostie came around, I asked her if this was right, but she did not know. She said she would talk to someone up in the front. Later on, a young girl, well no more than 30 years old, wearing the uniform of a First Officer, came to me and said, "John?" "That's very friendly." I thought. "You were asking about our latitude going across?" I said yes and that I thought it would be low enough to see the ice shelf. She agreed with me and then said that it was her first trip, and that she too could not wait to see the icebergs. She promised to come and wake me as soon as she saw them. I could not sleep that trip. I stayed awake and waited, and sure enough, they were there. Some massive icebergs, contained in a sea of ice. The First Officer came back to see if I was awake, and we chatted about what was below. Then she had to go back up front. I could see this very dark line on the horizon and wondered what it was. Very strange! Then I twigged. It was the shadow of the aircraft's con-trail.

On another occasion, we had taken a couple of the engineers with us and made a point of visiting some of the companies that would be supplying equipment to the project. Karen Morgan, a Process Engineer, and Victor Umanzor, an Electrical Engineer, also came over to Maputo to give an update on the progress of the design and to answer any questions the client had.

That evening, after dinner, we all settled into the lounge bar for a drink. I think it was Jim who said, "Lets have a single malt scotch." He suggested "the Balvenie". He had seen the full bottle sitting on the shelf behind the bar. That was it, the start of a good night. Next morning after breakfast, we were about to go to the client's office for more of the meeting and there was no Jimmy. I went up to Jim's room and pounded on the door. After a while it was opened by a person who had experienced a very good night. He recovered very quickly and away we all went.

Jim returned to the same bar at the Avenida Hotel on his last trip to Africa. (I was not with him on this trip). The barman saw Jim come in and asked him if he was going to finish the Balvenie, as there was still a little in the bottle. Jim being a very good and patriotic Scotsman said, "Of course I'm going to finish it!" And he did.

When we got back to Joburg, the engineers who had come to Africa with us wanted to see Multotec, a company that would be producing products for the new plant. While the engineers were talking with the Multotec engineers, the Manager told Jimmy and I that they would like to take us to see a Rugby match, if we were interested. I then mentioned that I was a Kiwi, and then it was on! We were definitely going to the match as it was between the Wallabies and the Springboks and the match was to be held at Ellis Park.

As we got to our seats, there were plastic replicas of a cooling tower sitting there. We had seen full-size cooling towers as we had driven around Joburg. They were painted in bright colours and really looked tremendous. What everybody had sitting on their seat was a replica, about 27cm high and 18cm in diameter. On the bottom of it was a plastic film, so if you tapped it, you got a sound like a bongo drum. You can imagine the noise when 50,000 of these things started up.

The best thing about it was revealed when our host got us a beer, half a litre of Castle draught, as cold as. He instructed us to place the bongo on the ground between our feet and place the beer into the top of it. It fitted perfectly. What a great idea. I managed to pack it and so I still have my 'bongo'. Unfortunately, the local team won the game, but what a day out.

On another trip we took a tour of Soweto. This was something not to be missed. The highlight was a very slow walk through the museum. Was that a story to be told? It was all in photos of the Apartheid period and the effects on the local population. Nelson Mandela's house was also worth seeing. In all, I did six trips to Africa and five to Mozambique that year.

Another Christmas and another year gone. The coal industry was in a big slowdown and a lot of jobs that Sedgman thought were coming up were being withdrawn and put in mothballs. Our job was going well, and a lot of engineers were signing off on their part of the project.

The design came to an end and was handed over to Vale before the due date and well under budget. I had no more to do on the Moatize project, but helped out on other jobs until the inevitable happened. On 9th June 2009, I was made redundant.

My Mum celebrated her 90th birthday on the 8th June 2008. She was still keeping in reasonable health, and was living in a nursing home at Manuwera, a suburb of Auckland not too far from Sis.

Risè said that she was going to put on a bit of a party for Mum and asked if we could go over for the occasion. So it was that we went over and stayed with Risè. Marc and Sam (plus Rohan) said, "We are coming." Tony and Beatriz, "Us too." They stayed with Tony's cousin Martin and his wife Irini, who also had James and Luis and Geoff. (Geoff was a "yes", but Michelle could not make it, and stayed with the kids.)

With all that lot, as well as Risè's daughter, Angela and Nelson and their two daughters, we had quite a roll up. This was to be the first time for Sis and I that all of our kids had been together since we had all lived in Nhulunbuy in the Northern Territory. It was a great day, a bit tiring for Mum, but she was pretty chuffed about making the 9-Zero. All the kids had a great time.

Another notable thing happened in 2008. My little girl retired. She decided she'd had enough. It is not an easy job to be a salesperson. They have to put up with all the shit that some people out there seem to want to hand out because they think they can. As well, they have to suffer an employer who expects that every person who comes through the door has to buy something.

Lyn was of the age that she could withdraw her superannuation, so we thought it would be a good idea to build a deck that would join with the existing one, continuing along under the master ensuite window to the corner of the house. This was to house a heated spa bath that would be accessible from our bedroom sliding door, which opened out onto the original deck.

I did the drawings of what we wanted, showing the attachment to the original deck and to the house, complete with the footing drawings. We submitted it to Council for a building approval. The drawings were returned with modifications to the footing drawing, showing I needed to make the footings two metres deep. I thought, "This is bullshit!" I took all the drawings to the civil engineer who had done the design for the house. He agreed with me that it was 'all bullshit' and said he would draft up a reply to Council and the job would be right. That is the way it was. I found out later that a new member of the Building Approvals Department was from the Old Country and was a bit of a problem.

The deck was built, the timber sanded and stained. Before the pool fencing could be attached all the way around, we had to get the spa into position. This meant we had to go and buy one.

We made a trip down to Springwood and found what we were looking for, a seven-seat spa with jets everywhere. It was delivered on the back of a ute driven by a big Maori bloke. He pulled the ute up alongside the back fence, and the two of us, mostly him, got the spa up onto the back fence and the two planks I had between the fence and the deck. From there it was a matter of pushing and shoving until the spa was in position on the deck. I finished off the fencing, filled it with water, and turned on the heater.

From then on, we enjoyed one of the best things we had ever purchased. Many an evening, when I arrived home from work, we would go and jump in the spa with a bottle of wine and discuss the day that had been, and what might be coming up in the next few days. It was so good to just totally relax and feel so warm. We used it most days, summer and winter. The winter was good, as we would jump in just before bed. Then it was out and dry off, and into bed while still nice and warm. (Sorry about that 'nice' word, it should not be used by a Bloke).

We also used some of Lyn's super' to purchase some 2010 Autodesk Inventor software. I was thinking seriously of doing some design work from home, working towards a business. This did not work, and I had to face the reality that I am not a business type person. The only good thing that came out of it was that Autodesk upgraded the package to Inventor 2011, within the first twelve months.

In April 2009, we had Jan Clarke, Lyn's school friend from Howlong in NSW, staying with us. My Sister Risè and her husband Phil had flown over from NZ to stay for a week or so. On the day before Good Friday in 2009, the three grandmas' as I called them, went shopping at North Lakes. At about 3.00 in the afternoon they decided they'd had enough, and it was time to head for home. They got out onto the highway north.

It had been raining and the roads were greasy and totally choked up, so Lyn thought, "Let's get out of here!" She took the Boundary Road exit and was heading for Lindsay Road. After going under the railway bridge, she started up the rise leading away from it. At that point a utility came flying over the brow of the rise and down toward Lyn. The driver panicked on seeing another car and jammed on the brakes. Lyn stopped the Benz, sensing what was going to happen, and the grandmas just hung on. The ute turned sideways and the rear side of the tray hit the right-hand mudguard of the little Benz. It continued along the mudguard and hit the windscreen pillar hard, shattering the windscreen instantly. The ute continued along the roof and over the boot. After bouncing on the road, it straightened up and continued down the road.

The driver turned around and came back to find the three grannies standing on the side of the road. All the doors still opened and closed, and the windows went up and down. I guess that's why I bought a Benz for her. The insurance company wrote the little car off, which did not make my girl happy. All because of a stupid driver going too fast in the wet.

After losing the little 180E, we found that we were left with a car that had only two seats. If we needed more, we were in trouble. We enjoyed the SLK. Driving with the top down was a lot of fun. Therefore, the replacement for the SLK had to be another cabriolet, and one that had four seats in case we needed them. Therefore, in the August 2009 we traded the SLK, and purchased a 2004 model CLK. It did not have a metal top like the SLK. It had a rag roof instead, but that still went down at the push of a button. It was goodbye to the little pocket rocket, and hello to a 3.0 litre V6, but I must admit it had a lot of power when you pushed the go pedal. I did once, when I needed to, and it surprised me. If the traction control had not worked, I might have been in trouble. Just as well, the boss was not with me.

Our CLK

We had joined the Mercedes Benz Car Club of Queensland on the 17th July 2008, and once a month went on a run with a whole heap of other people. We would meet for morning tea, and then start the run, following an instruction sheet although we all knew where we were heading. We would have lunch somewhere, an old country pub, or something.

Then we would find our own way home. We enjoyed the CLK and went on a lot more Club runs. We had many good times and made friendships that we still enjoy today.

Tony had also moved on from Sedgman and was now working for Origin Energy, as a draftsman, He was doing a lot of different stuff but the focus at Origin at that time was APLNG (Australian Petroleum, Liquefied Natural Gas), Australian Petroleum being another Origin Energy company. Origin Energy, in partnership with Conoco Phillips, an American company, were to explore and gather coal seam gas and pipe it to the Gladstone area, where they processed it in to Liquefied Natural Gas for export. Apparently, they needed to review all of their coal seam gas standards and specifications. The Drafting Manager was a Natalie Thorne. I had met Natalie previously at a café in Milton not far from the Sedgman and Origin offices. I was having a coffee with some guys from work, and another group, including Tony and Natalie, were on their way back to work. Tony stopped to say G'day and introduced me to Natalie. Much later, when Tony mentioned to Natalie that I had been made redundant, she said, "Well, that's who I need to do this review."

After an interview, I was employed as a Senior Design Drafter, through an agency, on a six-monthly contract to do the review for them. They would pay me $85 an hour. I started in July 2009. This was a much bigger job than I first thought. It was a matter of gathering all the information on coal seam gas that Origin had, in every State that had anything to do with coal gas. Then I had to sort it out into each of the disciplines that made up the process; finding the gas, getting it to the surface, piping it 600km, storing, refining, further storing and loading.

Once I had the information sorted, I then had to review the data, and condense it into a single document that would cover all states to create an Australian document. There were many drawings to reproduce, giving new title block and stuff, but it was mainly simple. As I finished each batch, I would pass it on to John Young, the Chief Engineer, and he or someone else would review it.

Anyhow, before too long, 6 months was up and I was nowhere near finished. They extended my contract for another 6 months. It's funny, but I hadn't finished 6 months later either. They must have liked what was happening, because they gave me a raise, as well another six months.

Something I haven't mentioned to this point are our investments, and I guess the reason why is that they weren't very good ones, meaning that we did not make a lot of money from them. We thought we were going to at the time, but there was always another factor.

Our first go at it was not bad. We were up in Gove and I had sold the yacht, so we bought some land on Tamborine Mountain, in the hinterland behind the Gold Coast. The sales people came up to Gove to sell the land, and thrown in was a trip to the Gold Coast to look at the investment. The block we looked at was one that, from memory, was about 5000sqm, on the top of a hill and covered in Macadamia trees. We bought this block. Later, when we sold it, we nearly doubled our money. We needed some money to buy the farm. We bought two other blocks down by Cedar Creek. We only made a pittance on those. The next investment attempt was the purchase of a unit at Nerang, on the Gold Coast, in the late nineties. I think we gave this about five years, decided that it was going to go nowhere, so sold it and lost about $60k.

About the year 2000, or maybe just before, Reiner told me that instead of giving me a raise he would give me one percent of the company's gross profit. This sounded all right to me, so I said "Thank you very much". In due course, I was able to add $50k to my super fund, only for it to disappear in the world financial crash. The lesson I learned from this was that I should have put it on the mortgage.

When we were building the house at 31, and were involved with Mike Ingamells and John Tasker, we spent a bit of time going over to Bribie Island. We were impressed with the way the Pacific Harbour development was going. We thought we might buy a block of land over there, as somewhere to go after 31. We put a holding deposit on three blocks until we could make up our minds. One was on the water and part of a development up an existing creek. It looked good, and we would be able to build a similar design to 31 there and it would look fantastic. The other two were on Marina Boulevard and were nothing special really, although one of them had a view down one of the canals. In the end, we purchased an ordinary block on the Boulevard. It had a flood-way beside it to keep the neighbours away.

We designed a house to build on this block. It was very different, with the outdoor living at the front because there was no room at the back. We planned a solid front fence. There was a three-metre spa pool in the middle connected to the house and outdoor living area via paving, with garden beds and some good old green grass. Inside the house, from the outdoor area was the usual dining, lounge, and kitchen, all connected to an atrium that was in the middle of them all. From the main entrance the immediate focus was on the atrium. Hidden behind this was a stairway that went up to the master bedroom with all the trimmings and a balcony that had a great view of the Glass House Mountains.

Further behind the stairway, on the ground floor, were two more bedrooms connected by an ensuite that serviced both. The garage and workshop on the side boundary had panel lift doors at the front and back so that a boat or van could be stored behind the garage.

We really liked this design and were looking forward to one day actually building it and moving in.

It was a little while after our purchase that Pacific Harbour decided to put the development emphasis onto the Golf Course and not the Marina. Therefore, the demand around our block dried up.

After I was made redundant from Sedgman, we decided that the block should go, and it did. We made a little on it, but the good thing was that it was enough to pay off the house and leave us debt free.

Chapter 14 - The Pinnacle

Another update on *HMS Victory*. My next job was to install all the standing rigging. Standing rigging holds the masts and fixed gear in place. It was a tedious job that really required small and dexterous hands. Mine are the exact opposite, so it just takes longer to tie the knots in the rat-lines and thread the blocks, but I got there. Therefore, in March 2013, I had the standing rigging complete. I left her like that for a while, just looking at her, and trying to decide whether to continue, and install the running rigging, or leave her the way she was with standing rigging.

Victory standing rigging.

I had an accident in the transportation of Victory out to Beachmere Sands. Of all the moves we have made over the years, it had to be the last move for something to go wrong. It wasn't too bad. The end of the bowsprit got in the way of the door, and it came off second best. Anyway, it was repairable.

In April 2010, we were invited to go on a cruise with some very good friends we had first met in Gove. In fact, Maria was our neighbour back then. Her new husband, Bill, owned a couple of prawn trawlers and fished the gulf every year. We met Bill a few times, through Maria and David, her then husband. We had kept in touch with Maria ever since.

Bill sold the prawn trawlers and designed a boat to cruise the Kimberley coast. He had it built and fitted it out with the best of everything. The maiden voyage was to the Kimberley Coast and they took David, (with whom they remained good friends) and the children, who were not really children at this stage. They spent a month going in and out of rivers, finding good anchorages, plotting the best course up the rivers and marking the points into the radar navigation system.

Later, Bill told me of an occasion when they were up some river and a guy came out of nowhere in a dingy. He yelled out, "G'day!" Bill replied and asked him aboard for a cup of coffee. While having the coffee, the chap asked what they were doing up there and Bill told him. The guy then said that he lived up the river a bit, and in all the years he had said G'day to different boats. Bill was the only one that had asked him aboard for a coffee. He then asked Bill if he would be in this spot for a bit longer? Bill replied "Yes, until tomorrow morning." With that, the chap got up and left saying, "I'll be back". Sure enough, the bloke returned later in the afternoon, and gave Bill a big pile of A4 paper. This pile of paper contained all the depth soundings of all the inlets along the Kimberley Coast, the best cyclone anchorages, and all sorts of info. Bill said, "I can't take that!" To which the bloke replied, "I like what you are doing, and you are going about it in the right way, and most importantly, you were the only one to show friendship and offer me a cup of coffee. So the best of luck, mate."

Back to the cruise. Maria rang Lyn one day and asked her, "How about coming on a cruise?" Maria added, "I'll give it to you at half price so we can fill the boat. We have the boat on the market and we want you guys to come with us before it sells." How can one refuse an offer like that?

At this point I will include the journal I wrote of the trip rather than try to recall it from memory.

Fri 09th April 2010 – *We caught a Qantas flight to Perth with a connection to Broome, arrived late in the arvo.*

Sat 10th April 2010 – *A very hot and humid morning. Went for a walk down town and did some shopping for stuff to take with us on board, had a look around town, (not that impressed). It was starting to get very hot, so we headed back to our Motel to cool off. In hindsight, we should have hired a car, and travelled in a little more comfort, and been able to have a better look around. We caught a taxi to take us down to the beach to meet The Lady M. We made it on board by 13.30, met up with Maria and Bill also the other passengers, four other couples. Left Broome at 16.30 and cruised overnight.*

(Note added) - The Lady M could only take five couples in ensuite cabins. As well, there were three other staff. This was advertised as a five-star cruise, and when you see five couples and five staff, you tend to agree. The trade winds had not turned that year, so instead of a following sea, we were beating into it. My little girl Nettie is not a good sailor, and before we got out of the heads, I knew it was going to be a long night, with a lot of strain on stomach muscles and a smell that never seems to go away.

Sun 11th April 2010 – Sunday morning means bacon & eggs on the back deck to start the day. After cruising through the night, we arrived at Silica Beach at 10.30, for a very welcome swim, as it was turning into a very hot day. Headed off again, arriving at Crocodile Falls at midday, another swim, this time in fresh water. Climbed up the face of the falls to find a very nice water hole at the top, some of the others joined me after finding an easier way to get up. We headed off again to arrive at Horizontal Falls at 16.30. (Note added) – Bacon and eggs were great for some, but a few passed it up. (Sorry about that).

Mon 12th Apr 2010 - Early start, 06.30 met up with the boys (some of Bill's friends who own the Horizontal Fall Seaplane Adventure), for a dinghy ride through the pouring rain to the Reef Hole to do some fishing. Back to the Lady M for some breakfast, then down to the falls, in the specialised boat the boys have for doing the falls, to see the incoming tide. The boat can take 12 people, and is capable of going through the falls on all but extreme tides. After lunch we all took a trip up Cyclone Creek in the Lady M caught some baitfish and attempted to catch some Barra or Mangrove Jack, but failed. Time to head back to the falls to see the reverse flow. This was much more dramatic. At a guess there was at least a three-meter height difference from one side to the other.

Tues 13th April 2010 – Left Horizontal falls at 08.00 heading for Montgomery Reef. We arrived at 13.00, and anchored, just as the tide was starting to clear the reef. Bill was expecting a 9-meter tide this day. At 16.00 we got into the dinghies and went up the inlet to see the waterfalls being created as the tide was running off this 1000-hectare reef. On our way back to the Lady M we could see a very big storm brewing. We all scrambled on board and headed for some shelter an hour away. We arrived at Doubtful Bay just around from Raft Point, at about 18.30. The thunderstorm was all around us, however our anchorage was dead calm.

Wed 14th April 2010 – Left in the dinghies, at 06.00 for a 2.5-hour round-trip hike to see some rock paintings. (Very good and very old) On arriving back on board we weighed anchor and set off for Ruby Falls. We arrived and anchored in Ruby Falls Creek at about 09.30. At 10.00 we headed up the creek for the falls. This was a magic spot, all had a swim, and I went rock climbing to get some photos of the pools above the falls. Arrived back on Lady M at midday, for a shower and a beer in that order, followed by a rest or a spa. We could see storms brewing in the distance and heading our way. At 16.00 it was time to do some fishing and crabbing, got some fish but no crabs, had to give up fishing early as the storm broke. We got 300mm in 2 hours, with a further 300mm overnight. I got my camera wet on the way back from fishing, and it died – bugger! Luckily, Maria had a spare, so that saved the day.

Thu 15th April 2010 - I don't feel too good today, some of the others have gone fishing, while I try to recover. The fishermen returned at 09.00 with a good feed. Bill went to put in some crab pots – trying for tonight's entrée. He got a total of nine, not quite enough. At midday we left Ruby Falls and headed for Camden Harbour, arriving at 17.00. We all went across to Sheep Island, a place where the early white settlers tried very unsuccessfully to farm sheep, it didn't work. We heard some very good storms all-around us during the night.

Fri 16th April 2010 – Weighed anchor at 02.45 and left for Kings Cascade Falls. Had some morning tea anchored in the river opposite the falls, and at 11.00 we headed into the falls area, which was a big water hole about 80 meters across, and The Lady M has a length of 31 meters. Bill did a very masterful job of manoeuvring the boat around in this very small area, to the point where he put the bow up to, and under the waterfall so that we could all have a shower. The tide however was still not in far enough and the boat bumped the bottom. So Bill backed off into deeper water. This was the ideal time for all to get into the spa with a glass of bubbles and wait for the tide. With the tide in enough, Bill took us back into the falls area with a great display of boat handling. We left the falls at 13.00 and anchored off Camp Creek and had the rest of the afternoon off. We did some reading, had a sleep, and watched some more storms brewing; all this hard work was helped with some nice cold beer.

Sat 17th April 2010 – Time for some more fishing from the dinghies up some of the creeks, also some crabbing, all while waiting for the tide to get up Camp Creek. At 11.00 hours we headed up Camp Creek, this was truly another magic spot, it had a greater flow of water than Bill and Maria could ever remember, (thanks to the storms we had the nights before). At times on our way up the creek we had to take to the creek, as the track was covered with the extra water, but at the end there were these ponds at the top of the waterfall, these were just made to lay in and soak up the beautiful day. By 14.30 we were back on board and sitting down to a wonderful lunch of crabs and good wine – more magic. At 15.30 it was time to leave for Careening Bay. Dinner was at 19.30, one of Bill's treats, spaghetti Bog, helped along with some good red wine.

Sun 18th April 2010 – *At sunrise we moved out of our overnight anchorage, for some fishing off a reef that Bill knew the location of thanks to the GPS. Got a good catch, Rob an 8kg cod and myself a 3.5kg snapper and a 2kg cod. After the usual Sunday morning breakfast of bacon and eggs, we continued to Careening Bay arriving at 13.00. We all went ashore to see the site where the explorer King stayed for 6 months doing repairs to his ship. We left Careening Bay at 14.30 and set course for the Hunter River arriving at 18.00, with the sky starting to clear.*

Mon 19th April 2010 – *Up at 06.00 to go and set some crab pots. After brekky we all went and did some sight-seeing up the Hunter River, very good. Back to check the crab pots and got six. At 11.30 we headed out of the Hunter to go around the corner to a place called Naturalist Island. We anchored off the beach and waited for a chopper to come and pick up 6 of our party for a ride along the Michel River to the falls. The chopper finally arrived at 13.00, and they all set off. They were back at 14.30, and we then headed off to Montague Sound, about 51/2 hours cruising. At 19.00 we found some shelter and dropped the anchor to have some dinner and stay the night.*

Tue 20th Apr 2010 – *An early start – 05.30, for Montague Sound. Anchored off the beach at Veranda Island, and all had an early swim. We did some cave exploring behind the beach, then another swim.*

We weighed anchor at 09.30 and headed for the Colosseum, this a formation of rocks that the wind, rain and sand has eroded to form these tall pillars of stone, all very close together. We explored these for a while, and then climbed back on board to move to another anchorage, and have an early lunch.

The afternoon saw us heading up the Sound to see some more artwork (not Aboriginal) that had been dated at 40,000 years old. Did some trawling on the way in and I missed a Barra, however coming back I got two Skinnies and a Barracuda. Mid-afternoon Bill set course for King George Falls, about 17 hours cruising away. At 20.30 Bill received a call from Discovery One. This was another boat that takes tours through the Kimberleys. They had run around on a sandbar and required assistance. We turned around and went back to assist them. We got to them after about a quarter of an hour, threw out some lines and pulled them off, we waited until they were under their own power and were OK, then at 22.15, got back on our original course for KGF.

Wed 21st April 2010 – We arrived at KGF to find "True North", (another tour boat) anchored off. We went straight past and continued up the river. At 10.30 we headed up the river in the dinghies to see some smaller falls – very good, Rob and Ken did some trawling on the way back – no luck. After a late lunch, we headed further up the river to the KGF. Bill put the bow under again. He said we needed a wash. The falls are very high, the cliffs surrounding them are really impressive. This was a great spot. At16.00 we left and went down the river a little for the night. (Note added) – When Bill designed the Lady M he gave it a shallow draft so that he could go further up the rivers than anybody else.

Thur 22nd April 2010 – The day started early, 05.45, before the sun, with a dinghy ride across the river. We all disembarked and climbed up the escarpment, quite a climb over rocks and loose gravel. We walked along the escarpment to the head of the falls and had a swim in the ponds above the falls. We took some photos; it was a great view from that height. Headed back down, and once on board, headed off down river for The Berkley River. At 14.00 we arrived at the mouth of the Berkley and found "True North" anchored off again, so we just cruised pass, again. We continued up the river and anchored for a late lunch at about 14.30, with Mt Casuarina in the background. After lunch we piled into the dinghies once again, and headed up a branch of the river, to the falls for a splash under the falling water. Back on the Lady M we headed further up the Berkley, about 12km, and dropped anchor for the night.

Fri 23rd April 2010 – A later start to the day, after breakfast, 07.30, we headed upriver for a swim, once again more water than Maria and Bill had ever seen, got some good photos, although the light was not too good. I saw 2 Brolgas in the distance but could not get a photo. Later while swimming hole we all saw them fly over. At 09.30 it was back to the Lady M for morning tea, and at 10.30 headed back down to the mouth of The Berkley hoping to reach it on the high tide. At midday we headed out into Bonaparte Bay and set course for Darwin, about 20 hours away – the sea was a little lumpy but OK for an overnight passage. The evening was our last on board, so there was a little party to celebrate a wonderful two weeks in the Kimberlys.

Sat 24th April 2010 – Saturday morning saw the Lady M arriving in Darwin as the sun was rising. It was time now for all the goodbyes and the last-minute photo taking, swapping of email addresses and phone numbers, of the friends we had all made.

Now it was time to order a taxi and head for the airport, and the flight home to Brisbane. This was the end of an absolutely marvellous trip that would go down as one of our best ever.

I did leave some!

Lady M

Flynn

On the 3rd June 2010, our third and final grandson, Flynn Jett Barraclough, arrived.

On the 11th June 2010, they all said that I was 65 years old. This came and went. After the 60th, I thought it should be a quiet thing, but the boys would not let that happen, and so we consumed a few too many reds.

20th August 2010 was a day like any other, but for one thing; it was to change my life into something that I had not thought about. The possibility that it could even happen had not entered my head. So, when it did happen, it was a shock that hit hard.

It all started at work on a Friday afternoon, just after 15.00. I wanted to get a couple of things done and I was running late. I had a train to catch, but I was cutting it very fine, so much so that I said to myself, "Forget Milton Station and go for Roma Street. That will give you another minute or two." I finished up, cleaned my desk by sweeping it all into the top drawers, lucky there was room, and off I went.

I went at the trot with my backpack strapped on but in shoes, not runners. I hadn't gone halfway and I felt different, I was running out of puff. I knew I wasn't as fit as I should have been, but I thought I was better than this. I had to stop for traffic lights, "Thank you, above!" Then it was on again. I made it to Roma Street Station, and as I came up onto the platform, my train stopped and I walked straight on. I made it, but I was buggered. I found a spare seat and sat down, still trying to regain some breath, and to stop the perspiration I got my water bottle from the backpack and had a long swig.

I said to myself, "Barra, you should have walked and got the next train". I started to regain some composure, so I got my book out and started reading. That didn't last too long, because I felt something was different, and I didn't know what it was. I put the book away and just looked out the window, trying not to think of what it might be, or not be.

Thinking ahead, when I got to Caboolture Station, I still had to catch a bus to get home. I rang Lyn, and asked her to meet me at the station. She said that was fine. That made me feel a little easier. The train got into Caboolture and I stood up to get off. I felt so faint I thought I was going to fall. I made a quick decision, sat down to wait for everybody else to get off, put my head between my knees and waited. When it was clear, I made a dash for the door, and headed for the closest bench seat. I sat there for a while, once again with my head between my knees.

After a while, I felt a little better, so I got up and started walking toward the stairs to get over the train tracks. I took no more than four paces and down I went. It was not pretty. I was in a heap, but slowly sorted myself out. Two young girls came up to me and said, "Are you all right Mister?" I said, "I think so. I just have to get out onto the street and my wife will be there." Then a chap came up and said, "I'm going to call an ambulance." I quickly said, "No! I just have to get out onto the street." With that he replied, "Can I help you there?" "Thank you." I replied. The girls then told us the elevator was out on maintenance, which meant it was up the stairs.

I climbed the stairs very slowly but made it to the top. We crossed over the two tracks and started to go down the other side. I had to grab the handrail once as I was about to go headfirst down the thing, and that would not have been good. But we made it, the chap helping me was a big asset and I could not have done it on my own.

We got onto the street and Lyn was over on the other side. We got there and I threw my backpack onto the back seat and then took the chap's hand and thanked him very much. I noticed that he had a name on the railway workers' shirt. His name was Graham. I said to myself, "Remember it." I opened the passengers' door and slumped in.

Lyn looked at me in shock, and asked, "Are you all right?" I replied, "No, but just get me home." She said, "No, you are having a heart attack, and I'm taking you to the hospital." I said, "No, I just need some Panadol." She started driving and heading for home, so I thought, but she slipped around a left-hand corner, heading for the hospital. By this time, I really didn't care one way or the other. We pulled up in front of the hospital at about 17.00.

Lyn rushed into the Emergency Department and called, "Please help, my husband is in the car, and is having a heart attack!" None of the staff moved, and so she repeated it again. This time a nurse moved and got a wheelchair, another nurse joined her and they started walking toward the car. I thought, "Bullshit!" I opened the door and got out of the car. That seemed to wake them up a bit, because they then rushed over to pick me up and put me in the wheelchair. They kept saying, "Please sit up or you might fall out." By this time the pain in my chest was so terrible that I was hunched over because of it. I guess I hunched a little too far because out I went. I was a mess on the ground, rolling around in pain, not knowing what was up or what was down.

The next thing I remember is looking at all these pipes running along under the roof, well I thought it was the roof because I was on my back. My little girl was beside me holding my hand, and I think she was calling me a "silly bugger", not sure on that though, things were a little foggy. I remember many people around the bed all asking questions, like "On a scale of ten how would you rate your pain?" I answered, "Twelve." I don't think they thought it funny. After a while, things settled down a bit and I was ready to go home. Then the next one started, and just kept going, no relief, just pain in the chest. No, everywhere. I had not experienced this sort of shit before, and I wasn't a fan. It went on, and on, and on. Then, like it had run out of steam or something, it started easing up again. I thought, "Beat you, you bugger!"

A doctor came over and said, "John, we are trying to stabilise you and then we will send you to the Prince Charles." I said "OK." Before they could do any of that, along came the pain again, same pain, same place, same length of time. Then it started to ease again. With the lull in pain episodes, they bundled me into a waiting ambulance, and we set off for the Charlie. They had looked up my hospital records to find that on the previous time I was in there, they had diagnosed Angina, but nobody had told us.

The ambulance did not muck around. I remember looking out of the rear doors and seeing red traffic lights, hang on, I was seeing them red out the back. We were on the wrong side of the road. Then it started again. I think it was getting a little worse each time and lasting a little bit longer. We got to the Prince Charles and it was still going strong. I remember a doctor leaning over me and repeating my name. I said "Yes."

He said, "John we are going to give you an angiogram right now, and if we find anything we think is the problem, we will stent it straight away. Is that alright?" I said, "Go for it".

The relief was instantaneous, from so much pain to nothing at all. Well, not quite nothing. The whole body was aching but I felt on cloud nine, I had survived it. They carted me off to somewhere and all was quiet, so I slept, and I woke to see my little girl beside the bed. She said, "The boys are here." I think I walked with Nettie to a room where the boys and their wives plus young Brendon and Emmily were waiting. It was good to see them. However, I got very tired, very quickly, and had to go back to bed.

The next morning, I was much better. I had a good breakfast. Not bacon and eggs, but a good breakfast for a hospital, or was it that I was just glad to be able to eat it. I recalled the lead up to the event and asked myself, "Why had I not been able to recognise what was happening?" Lyn knew as soon as she saw me. Maybe I just did not want to go there and admit what was happening.

I saw the surgeon later that morning and he said a small piece of plaque had dislodged itself from the wall of the artery and blocked one of the coronary arteries. They inserted a stent and that should be okay for quite some time. When I got out of hospital, about three days later, I went back to the Caboolture Railway Station at 16.30 and looked everywhere for a guy named Graham. He didn't get off the 16.30 train, and I looked everywhere. Finally, I went to the Station Master's office. I quickly explained why I wanted to find this guy. I just wanted to shake his hand and thank him for saving my life. But they had not heard of a chap named Graham.

I went back to work after ten days at home, but after three weeks at work I was buggered. I felt very tired and lethargic. One day, I rang Lyn from work and she suggested I take some time off work to recover. I suppose that any fitness I had before had been drained out of me by the heart attack. I just had not given things time to recover properly. Maybe I could go back after Christmas. I thought this was a great idea, so I saw Natalie and had a chat. I went home thinking it was to be three months or so, but I liked this not having to go to work thing. I enjoyed the relaxation and the break from the hectic routine, and I enjoyed the relief of not having to go to work. I was at the stage at work when I was not enjoying it anymore. It was hard going, and I really felt that I was doing a job that was above me, that required more than I could give it, and I was afraid that I was not doing the job as it should've been done. I thought, "This is a job for an Engineer, and I cannot get away with doing their work any longer." It is strange that you don't think of these things until you make time to think about them. On the 15th October 2010, I retired from work.

Late January 2011, we took a trip over to New Zealand. It was just a quick trip to see my Mum and Sis. My Mum was 92, and she was keeping reasonable health, just getting old and tired. She was now in a nursing home in Manurewa, close to Risè, as it was too risky for her to have to bother with the chores of living.

We wanted to spend more time with her as we felt she may not be around for much longer. I remember I used to wrap my arms around her and give her a big hug. She sighed and whispered, "I miss hugs like that." After my Dad died back in 1973, Mum was at a bit of a loss having to sell the hotel, and being diddled out of some money. I'm not sure whether it was a lawyer thing, but that was in the past. I know Mum was very lonely, and when she met Hugh Saxon, she found somebody that could help overcome the loneliness. Hugh, who was a good, quiet guy, had lost his wife not long before Dad died , so the two of them helped each other.

Mum and Hugh Saxon.

Hugh died a few years before 2011, and Mum was once again on her own. I was fortunate that Risè was close by to bear the brunt of things, as Lyn and I are for Lyn's mum.

After a lot more hugs for Mum, we returned home at the beginning of February. When Risè went to see Mum the day after we left, Mum muttered to her, "I've seen my Johnny, now it's time to go". Mum died peacefully on the 22nd February 2011, aged 92 years, the day of the Christchurch Earthquake.

My sister Risè was not keeping in the best of health, having been diagnosed with bowel cancer. She was not coping very well with it. They operated and removed part of her bowel, but she steadfastly refused to have any of the follow-up chemo-therapy. She said it would only delay the inevitable, and besides, it was not nice stuff.

After the heart attack, when things had settled a bit, I went back to my doctor. He wanted blood tests and stuff, just to check. I had been on 12-monthly blood tests since the ripe old age of 60yrs. This time he found that my PSA reading was a bit higher than normal, I think it was about 2.2 or something. He said, "This is not good. We will get another test in 6 months." After 6 months, it was up to about 3.0 or something. I told Rob that Lyn and I had a trip to Europe planned for June–July, and asked if this thing would make a difference. He said, "Go and have the trip. As soon as you get back, have another test." With that, he gave me the appropriate form and away we went.

June and July 2011, saw our first and last trip to Europe, not because we did not enjoy it. On the contrary, we did and had a great time. It's just that as I write this, our passports have expired, and I have done enough flying around the world. I need no more. I don't like airports either. Too many people in a small space. There are too many silly people over there on the other side of the world, with bombs.

Anyway, let me get back to something more interesting. We started our trip planning by making a wish list, and on it were;

1. Visit our friends, Peter and Draha, in England.
2. Have a quick look at the UK
3. Visit the Mercedes Benz Museum in Stuttgart, Germany.
4. Florence, Italy.
5. Tuscany, Italy.
6. Rome, to see the Sistine Chapel and Leonardo, Italy.
7. The Amalfi Coast, Italy.
8. Naples and Pompeii.
9. The Cotswolds and the Lake District, England.

They were the main ones, so we planned three and half weeks in the UK, and four and a half in Germany and Italy. We booked the flights for the beginning of June, returning late in July.

At this point, I will include the Journal I wrote of the trip at the time, rather than try to recall it from memory.

Journal of the European trip June – July 2011.

Thur 2nd June 2011 – *Travel Brisbane – Singapore, in a Qantas 747-400 (still a damned good aeroplane)*

Fri 3rd June 2011 – *Did a coach tour that included the Singapore Orchid Gardens, the Singapore Flyer and sites around Singapore city.*

Sat 4th June 2011 – *Travelled Singapore – London in a Qantas Airbus 380 (not that impressed), arrived London 07.00. Then transferred to our hotel, the Ibis Earls Court. Met Cheryl and Sandy (Cheryl is the wife of my old workmate from Sedgman days Jim Hughes, and Sandy is her girlfriend, they were doing the UK thing). We used their room for a shower etc. Took the 74 bus to Marble Arch and went for a walk down Oxford Street. Left Cheryl, Sandy to do some more shopping, and we went back to our Hotel to check in. Later met the girls for a drink and dinner.*

Sun 5th June 2011 – *After breakfast went to Marble Arch again and got the Hop on Hop off Bus for a look at the city of London. Transferred to the river cruise on the Thames and went down to Greenwich, then back up to Westminster, then back to the start again. (Good trip)*

Mon 6th June 2011 – *Got a Taxi to the bus station and caught the National Express Bus to Ringwood. Pete and Draha were there to meet us.*

Tues 7th June 2011 – *Pete and Draha took us on a drive through "The New Forest" to Milford on Sea for Lunch. From Milford we could see "The Needles" on the western tip of the Isle of Wight.*

Wed 8th June 2011 – *Market day in Ringwood, had a good look around, tried the coffee, tried the pub, all very good.*

Thu 9th June 2011 – *Left mid-morning for a drive to Brighton, visited the Pavilion (impressive) then drove down to see the Pier then on to Grawley where we had lunch at Gatwick Manor. Then it was time to head back home.*

Fri 10th June 2011 – *This was shopping day in Bournemouth. And a look around.*

Sat 11th June 2011 – *Pete and Draha had friends over for early drinks, which turned into a surprise birthday for JB. It was a really good day and we met some very nice people.*

Sun 12th June 2011 – *BBQ lunch (in the rain) we sent young Pete out to do the cooking.*

Mon 13th June 2011 – Early start 05.45, drove to Dover and the Euro Tunnel, loaded the car onto the train and sat back and let them take us to Calais. Back to driving again and onto Reims for a late lunch and a two-night stay. Went for a walk to the Cathedral, 800 years old, and just finished some renovations.

Tue 14th June 2011 – Went supermarket shopping, then drove to Epernay for a tour through Moet & Chandon. Back to Reims and tried Entrecote for dinner. (Very good stuff)

Wed 15th June 2011 – Drove to Lisieux to stay two nights, arrived mid arvo. Visited the Basilica and Crypt (both very good) had dinner back down town. (A very full day.)

Thu 16th June 2011 – Drove to Bayeux, went and saw the tapestry (very impressive), (hell of a way to tell a story) visited the Cathedral then had lunch, crepes I think. Drove to Coleville and the American war cemetery, then along the coast to the British and Canadian sites. Back to Lisieux for dinner at the hotel.

Fri 17th June 2011 – Returned to Ringwood from Lisieux, it was a very wet and cold day. Had a great lunch in Calais, tried some French boutique beers and some wines, (not bad). It was a long day starting at 08.45 when we left Lisieux and arriving at Ringwood at about 21.00. This was the end of a great and very full four days in France.

Sat18th June 2011 – Went shopping to Ferndown (halfway to Bournemouth). Purchased some Kiwi Wine for our own consumption. Young Pete and family came over for lunch and dinner and shisha. Another wet day.

Sun 19th June 2011 – Quiet morning, out to lunch, with Geoff and Chris, to the Castlemaine Hotel in Chettle, in Dorset. Great food. Back to Chris and Geoff's for 10 minutes, then home at 16.00. Young Pete and Family came over for dinner and Shisha.

Mon 20th June 2011 – Headed off at 10.00 to Portsmouth to see the HMS Victory, the Mary Rose and the Warrior. Made it home by 15.30. Good day with heavy rain on the way home.

Tues 21st June 2011 – Drove over to Corfe Castle (the other side of Bournemouth). Walked through the ruins of the castle, then the village. We then caught the steam train to Swanage, the town with 10 pubs. Had lunch and a good look around the town, then caught the train back to the car park near Corfe, and home.

Wed 22nd June 2011 – Today we went to the National Motor Museum at Beaulieu. A Great museum with some very good cars, it was much bigger than I thought it would be. We also walked through the Beaulieu Homestead; which is still lived in by the Montague Family, also saw the ruins of the Abbey and a display of some very good tapestries.

Thu 23rd June 2011 – Was the day we went to Stonehenge, Sarum Castle, at Old Sarum, and Salisbury Cathedral (tallest spire in the UK). All good Stuff. (Read the book "Sarum" to get a full insight to this place) Over to Chris and Geoff's for dinner. (A full and very good day)

Fri 24th June 2011 – A rest day for washing and updates.

Sat 25th June 2011 – Left Ringwood at 14.00 for Heathrow, for our flight to Stuttgart. The flight was delayed ? hour, which made for a late arrival at our Hotel in Stuttgart.

Sun 26th June 2011 – Mercedes Benz Museum all day. Met up with Oliver Whittag, (a liaison guy) between car clubs of the world and the Museum) at 10.00 and got the tickets for the "Cars and Coffee" function that Mercedes had invited us too. This was a great turn-out of all types of vehicles, with the drivers enjoying a chat and coffee. About midday the assembled cars started leaving, and about 13.00 a few SLS's started arriving. Later when I went to get some photos, I counted 22 of them. Not bad considering the price tag. The pick was the odd one out a 1955 300 SL Gullwing, in yellow paint, very nice.

I did the Museum 3 times, twice while Nettie was having coffee. A very impressive building, 8 separate floors each connected by a wide ramp walkway, that enabled you to look over the floor you were going down to, and yes, it was recommended that you started at the top and came down.

Italia

Mon 27th June 2011 – Picked up our Rental car from Stuttgart Airport, an A-Class Benz. We had purchased it a GPS in the UK, which we called Thomas Tom. We set it up and headed for Lake Como via Zurich. Missed a turn (driver error) so went through downtown Zurich in peak-hour. We stopped for lunch before the Alps, (1 hr). Set off for the tunnel just to meet up with a delay of another hour. We finally got to the tunnel, all 16 km of it. Arrived at Lake Como at about 17.30, took a wrong turn (driver error) and therefore entered a one-way street the wrong way.

Found reverse gear very handy in that situation. Got settled in the Plinius Hotel, and went for a walk, found an outdoor restaurant for some dinner, all at a pleasant 28Deg.

Tues 28th June 2011 – After breakfast we went for a walk and saw a little of the Lake Como shore-line, took some photos, etc. We went back to the hotel to check out and start the trip to Florence. It was a good drive; the roads were good, but not as good as Germany. Paid 28.60 Euro in tolls for the trip and arrived at our Hotel at 15.30. We were given an upgrade to a suite overlooking the Arno River, which runs through the heart of Florence, (very nice). So settled in, then went for a walk. Too many people!!! (Bloody tourists) it seems they start at about 08.00 and doesn't stop till midnight. Temp around 28.

Wed 29th June 2011 – Sightseeing in Florence – used the "Hop on Hop off Bus", it was a bit hot in the sun on the top deck but got a very good view, and spent about 2 hours in total driving around Florence. Went back to the hotel for lunch and to cool off, (temp about 30deg). Headed back into town about 17.30 for the Wine Tasting part of the day, not bad but not very informative.

Thu 30th June 2011 - "Wanna Be Italian Cook" - This was a good day – it started at 10.00 with a walk through the markets as a group, then the indoor food markets – impressive – all the time collecting and tasting food for cooking later. Then walked to the venue for the cooking class and proceeded to be instructed on how to be a good Italian cook. The class did not finish until 17.00, which meant that we missed the "David" tour; we decided we would try that tomorrow.

Fri 1st July 2011 – Went on a half day Pisa tour, took a cab to pick up the tour which was a 11/2-hour bus ride to Pisa. Unfortunately I could not take any photos inside the buildings. On our return to Florence we were caught in a thunderstorm. It was only water. Went to a cafe in the Piazza Della Repubblica and had coffee and a late lunch before joining the "David" Tour at 17.00, this lasted an hour, knew most of what she told us, but still, not a bad tour.

Sat 2nd July 2011 – Florence to Perugia, took a slow drive to Perugia, did some supermarket shopping at Castiglione del Lago on the shore of Lake Trasimeno. This was to be the first part of our timeshare stay, so needed food. Checked in at about 15.00, but we were a little disappointed. It was just average. I guess we expected more. It rained in the late arvo.

Sun 3rd July 2011 – Drove toward Assisi to find a shopping centre (Calistrada), but missed the turn (driver error) eventually made good by accident, got some more food, booze, etc. A Glenlivet 12 for me and a Bombay Sapphire for Nettie. Also got some wine when we got back to the Domus Volumna, our timeshare. It had their name on the label so thought I would try it, not bad.

Mon 4th July 2011 – Went for a drive to Assisi to see the town, took another wrong turn, (another driver error), and wound up in the country, got some good photos and eventually found Assisi from the other direction, which was the back of the town. However, we got some good photos of the Basilica of Francesco, that we would not have seen if we had come in the normal way. We spent a few hours going through the Basilica and looking around the town, had a late lunch and went home.

Tue 4th Jul – Stayed home today to recover from a cold. Nettie was starting to cough as well. Some light rain in the evening.

Wed 6th July 2011 – Drove to Dian di Masciano (Masciano Station) and caught the Mini Metro. It cost us 6 Euro for a return trip for 2 to Perugia. Perugia is on a hill, and is walled all around for protection (like Assisi), and was founded about 300 years before Christ. The Mini Metro is a light rail system that runs from below Perugia up into and under the city centre. At the end of the line escalators (3) take you up into the city. We went to the Museum and walked around part of the city.

Thu 7th July 2011 – Drove to Cortona through the country and up the hill, eventually found a park for the car, and then walked into the city.

This is where the movie "Under the Tuscan Sun" was filmed. Slowly walked through the town and had lunch; a pizza for me and ravioli for Nettie. Drove on to Arezzo, drove around the city and could not find a car park, so headed back toward Perugia. Drove through some great farming country, neat, clean, wonderful crops and houses in a good state of repair. On the way home we went by Castiglione del Lago again and did some shopping at the supermarket. Driving around looking for a pharmacy we found more of the city worth looking at, so decided to return on Saturday morning for a further look.

Fri 8th July 2011 – Returned to Perugia via the Mini Metro to do the city site seeing on an open-top bus. For 50 minutes we were driven around the city, both inside and outside the walls. Did some more window shopping then returned to the Ristorante, we had lunch at on Wednesday, for a Napoli Pizza one of the guys recommended, (it was OK). After lunch we went for a walk and listening to Jazz music (part of a weeklong Jazz festival called Umbria Jazz). Returned home mid arvo to pack, ready to leave the next morning heading to Rome.

Sat 9th July 2011 – Drove to Castiglione del Lago, looked around the markets and the old fort then the Museum, after walking down the inside (middle) of the outer wall (100 meters of it). The Museum had some very good artwork, but we could not find any info to explain it. Went for a walk down to the shore of the lake, had some lunch in a little Ristorante. Went uptown and got some fuel and Sangovese wine 3.99 each. We then drove to the Roma Golf Club (our next timeshare), about a 2hr drive through the country to start, then onto the Toll Road. Got the sound working on Thomas Tom once again, (makes it a little easier driving).

Sun 10th July 2011 – Day of rest. Did some shopping for extra food, picked up a six-pack of Peroni for E5.49 660ml bottles, 4.7%? Very hot day, it was a good day to do nothing. Good to talk to all the kids this morning, Rise", Marc, Tony, tried Geoff but only got message bank.

Mon 11th July 2011 – Drove to Lake Bracciano, had some lunch on the lake shore, (the water was so clear), can imagine this place would be packed at weekends. After lunch drove around the lake through Trevignano, (nice place possibly better than Bracciano), then headed back to our timeshare.

Tues 12th July 2011 – Drove to Tivoli, saw the waterfall on the way to into town. When we got into town we found it full, no parking anywhere, very narrow streets and some very crazy drivers. Because we couldn't find a park, we kept on driving through town and back home. Went for a walk to the Golf Club. The place seemed dead, found out later that it was closed on Tuesdays.

Wed 13th July 2011 – We enquired at reception the day before about a wine tour, however the info still had not been faxed through, so we did not do much – like nothing.

Thu 14th July 2011 – The info came through last night, so this morning we headed off on a personalised tour of two wine facilities, with lunch included. Total of four hours for E98.00 ea. drove to Frascati, (in the Roman Hills overlooking Rome from the south). We were due to meet up with Veronica Trasmondi, a winemaker and the owner of "Wine in Tour". She was a very nice person, very passionate about her country and their wine, soil, past, and future. Spent a great day all based on wine, but included the history of the The Roman Hills district and finished with ice cream while sitting on some steps overlooking Rome. Veronica's husband was a very nice guy also and showed us around his wine processing and bottling company. All Good, a lot more that the four hours we had paid for.

Fri 15th July 2011 – The Amalfi Coast – Drove along the highway to Solerno, then along the Amalfi Coast Sorrento, saw the Isle of Capri in the distance. Drove to – drove along – drove home. No, not that bad but once again no parking anywhere.

Sat 16th July 2011 – Returned the car to the airport early, and met the transfer to our hotel in the city where we were to spend the next five days. After getting settled, we went for a walk, went outside the city wall, and found a big park & Zoo. It was a much cooler day, quite pleasant. Had a great dinner in the very plain hotel Ristorante. Met the hotel manager and had a good chat about Italian wine.

Sun 17th July 2011 – Early breakfast, after which they informed us they had a new room ready for us, so we moved in straight away then met the "Classic Roman Tour" at 08.00. Had a good look at most of the major sites of Rome. We got dropped off in Town so we could have a further look around seeing the Piazza Navona and the Pantheon and the Fontana Di Trevi (Trevi Fountain). We had some lunch somewhere along the line and finally caught a taxi back to our Hotel.

Mon 18th July 2011 – Early start again, the pickup was at 07.00 for the "Napoli – Pompeii Tour". Naples was what I thought – a dive. Pompeii was much better, had a good lunch then into the old city – some place, great planning for something so old, the layout was North-South for the major streets and East-West for the minor. Mt Vesuvius is to the North and is almost the backdrop when looking up the main streets. The acoustics in the theatres was amazing. Water was piped around the city, using lead pipes, I guess that's why they seldom lived beyond the age of 55 years, but they lived very well with a lot of mod cons, even toilets in the house, not bad for 79AD.

Tue 19th July 2011 – Another early start, 07.30 (they were late). This was the Vatican & Museums Tour. All good stuff, the highlight of course was the Sistine Chapel. Spent 20 minutes just standing there looking at it, (along with the other 27,000 other people) one of the things I had always wanted to do since I was very young and had read about Michelangelo. What a brilliant man he was. We got dropped off near the Spanish Steps, walked around, then had a look at the Villa De Medici then walked back to our Hotel.

Wed 20th July 2011 – This morning we jumped into a taxi and went to the Palazzo della Cancellerio to see the Leonardo Exhibition. This was very good, with full size models of many of his inventions, as well as copies of most of the famous paintings. We then walked over to the Piazza Navona and the Pantheon again. Had some lunch, then took a slow and very long walk back to our Hotel, to pack for our trip back to Aus.

Thu 21st July 2011 – Got our transfer to the Rome Airport and picked up our flight to Heathrow. We spent some time at Heathrow waiting for our connection to Singapore with British Airways 747-400. It all finally happened, and we made Singapore for an overnight stay, before heading back to Brisbane the next morning.

I had forgotten about the blood tests I was to have. When I saw the form hanging on the fridge, with the things that are to remind oldies that they should do something, it reminded me. I had the tests, only for the doctor's nurse to ring two days later to say that Rob wanted to see me, and made the appointment there and then. When I saw Rob, he told me that the PSA was now at nine and it was time to do something about it. He suggested that I go to see John Yaksley, a specialist in that sort of thing. I saw the man, and he said, "The first thing we need to do is get a biopsy done of your prostate, to tell us if it is cancerous."

This was all taking time, as one would expect. I think it was around the end of September before the biopsy could be done. Then there was a call back to see Mr Yaksley for the result of the biopsy. Nine of the eighteen samples taken showed signs of cancer, which was not good. He then informed me that there was a research program taking place. It was to compare the results of the robotic surgery to "the slash", as he called it. He said he would like to recommend me to the controlling team, to be considered for the trial. I said that would be all right by me.

He also told me that the candidates for each type of operation would be selected by computer. If I was chosen for robotic, it would be carried out by his good mate Geoff Cogland, and he was the best in the country and if it was to be the slash, he, Yacksley, would do it, and he was the best. How could a bloke argue with that?

The very smart computer decreed that I should go visit the robot and Geoff Cogland, and that this should all happen on the 29th February 2012. The operation took place on the 29th.

In the recovery room, a chap called Peter (cannot recall the surname), came to see me. He was the Registrar, and the one who had carried out the procedure under the guidance of Geoff Cogland. He explained that the cancer growth was all on the outside of the prostate. Because of that, they had also removed 25 lymph nodes that they would test in the lab.

Apparently, I also gave them all a bit of scare. I stopped breathing a couple of times. But that was all right because the heart did not stop, although it was down around the 40 beats per minute. However, that's OK.

My Old Fella did not improve in his performance, if anything he got a little lazier. They sent me to a specialist who was supposed to know all about these things. That was a bit of rubbish, because he did nothing to help my Old Fella, but he did take a lot of my money while he was trying.

September 2011, another trip to NZ. This was a special trip to take Mum to be with Dad. Mum had said all along that if she outlasted Hugh, then she would like to be buried with Dad at Pihama.

We arrived in Auckland and spent a few days with Risè and Phil. Risè put on a brave face. She invited their children, Angela and Nelson, Taylor and Kaia, and Martin and Irini, and their two boys, James and Luis, over on the Sunday for lunch. It was a very good get together, but I think took its toll on Sis.

We borrowed Risè's car and headed south for New Plymouth. We stayed with Paul and Margaret Wadsworth, and the next day went down to Eltham, to Brother's place. He had organised that his son, Barry and daughter, Linda, would be there and we would all go out to Pihama to Dad's grave and put Mum with him. Hilton had pre-organised with the cemetery's caretaker that we could put Mum there. It was a freezing day, but I suppose that's normal when you do that sort of thing.

Leone and Brother Hilton with Lyn.

Mum and Dad together at last.

On the way back to New Plymouth, we had a good look around Opunake, and at all the places I used to go as kid. They had all changed, but that is normal. The next day we had lunch with Judy Allen. She had lost Doug a few years earlier and it was a bit of a blow, but she was coping OK. When we left to return home, Risè was in bed and did not look all that good at all.

Doug Allen and I in 1968.

A week after we got home, Phil rang to say that Risè was in palliative care, and was not too good. We flew over the next day. I went to see Sis as soon as we got there, but found she was in a coma. The following day, Phil and I went down to see her, and nothing had changed. After a while, Phil asked if he could just return home to get something he had forgotten, I said, "Of course, go for it."

About twenty minutes later, Risè gave a big sigh and moved just a fraction. I said, "I'm here Sis, It's alright". A little later, her breathing changed again, and she seemed to be trying to say something. I repositioned her hand in mine and lent forward to her ear and said very softly, "Sis, it's OK to go. As you said to Mum, it is OK to go." With that, she gave one big sigh and breathed out. My Sis had gone. At that moment, Phil arrived back, but a fraction too late. It hit Phil very hard. I got up and walked out into the garden, just to be alone. Risè now rests forever in the Mt Eden Botanical Garden, where she has a plaque under a red camellia bush.

In early June 2012, we decided to take a holiday to New Zealand, and use some timeshare. It was a toss-up between The Bay of Islands and Lake Taupo. Lake Taupo won the toss. We rang and checked with Phil, and told him we were thinking of it, he said "Good Idea."

I include once again the Journal of the trip.

1st June 2012 – *Arrived Auckland from Brisbane, Phil picked us up at the airport. And we went to his place at Manukau City.*

2nd June 2012 – *Borrowed Risès car, (Phil had kept it for us to use, any time we went over) and went for a drive to the Botanical Gardens at Mt Eden. We were looking for the resting place of Risè, we found it right where Phil said it would be, but for us it still took a bit of looking. That afternoon, Phil took us up to his son Martin's beach batch, as they called it. It was at Orewa, north of Auckland.*

3rd June 2012 – *Went for a good walk along the beach, had a look at some other new housing around the area of Martin's Place.*

4th June 2012 – *More walking, and relaxing, Lyn and I had a spa that evening, it was ok. It made us think back to the spa we had at 31 Riverside.*

5th June 2012 – *Martin and Irini and the boys arrived just before lunch. It was a Hi and Bye thing, as we had to return to Auckland.*

6th June 2012 - *left Auckland in Risè's car, and headed for Lake Taupo, there was no real rush, as we could not check in until 16.30*

7th June 2012 – *Today was relaxed day. We had done some shopping in Manurewa before we left Phil's Place. Had a very long Spa that evening, and it was very good.*

8th June 2012 – *Went for a drive down around the lake heading for Turangi, and to look up a guy by the name of Ross Baker. Ross is an old friend and schoolmate of Brent Purser's and was a groomsman at Brent's wedding, when I was the Best Man. Ross and his wife Pip, had bought a Motel in Turangi, a few years before after selling out of the "Kiwi Fruit Wine Company". Ross had founded this very lucrative business, utilising fruit that could not be sold as fresh fruit. He had contracts with Air New Zealand, who used it as a promotional thing for New Zealand. Now he was running a motel and doing quite alright. Once or twice a year Brent would come over from Australia and run Trout fly-fishing tours up the many rivers in the area. But mainly on the Rangatiki. Which run through to the lake just north of Turangi. It was good to catch up with them again and talked of old times over a cup of coffee.*

9th June 2012 – A day for some sightseeing around Taupo and the Huka Falls. They have not changed, sill a heap of water going through a small space.

11th June 2012 – went up to the De Bretts hotel. We used to go there a long time ago when we were courting, this time however it was just for a quiet lunch and called it my birthday present.

12th June 2012 – Time to leave, so checked out early, and headed south. At Turangi we turned and headed west for Taumarunui, and then down the "Forgotten World Highway" to Stratford. It was not long down the road when I stopped and looked back. They were still there Mt Ruapehu on the right and Mt Ngauruhoe on the left, but straight ahead of us the best of them all Mt Egmont, (now Mt Taranaki). It was a good drive and one that I had not done since I was a boy. We got to Stratford and turned left and headed for Eltham, where I would find my brother Hilton. We all had a coffee and a bite to eat and then it was off again, heading for Pihama, where my Mum and Dad lay at rest, in the Lizzie Bell Memorial Cemetery. Then it was on our way to New Plymouth. We had arranged to spend a couple of nights with Paul and Margaret Wadesworth.

13th June 2012 – Had a look around town and went out to Bell Block with Paul and Margaret to visit some friends.

14th June 2012 - It was time to head back to Auckland and spend the night with Phil. Lyn had to pack some bags and stuff for the trip home tomorrow.

15th June 2012 – Phil dropped us at the airport, and we said our goodbyes and thanks.

After the big "fall over incident", Lyn and I were having a real "D & M" one day, and I said to her, "What would you do if I had another of those things and did not make it back?" She said, "Don't talk like that!" That was a standard answer to anything that she did not want to talk about. I then asked, "Would you stay here in this house?" The answer was, "No, there would be too much maintenance with a house this big and the garden." I then suggested that we should look around for something else and make the move while there were two of us to do it.

In September 2012, we were about to leave on a trip up to Port Douglas. It was to be a couple of days on the road, followed by a nice relaxing 7 days at the Ramada Resort, using our timeshare once again. Lyn was looking at the local Caboolture newspaper and saw a big advertisement for Palmlake Resort at Beachmere.

She showed it to me and said this was the one we had tried to find a year before. We took a trip to Beachmere and looked at the place. It was not what I had expected. We had been down to North Lakes to look at a retirement village, and there were miles too many old people there for this little black duck. This one seemed different. There was plenty of room around. The villas were a good size and there was an area called The Farm, a sort of common area that had gardens and caravan storage and stuff. We thought enough of it to take all the info away on holidays with us to digest it a bit more.

We did that and, when we returned, went back to Beachmere and had a look around the once fishing village. We went to Palmlakes and looked at the overall layout of the place. We liked the look of one villa in particular, as it had a good size backyard, so we paid a deposit on it. As we were buying it off the plan, and they needed 3 months to get to that stage of the development, we told them it was okay, as we had to sell a house and a pile of rubbish we wouldn't need anymore. Our home at 31 Riverside officially went on the market on a Monday. By Wednesday it was sold. We signed two separate contracts, both with settlement in three months.

The next three months were spent on the normal tasks of garage sales and getting rid of this and that. A week before we were to move in, Palmlake informed us they needed another week. Luckily, the people buying our place agreed. So, on the 17th December 2012, we arrived at the Funny Farm.

Early in 2013, the Manager, Keith Arnfield, asked for a group of guys to look at what they would require in a workshop. John Broderick, one of the residents, had raised the possibility of having a workshop like other villages. Therefore, a steering committee was formed to look at what they would require. Walter Elliott (the owner of Palmlake Resorts) had said part of the old blue shed could be used for the purpose.

The group had a look at the Deception Bay workshop, just to give us an idea. I asked the group if they would like a drawing of the shed and the equipment we wanted in it. The group agreed that it might be of benefit. I started by measuring up the blue shed. I did not think that part of it would do the job, so I drew the lot, then I started drawing up the equipment and placing it in the shed. I included benches and work areas. I even detailed the kitchen and toilet. One of the other guys put some text together justifying the equipment and what we wanted. The finished cost of it all was $61k. We thought if we aimed high, we could always come down but it is very hard to go up from a low starting position.

When finished, the proposal was given to Keith Arnfield to pass on to Walter Elliott. The next we heard was that Walter was very impressed with it and had okayed the lot. It was full steam ahead to get the whole thing set up for a great opening day.

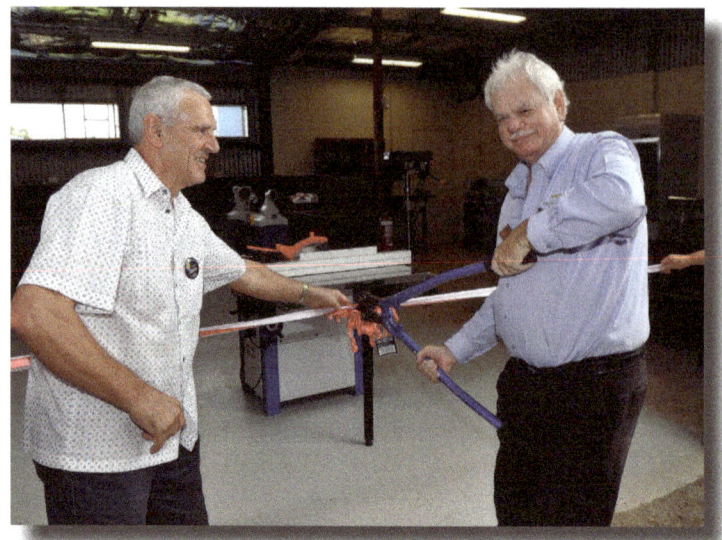

Keith cutting the ribbon with some bolt cutters.

Workshop on Opening Day.

In June 2013, they persuaded me to join the Residents Committee here in the Village. I thought I might be of some help to get things going somewhat better. There seemed to be a lot of friction between the older residents and some of our newer ones. The older residents also "had it in" for the manager, as he was the one who put a stop to the free rein that the older ones had held since the village had been in receivership, about three years before. To cut a long story short, I was elected onto the committee, and that was fine, but as we would decide on the portfolios we were to have, someone said "John, I will nominate you for the Chairman's position." Someone else said, "And I'll second it." When we actually got to take a vote, it all happened very quickly. I was suddenly the new chairman. At our first ResCom (short for Residents Committee) meeting, one of the chaps elected had to resign, so I now needed another Treasurer. Lorna Mackay put up her hand and said she would do it. That was good, until I found out that she could not use Excel software. Therefore, I said, "You do all the day-to-day stuff, and I'll do the spreadsheet stuff and the Monthly Report". She was okay with that, and it worked well.

When the first General Meeting came around, I had been in the job for three months, and things were going okay, but when it was time for the meeting, I was not a happy camper. I had been to a lot of meetings in the past, with Round Table and Apex, so I knew about the procedures, how a meeting should be run and all of that. Nevertheless, I had never been the Chair of a meeting, and it scared me stiff. I wanted to hide somewhere, but I couldn't. I wanted to have a couple of good whiskies, but I couldn't. I wanted to run away, but couldn't do that either. So I had to face the music. At the end of the day, it wasn't so bad. They hadn't lynched me or anything. Mind you, there are always those who cannot help but tell you how things should be done, instead of allowing one to do what one believes is right.

A little while after the second General Meeting, I resigned from the Chair, but stayed on the committee. I stood again the following year and unfortunately was elected again. This time I got roped into the job of Secretary. I continued to do the Treasurer stuff for Lorna, who did it all again, like me. I did not stand again, but in hindsight, maybe I should have. We might not have the stupid voting we have today.

Around February 2014, some people here were going up to Kenilworth for the weekend, and asked us if we would like to come? The immediate answer was "Yes, but we will be in the tent." "That's all right," they said. By 'they', I am talking about Ron & Brenda, Ross & Lesley, Peter & Trish, Rod & Pat.

We all arrived up at Kenilworth, they with their caravans on the back, but we of course were in the CLK. We waited back a bit until they had parked their vans, then I asked, "So where should I put the tent up?" I started unloading the CLK, and they all stopped to see how much stuff was coming out. I put the top down to make it easier to get the stuff on the back seat. I soon had it all out. then pitched the tent and was ready for Happy Hour along with the rest.

Camping in a sports car.

However, that was not good enough. All weekend long, Peter and Rod, with the occasional Ross, were on about going camping in a bloody sports car. I replied that it was a good sports car, so bugger off. Then it was the tent versus the caravan, getting down on the dammed ground to go to bed, and all that sort of thing. Apart from the ribbing, we all had a good weekend. It was on the way home I took a detour to "Mercedes Benz Sunny Coast".

We looked at some 4-wheel drive vehicles. They had a couple there, one had a tow bar fitted already, so that saved a couple of thousand. Anyway, we did a bit of dealing about the trade-in value, and a couple of other minor things. Bottom line was, we went back the next day and picked up an ML320.

The ML320

When I got home, I got it in the ear about getting a Benz instead of a real 4-wheel drive. My answer was, I got the Benz because if any bugger hits me, I want to be able to walk away. That shut them up, and we had a little bit of peace and quiet for a while. That all lasted until one day we came home with a camper trailer. Then it all started again, "Why did you waste your money on that, instead of getting a caravan?" I replied, "Because we like to sleep under canvas." That shut them up for a little while, but the undertones were still there.

We all went up to the Bjelke Peterson Dam for a week away. It was a good week and we found the camper worked very well. The three other couples had accepted the idea by now, and did not keep giving us a hard time about it, so that was good and we all enjoyed the long weekend. (Must go back one day soon.)

Ready for Bjelke Peterson Dam.

Lyn and I had decided that we had to use up some more timeshare, so we booked another week up at Port Douglas for late in May 2014. On telling Warwick and Carole that we were going up there, they said that they would be at Sapphire so why not call in on our way home? We had never been to that part of the country before, so thought, "Why not?" They said that they would book the cabin for us, as they knew the owners of the park very well. We'd only had the ML a short time and had a couple of runs with the camper, but no decent ones, so thought this would be a good test for it. That did not last long. I couldn't even get the beast out of the garage. I thought, "The bloody thing doesn't want to do any work!" The problem was a flat battery. I'd done something stupid, and it was paying me back. Anyway, Ronny from over the road came to the rescue with some very long jumper leads that would reach into the engine bay of the Benz, and he jump-started the thing for me. It is something I don't remind him of, because if I did, he would make me pay, and I don't mean with money, I mean the need of a Toyota to start a Benz.

We got away a little later than we had hoped, but that was ok. First night was Rockhampton, second night Townsville, third night Port Douglas. We spent a week of relaxing and doing not much, although one day we went up to Mossman and the Mossman Gorge. We walked up the gorge to the moss-covered rocks and came back. It's still a good walk, for old people.

Too soon the rest had to end, and we were on our way to Sapphire. We left Port early, had a good run down the coast, and stopped at the Big 4 in Bowen. We spent another week there, in a cabin only a few metres back from the seawall, most enjoyable.

From there it was down to Mackay. We turned west along the Downs Highway. After about 275 kms of this, it was on to the Gregory Highway and down to Capella. There we turned west again and headed for Rubyvale, then Sapphire.

We found the caravan park on the hill and checked in, caught up with Warwick and Carole, and had a good night with some red wine. A couple of nights later, it was my birthday, so some more red wine, and a very nice evening meal. Over the next week, we went out every day to do some hunting for sapphires. We paid $10 for a bucket of gravel that had been brought up from a mine. We washed it, sieved it, and then searched in what was left. If you were lucky, you could find some good ones, small but good. Warwick then took us to meet Darren, who was a very good gem cutter and polisher. He was the man if you found a good stone.

When our week was up, it was time for home. Once again, we left on the early side. We turned south near Rockhampton and kept going. 9 hours later we were home. It was a good trip, and I almost forgot the flat battery in the beginning.

Sometime later, in September 2014 I think, the Resort Manager, Keith Arnfeild, came up to me and asked if I could help him out with a proposal he was putting together for the expansion of the clubhouse, and maybe a golf course with a separate clubhouse close by. We talked about this for a while, and I went away to think and get some ideas. I started to draw the clubhouse first, and used the same theme used in the original, that being the octagonal corners. It all turned out very well and I was pleased with the whole thing and the way it tied in with the existing clubhouse. It made it look as if it had always been that way.

Not many people in the village realised that it was Keith who did the groundwork for the extension, but that is another story. Keith put the proposal forward. They built the whole thing as per the drawings, and today we have the new clubhouse.

The outside is as I had drawn it, but they changed the layout inside a bit, mainly doing away with the bar where I had it, and made that space the library, leaving the original one in place for us to use. A little later on, the leader of the bar group approached me to ask if I could help them out with some drawings, as Palm Lake had decided to extend the original bar. This I did, and gave them several options on what I thought they needed. One option was finally accepted, and they built the new bar. I am now in retirement.

Not long after arriving at the Sands, I got myself a plot in the residents' veggie garden. This meant that I could grow a few vegetables for us. I had to enclose the garden with bird netting to keep the pukekos (swamphens) out. I had to go a little further than that because I found that there were a few light-fingered residents in this place who would help themselves to the produce. So the garden got a lock on it.

In 2016, after Keith had left and Patricia was appointed our fill-in manager, I approached her with a proposal to utilise six concrete tubs that had been part of a water recycling process and were no longer used. I told her that if I could use the six tubs, I would give back the gardens I had in the compound, plus two other guys would give up their gardens, totalling five gardens returned between us. We would use the tubs after I set them up outside the fence. She agreed to all of this, so it was on. I borrowed Warwick's hammer drill and drilled a ring of holes in three places along the bottom of the tubs, then smashed a bigger hole with a big hammer. A chap by the name of Daryl Groves could drive a small Kubota tractor that had a front-end loader on it, so I got him to help me turn the tubs over and sit them on a bed of sand that he had obtained for me. Then he went and found some good soil to fill the tubs. I fenced the area in and, with the help of Warwick, we covered the whole thing with bird netting, the sides as well. That stopped the birds, and the people, as I had put locks on both gates. With the help of Warwick, we have made up some low garden beds as well. Between us we now have about 46m2 of garden beds. We grow everything we can and all year round, as the climate at Beachmere is frost free. Last year I very successfully grew tomatoes up a string. I had productive plants for 12 months, and they had grown over 4 metres in length.

Chapter 15 - Enjoying Life.

Another update on *HMS Victory*. I decided to continue with the rigging and install the running rigging. If I thought the standing stuff was difficult, it was nothing compared to this running rigging.

Throughout the building of the model, I had tried to maintain the moment in time, so I decided that everything was to relate to a time when she would be in port. This meant no sails and no open gun ports. I failed on this because I have some of them open. But without sails, it was a little easier.

I also started thinking I had to make a glass or perspex case to keep the dust and stuff off it when it was finished. I started hunting around for some timber to use for the baseboard and asking the guys for help. One day, Trevor Harris said, "Would Silky Oak be any good?" "Almost perfect." I replied.

The Finished "Victory"

I made the baseboard from Silky Oak, and decided on perspex for the enclosure. I kept plodding along until, on the 30th November 2017, *HMS Victory* and her display case were finished. I then had to put it somewhere. Well, that is another story.

The Beachmere Sands campers decided on a holiday down to Nambucca Heads. We had planned a trip to the 2015 Melbourne Flower Show in March with Warwick and Carole. However, the timing allowed us to have a couple of nights with the mob at the heads, on the way down to Melbourne. The mob were already in camp when we arrived so, when it came time for The Barra to set up the camper, he had an audience. They were all seated in a semicircle around the campsite, waiting to see me do the job. Then started a light drizzle of rain. Damn it! They all stayed there to watch.

Well, away I went. All went smoothly, and everything just popped into place. Peter actually gave me a hand, and that was good. We stayed a couple of nights at Nambucca, and then it was time to head off to Mittagong for the night. On the following day it was a couple of hours to Howlong, where we would leave the camper with Jan. It was good to see Jan again.

We stayed a couple of nights, and I half-jokingly said to Jan, "The camper is on the market, if you can find a buyer." Then it was off to pick up Warwick and Carole from the Tullamarine Airport. They had flown down from Brisbane.

Lyn had booked some timeshare at the Clarendon in the city for a three-night stay. We all enjoyed that, and the following day we all went off to the flower show by bus. It was all good. At the end of the city stay, we dropped Warwick and Carole off at the airport. They went north and we went west.

We spent about three weeks travelling, which included Easter. We visited the Coonawarra wineries, then drove over to Robe, down to Mount Gambier, then across to Warrnambool. Lyn caught up with two of her sisters, staying overnight with each, (to give more talking time) and a real old friend, Kris Harris, who had been Kris Ormsby before that, then Kris Rose, and later would be Kris Rose again.

We did the trip along the Great Ocean Road. We were a little disappointed that we couldn't stop anywhere, as all the car parks along the way were full with a great influx of Asian Tourists. They were in buses, cars, campers, anything that was mobile, and they stopped where and when they wanted.

We kept on going and made it to our week of timeshare at Bellbrae. We had a good look around, going out to the Bellarine Peninsular and Geelong, stopping off and looking at new caravans whenever we saw any. Then we were on our way back up to Howlong.

When we arrived back at Jan's place, she told us she thought she had a buyer for the camper. We said, "Keep working on it. We will be back in a few days after more visiting." Next day, we caught up with Marie and John Thomas over at Porepunkah. Then over to Walwa, to see Lyn's brother Graham and Julie, stayed the night, then onto Frank and Judy, who we hadn't seen for a long time. Then it was back to Jan's for another three nights. This is when we heard the full story on the camper trailer. Before we left Jan's the last time, I had put the camper up, so the prospective buyer could see what it looked like assembled. On seeing it up, he liked the layout and thought it would suit his needs. There was a bit of a shock when he said how much he wanted to pay for it.

To cut a long story short, we no longer had the camper and had to find something else. We went to the local Jayco dealer and started looking around and comparing prices. Another long story, but at the end we were heading north with a caravan following. It was a Jayco Journey with tandem axles.

Our Jayco Journey

The weather forecast was looking terrible along the coast, so we rang ahead to cancel the bookings we had and started for home, travelling up the centre. We stayed the first night at Dubbo. The new van had towed well, and most of the time we didn't know it was there. The next day it rained just north of Moree and was drizzly through to Goondiwindi, where we stayed the night.

Next morning, we were about to leave, only to discover I had no lights on the van. This problem would haunt us for a while, as the car was incandescent and the van was LED.

Eventually, we got it fixed but it had delayed us by over two hours. This turned out to be critical at the other end, as that delay stopped us from getting home before the roads flooded. It meant that we spent the night sleeping in the van, on the side of the road outside a MacDonald's store. However, that was just the start of the caravanning. So far, it has all been good.

The year was 2015, and we headed north, with the brick on behind us. We spent the first night at Cania Gorge, didn't think too much of this place, but we didn't see much either. Another week prospecting for that elusive big stone. This time, after Sapphire we went west to Ilfracombe, and stayed at the famous van park where the owners put on one of the best Happy Hours you will ever come across. From 17.00hrs for an hour they pack it with stories, jokes, and a general good time, put on by Jessie and Cath. We stayed three nights there. The next day we visited the Stockman's Hall of Fame and the Qantas Museum, both just down the road a bit, in Longreach. The next day we went for a walk down the Mile of Machinery. This is in the main street of Ilfracombe and is a collection of farm machinery from the farms around the area. Next day it was off through Longreach, to Winton, Hughenden, and on to Charters Towers, where we stayed one night at the Big 4. The following day would be a long run north up to Carol and Warwick's place at Mareeba.

We did not know this, but Carole had made some bookings. In the late afternoon of the 11th, she suggested that we pack an overnight bag as we were going out. We got in their car, and they drove us north to Port Douglas, where we found the apartment that they had booked for us. Carole and Warwick were just down the hall. They told us they would pick us up at 19.30hrs. At 19.30 there was a knock on the door. As we were ready, we headed to the Nautilus Restaurant, where our table was waiting. The surprise was for my 70th and Carole's birthday that had been on the 20th May. The red wine for the evening was a couple of bottles of Chris Ringland Shiraz, which is one of the best going. It was a great night and we will always remember it. When it came time to come home, it was a quick trip with stops only at Ayr and Yeppoon.

Late in 2015, Carole and Warwick were talking to Lyn about the "Stairway to the Moon", an event that happens over in Broome only a couple of times a year and which they were going over to see, It is a phenomenon that occurs when the rising moon is reflected from puddles of water left behind on the sand at low tide. They would travel to Broome at the end of October."

Lyn said, "We'll be in that!"

Carole and Warwick booked a twin double room at a resort that had all the mod cons, including a personal swimming pool.

On the 26th October, we are all off down to the Airport to catch the flight to Perth. Bill and Maria made the trip up from Mandurah and we all had lunch at the airport while waiting for our flight to Broome.

We arrived in Broome late in the evening, picked up the hire car, and drove to the resort. It was all good, very spacious. We spent the days looking around Broome, Cable Beach, and the Wharf.

In the evening we went down to the observation place to see the "Stairway to the Moon". There is now a big hotel catering for all those wanting to see the sight, so it was simply a matter of getting a good table and a bottle of wine and waiting for the show to begin.

To get a clear night on a full moon and a spring low tide is a big ask. We *did* ask, but nobody listened. We saw part of it, saw the reflection, but the moon stayed behind the clouds.

We came, we tried to see, but it didn't happen. The trip home was via Melbourne, and the flight took us over Lake Eyre, and I got some good photos out of the window.

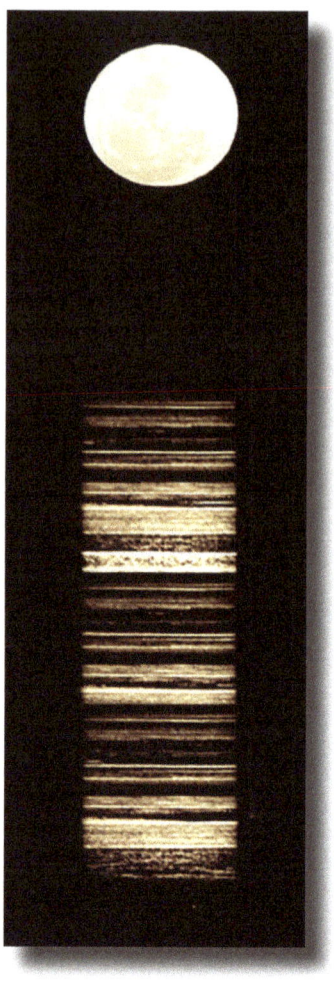

Stairway to the Moon.

One of our friends at Beachmere Sands suggested that a few of us should go down to Tamworth in January for the 2016 Country Music Festival. We would take the vans and camp at Kootingal, just north of Tamworth, in the Pony Club paddock. As it turned out, there were eight couples with vans wanting to make the trip, including us. We did not leave with the mob, as they would stop for a night on the way. I said we would go later.

On the 16th Jan 2016, we headed for Tamworth. As we got close, we gave Ron a ring and he guided us to the campsite.

The next day, we all piled onto a bus that Ronny had hired and off we went out to the Nundle Woollen Mills. We had a good look around and the girls did the usual thing and were happy. For lunch, it was off to the local pub where they had live music. It might not have been Tamworth, but there was music going on. After lunch, it was back to the park and a little bit of watching the sun go down.

On the following morning, we again piled into the bus for a look around town and drove up to a lookout that gave a good view over Tamworth. The next day Ronny suggested we should all go out to have a look at Bendemeer. We did, finishing with lunch and music at the local pub again.

On the following day, they held the Grand Parade in town, so we made an earlier start in order to get a spot with a good view of the parade, and to beat the traffic.

The parade was spectacular and long. In the middle of the parade, it started to rain, and rain it did. That night we all watched the sun go down and the full moon come up. It was pack-up time for some of the mob, as they were heading home.

 Those who stayed on went out to Werris Creek, to the Rail Museum. It was well done, and had some great exhibits. The next day, the four remaining vans packed up and headed for Mudgee. We stopped off on the roadside, at a clearing, and had a leisurely lunch. Then it was off to the Mudgee Racecourse free camp area. We found a spot and parked for the night.

In the morning we took a drive out to the Robert Oakley Winery and bought some needed supplies. It was going home time for the Benz the next day, so we had an early start. We didn't know where we would spend the night. I thought we would keep driving until we found somewhere good. That happened, we slept in our own beds back in the village. We drove straight through to home.

In May 2016, somebody suggested that we make a trip up to Darwin, going to Alice Springs on the way down. They invited four travellers to undertake the journcy, and all accepted. The planning got down to detail with a departure date set for Wednesday 8th June.

As with the previous trips, I shall use the trip journal for information.

The Darwin Participants - in travelling order left to right.

K & S in "Paj with an Option" Call Sign 39

R & L in "The Travelling Vee Dub" Call Sign 76

R & B, in "The Sterling Prado" Call Sign 75

J & L, in "The Merc on a Journey" More commonly known as "Benjie and the Brick" Call Sign 79

G & C joined us for the first week in "The Jeep Crusader" Call Sign 78 (Not in the photograph)

Day 1 – Wed 08.06.2016.   Beachmere to Miles Free Camp.

Left the village at approx. 08.20 with G & C leading out, followed by K & S making the first group. The second group of R & L followed by R & B, and J & L, being the "Tail End Charlie".

All Stopped at Yarraman for a coffee at about 10.30, with J & L having made up a lot of ground after being split from the group by a lot of very slow trucks and motor homes and traffic lights.

All arrived at Miles around 13.45 topped up with fuel, before going on to the free camp site just north of town. By popular demand happy hour was moved forward to 16.00, anticipating the very cool evening that was on the way. With the cool moving in, stumps were called on the happy hour at around 17.45, and all returned to their own vans for a warm evening meal and nightcap.

Day 2 – Thu 09.06.16   Miles to Carnarvon Gorge [Takarakka Bush Resort]

G & C left before the mob as they were going on to spend the next night at Springsure, but changed their minds and went straight through to Sapphire. The rest getting away at exactly 08.30; it was exactly 08.30 because somebody made it so.

It was an uneventful trip; the traffic was not too bad, but still with its fair number of slow ones. Coffee time arrived at about 10.15, just north of Roma. Who do we find also having coffee but G & C? They went on their way again, with the rest leaving at around 10.45. On to Injune for fuel and lunch. The road from Roma was a bit lumpy, but the traffic was lighter. After lunch we headed for Carnarvon Gorge, J & L having to make a quick pit stop to check the doors in the van (not locked), then had to play catch up with the mob.

Got to the turnoff around 13.45 and headed for the gorge, Saw a bunch of Emus' in a paddock on the left, all good until the dirt road. Ron was going to turn back rather than get the rig covered in dust, as it turned out Ron didn't turn around but did get covered in dirt like the rest of us, especially the "tail end Charlie" who coped the lot.

All got checked in and set up. Called the happy hour for 16.00.

Day 3 – Fri 10.06.16   Carnarvon Gorge [Takarakka Bush Resort]

Left camp just after 08.30, and drove up to the Ranger Station, a little further up the Gorge.

Started the walk to the "Moss Gardens", a walk of about seven km return at around 09.00.

An interesting walk. And tested the endeavour, courage, and fitness, and ability of all. The end result was very satisfying, I think, to all, and was enhanced by the fact we were able to tag onto a tour group and got some good info and to how the "Moss Gardens" came about. We arrived back at the Ranger Station, at around 13.30, and after a short sit down and toilet stop, headed for camp.

After a lunch of Annie's soup and bread, and a rest period, it was into happy hour once again, to discuss the events of the day, and others.

Tomorrow means on the move again, heading for Emerald to fuel up, both for body and auto, and head for Sapphire.

Day 4 – Sat 11.06.16   Carnarvon Gorge to Sapphire [Sapphire Caravan Park]

The departure from Carnarvon was delayed for 15 minutes, due to some members of the group having to frequent the toilet block often. This delayed the packing up of the van. The cause of this, I believe, was a previously consumed meal. However, once on the road it was a good trip through to where we stopped for a coffee at 11.00.

Next stop was the Woolworth's carpark at Emerald, got there at around 12.00, did the required shopping, lunch, and all topped up with fuel. One particular member decided that he'd had enough of looking at his very dusty truck and trailer (a gift from the dirt road we had to travel on to Carnarvon), so went off to find a car wash, this was successful and so two other members used the facility as well. With three clean and one dirty, we headed for Sapphire, arriving at around 15.00.

After check-in we caught up with G & C, and also Warwick and Carole, who had left the village the day before the rest of us. This brought the number of Beachmere Sands residents up to twelve. We all enjoyed happy hour, with a BBQ to follow. A quiet celebration of John's birthday followed this.

Day 5 – Sun 12.06.16   Sapphire [Sapphire Caravan Park]

How better do you start a day, than with a bacon and egg cook up? It happened on this Sunday morning and was enjoyed by all.

After lunch we all went for a drive out to the Heritage Mine for a look, with a couple of members going underground as part of a tour and information thing. During the drive, we passed three Brolgas feeding by the roadside, so had to get some photos of this rare site.

After returning had a happy hour at our site, but because of the very cool evening we pulled stumps early.

Day 6 – Mon 13.06.16   Sapphire [Sapphire Caravan Park]

We woke to the sound of rain on the roof. Not heavy, just annoying. It reduced the light enough to make trying to find Sapphires very difficult. So the morning was declared free to do whatever.

That evening R & B did a nice roast beef, with the other girls doing the vegetables, etc. We went up to the BBQ shack and set the tables early so we could guarantee some good seats around the open fire. On the hour of six the food arrived and so started a very pleasant evening meal, with dessert to follow. All of this in front of one of Warwick's roaring fires, with the sound of rain on the iron roof. In fact, it was so comfortable that one member removed her shoes and held her feet to the fire with a very satisfying sigh.

Day 7 – Tue 14.06.16   Sapphire [Sapphire Caravan Park]

The rain had gone and the sun was trying to shine, and today was the day when we were going to find our sapphires. After morning coffee, we headed out to the Miners Cottage to meet Gay. Warwick had already for-warned her that the mob was on the way.

After Gays' initial explanation of how to go about the finding of these little shiny pieces of stone, it was on and everyone set to finding as many stones as possible. Warwick took G & C down to meet Darrin, the local gem cutter, to get some good samples to take home. The rest of us took a little longer with Gay and got home around 16.00. Happy hour started in earnest at around 16.30, for another good evening.

Day 8 – Wed 15.06.16   Sapphire to Ilfracombe
[Ilfracombe Caravan Park]

G & C left camp at around 08.00, to go and pick up their cut stones from Darrin, and then head north towards their destination of Airlie Beach. The rest had a leisurely pack up and left camp at around 09.45, leaving behind Warwick & Carole, who were staying on till the end of the month. After a 30-minute stopover at Alpha for coffee, we headed directly to Ilfracombe, arriving around 14.20. At check-in, we found that we had to split up because of caravan size etc., which meant that J & L were out on their own away from the mob.

Happy hour at the Ilfracombe Caravan Park is different from anything, anywhere. Absolutely entertaining, by our hosts Jessie & Cathy. A good night then home for dinner for those who did not eat at the Shed.

Day 9 – Thurs. 16.06.16   Ilfracombe [Ilfracombe Caravan Park]

The group split up with R & L taking their truck, with K & S as the passengers, and off to the "Stockman's Hall of Fame", and R & B in their truck taking J & L and heading to town, for shopping. All was quite uneventful until one member of the group got stuck in the public dunny. I ask you, how does that happen in a place like Longreach, the is answer is simple, it is because there was no maintenance on the dunny door lock mechanism. Luckily some good Samaritan came to the rescue, freed the member and reported the incident to the local Council and Police department, who I might add, offered to shoot the lock off the door and therefore do away with the problem.

Apart from that it was an uneventful day, until a "Road Train" parked on the roadside not 20 metres from the van of J & L, then the load of big fat bullocks decided to relieve themselves, this of course ran out of the trailer and over the road and down the gutter. To find out a little later that the driver of the road train was Cathy's brother, who just stopped to say g'day. That's the way it is out here, like it or lump it.

Happy hour was at 17.00 at the van of R & B. The camp happy hour was doing a Karaoke thing that we were not that interested in.

Day 10 – Fri. 17.06.16   Ilfracombe [Ilfracombe Caravan Park]

Day started out overcast and cold, and looking like rain, but as the day progressed it became a little brighter, and warmed up to around 24 deg.

K & S went for a drive to Longreach, the rest headed for the "Machinery Mile", to view the old equipment and machinery used to make this part of the country farmable. It was quite a display and worth seeing. On the way back to camp, and on the other side of the road, is the "Wellshot Centre" worth a look with a good video on what "Wellshot Station" was all about and how it came to be. In its heyday it used to carry in excess of 400,000 sheep, being the largest in the country. Further down the street it was decided that, as it was after midday, a beer at the "Wellshot Hotel" was in order.

Tonight, is back to happy hour at the shed, with Cathy entertaining us this evening, along with a roast pork dinner at 18.00.

Started packing up around 15.00 just in case we got some more rain this evening, and we need an early start in the morning.

Day 11 – Sat. 18.06.16   Ilfracombe to Kynuna [Free Camp]

The day started overcast and remained overcast, with rain before Longreach, and after Winton.

All fuelled up at Longreach except Ronny, who had done it a couple of days before. The trip was uneventful to Winton, and we found parking for all, then went for a walk to into town to find some lunch. This we did at the Tattersall's Hotel, where the Ronny and the Barra had lamb's brains, something Ronny had wanted before we left home.

More fuel was taken on at Kynuna. Then we looked for the free camp for the night. Rosco did the job again and we pulled into a site 30 kms north of Kynuna.

After setting up, we had some light rain that was on and off. One member decided to go bush and point Percy but forgot how soft the mud could be, after pointing he came back to camp wearing two-inch platform sandals, only to get told off by she who must be obeyed.

Happy hour was a must, so all eight of us piled into the Traveller that gave not a lot of room for drinking, but a lot of room for laughter.

Day 12 – Sun. 19.06.16   Kynuna to Mary Kathleen [Free Camp in old Town site]

Headed off from the free camp around 08.45 headed for McKinlay., stopped to take a photo of the Croc Dundee Hotel, found the local dunny and a dump point, used both and made a note for next time. Heading for Cloncurry and the info centre on know what was worth looking at and what was not. This was a reconnaissance thing for the return journey (that word again). Some members had to get bread, others had to get gas. One wonders if we will ever get on the bloody road again. Anyway, we did, and we headed for the old Mary Kathleen Mine site.

We made it, but the debate started as to whether we should go in, go somewhere else, or whatever. After about an hour, we finally parked the vans and said this will do. In hindsight, it was not a bad site; I say site, but really, we could have gone anywhere in the old town. All the old houses had been removed of course, but the concrete slabs of the garages were still there, and it was great to park the van beside these. After lunch it was a bit of a relax, or some chose to go for a walk and take some photos.

Then came the happy hour, and to top that, came a visit from the Avon Lady, yes the Avon Lady, out in the middle of nowhere, a deserted old mining town, came the Avon Lady, with the bloody door chime and all, but it made Ronnie's day, he was able to buy some hair shampoo; I ask you. After dinner it was time to look at the moon and stars to find out exactly where we were, tracked a few aircraft, and saw a satellite, then was time for bed. However, some of the girls had to watch a TV program about some gardens.

Day 13 – Mon. 20.06.16   Mary Kathleen to Mt Isa [Sunset Top Tourist Park]

The day started a little early (06.00) with a certain member of the group banging on a caravan door saying something about lights being on. He then decided to do a wake-up call for the whole camp at 07.30.

This was not appreciated at all, and he was told by all.

It was later discovered that the lights had been on all night (operator error) and a battery was very, very flat. After a jump start, all was well.

Left Mary Kathleen around 09.30 and headed for Mt Isa, approx. 60km away. Got set up in the Top Tourist Caravan Park before lunch, with time for some to go to town, and some to stay home, the air in the Isa is quite cool, but if you are in the sun it is quite pleasant. We have three nights here, so a couple of days to look around.

I think next time we might look for a better park, this one is a little ordinary. It is hard to pick a good one from a bad one out of a book.

Day 14 – Tue. 21.06.16   Mt Isa [Sunset Top Tourist Park]

This morning was a start at around 09.30 and we were heading for the "School of The Air". (not for some last-minute education, but a look at what and how they do it) Very interesting set up. From there it was off to the information centre to book in for the underground tour, the next day. Then on to the Coffee Club, where a member of the group discovered that a pair of sunnies was missing. After quite some time and thought on the subject, it was decided that a trip back to the information centre would solve the problem. However, this was not to be as the glasses were discovered it somebody else's handbag.

Day 15 – Wed. 22.06.16   Mt Isa [Sunset Top Tourist Park]

Down the mine all the blokes went, and the girls were off to the underground Hospital. All had a good time with nothing lost or misplaced. The afternoon was set aside for shopping, refuelling, and car washing was optional. Started packing up late afternoon, but making sure that it did not interfere with the happy hour thing.

Day 16 – Thur. 23.06.16   Mt Isa – Wonarah Bore [Free Camp.]

Left Mt Isa at 08.30. and headed west, I think that the Isa has more smoke and more dogs that anywhere else.

Stopped at Camooweal for coffee and Kevin got some fuel. Got going again half an hour latter heading for Rosco's Wiki Camp site. Could not find the campsite so kept driving on to the Wonarah bore. It was a good run, not a lot of traffic, and the country was changing all the time.

Not a bad spot for an overnighter, somebody even made the comment "Gee, I've got a room with a view".

Had lunch, and waited for the party. That was to celebrate the new State we were now travelling in. Good party, a lot of laughs and merriment. After dinner, some members of the group were lucky enough to have Beachmere grown lettuce, cabbage and beetroot in their salad. Then it was star gazing time. The size of the Milky Way is incredible, totally different to what you ever see in the city or anywhere on the coast.

Time for a short read, then bed, as we have an early start in the morning.

Day 17 – Fri. 24.06.16 Wonarah Bore – Taylor Creek [Free Camp]

Got away 07.45, a good time considering the constraints. It was a good trip, with plenty of changes in the countryside. It was noted that there were very few insects on the windscreen and very few Kangaroos on the road.

Arrived at the Three Ways the junction of the Barkley Highway and the "Stuart Highway". Coming into the Northern Territory the road was a little rough, but after about 15Km's it changed for the better, and ever since it has been really good.

The Three ways can be noted for about only one thing, that is the price of fuel, at $1.68/ Litre, not good. We took on what was needed and headed south for the" Devils Marbles". When we got there, the campground was full so decided to move on down the track and see what we could find.

Day 18 – Sat. 25.06.16 Taylor Creek – Ormiston Gorge [Campground]

Got another good start to the day and headed for the Alice. Stopped for fuel at Ti Tree, but JB was the only one silly enough to purchase at $1.75 per litre. Then continued on to the Alice. We arrived around midday and pulled over and parked to check out directions and fuel sites. Decided to have lunch, then top up with fuel and head for Ormiston Gorge. All of that happened as planned until the tour leader overshot the turnoff to Ormiston and took the whole group to the Glen Helen Turnoff before we could do a U turn and head back to Ormiston Gorge.

We were lucky enough to get parking for all 4 vans, so did so, then found there was a fee, well, donation really, but with a bonus attached, in that we could order a pizza for dinner. This we did and had a very good night.

Day 19 – Sun. 26.06.16   Ormiston Gorge – Alice Springs [Wintersun Cabin & Caravan Park]

We had light rain on and off on during the night, not a lot, just enough to settle the dust a little more. Before breakfast I took a walk up the hill behind the Gorge, to get some more photos. It was all good, but it would have been better if the sun was out. After breakfast it was down to the Gorge itself for some more photos.

Things have changed over time, with the campground we used 35 years ago is now unused, with all the infrastructure being moved back up the hill. With the light rain still coming down, it was decided to head for the Alice and get set up for a four-night stay. Half way back the rain had stopped and the road dried up.

Day 20 – Mon. 27.06.16   Alice Springs [Wintersun Cabin & Caravan Park]

Today was a day when we had to do our voting for the Federal Elections. We had all organised for postal votes to be delivered the Alice Springs Post Office, but when we arrived to pick up the posted info, it had not arrived. So, enter plan "B" find the "Electoral Office", and just do it. So we did. After we went back to the Woolworths Shopping Centre and had a coffee. Of course, K & S were exempt from all of this because they had done all this in Mt Isa.

Back to camp for lunch, and then off to the Transport museum, on the South Side of Town, while the girls were off to the Beanie Expo. The transport was very good, and the blokes really enjoyed looking at all the memorabilia, until one member of the group displayed, that he was still a child, when he tried to ring the bell on a fire engine, to find that it was child proof. The girls said they enjoyed the Beanie thing, saying that they would like to return, to see some of the other displays that were on offer.

Day 21 – Tue. 28.06.16   Alice Springs [Wintersun Cabin & Caravan Park]

This morning was BC. (Bloody Cold), like 3 Deg. This did not deter the intrepid travellers, and they prepared to go to Standley Chasm. K & S decided not to go on the walk, so six of us headed out.

The Chasm had changed a bit over the 35 years since the last visit, with infrastructure being built and a Kiosk and gift shop, now operating.

The car park looked different and the walk up to the chasm was now on a made track, whereas before it was up the creek bed. Up at the Chasm itself had also changed with a lot more gravel, and less water from what I remember. The rock formations were still memorable and we got some good photos. Back at the Kiosk we had a coffee and Lesley said she would like to visit the Royal Flying Doctor Centre. We all agreed, so it was we follow them. I do think that the navigator aboard the Vee Dub should turn the map up the other way, or learn to program the unit that is connected to the satellite. In time we all got there and thought that the RFDS was very good, and very well worth seeing. Then it was time for some lunch, and an afternoon of not much.

Day 22 – Wed. 29.06.16   Alice Springs [Wintersun Cabin & Caravan Park]

A free day for all, so time to catch up on the washing and ironing.

Went out to The Culture Centre, as Lyn wanted another look around, and the blokes could take in the Aviation Museum.

Another car load went off the Telegraph Station, and had a good time, said it was well worth it. They even sent a Telegraph message back home.

It was then time to stock up on some food, for the next few nights of free camping, give the cars a wash. And start packing up in prep for the next morning.

Day 23 – Thu. 30.06.16   Alice Springs – Bonney Well [Free camp]

The day did not start well for someone when he discovered that the black machine would not start. So, after much humiliation, especially after having to be jump started from the Mighty Merc. On analyses, it was thought to be non-adherence to correct procedures, in other words "Operator error" on the part of the pilot. All that aside, we got away 15 min early and headed for Bonney Well, for the first night of free camping since Ormiston Gorge. Topped up with fuel at Wycliffe Well. Then on to get set up early, before the rush.

Day 24 – Fri. 01.07.16   Bonney Well – Elliott [Free Camp, Longreach Waterhole]

Got away 10 minutes early. And headed for a fuel stop at Tennant Creek. Did a coffee stop at around 10.30. at Attack Creek. Would have been a good free camp site. After coffee we headed for Elliott and the turnoff to the Waterhole. The 11Km Sandy track in did not please everyone, but we made it, and set up camp a little back from the water's edge. Had a happy hour at the normal time or thereabouts, with some friends of Sue, Clive and Judi. A good night, seeing the sunset across the waterhole. The birdlife at this place is incredible, a lot of Pelicans and Capped Turns. It was an early night for all, with no Road Trains, no trains, no cars, all trying to do 130kph or more, in the night.

Day 25 – Sat. 02.07.16   Elliott [Free Camp, Longreach Waterhole]

A nothing day planned, so a sleep in, even I missed the Territory Sunrise. After the usual things, like breakfast with a good coffee. It was a do what you want day, most read, some had to write a book, (so others would have a record of what they did on this trip). This was the day of the Federal elections, and the technocrat of the group set up the satellite dish, rigged the tele outside, so that we could all watch the Election results live. In hindsight, I think it was a waste of time, because we all went to bed, not very happy with how things were going, and may well have been better off not knowing anything.

Day 26 – Sun. 03.07.16   Longreach Waterhole – Mataranka. [Mataranka Cabins & Camping, Bitter Springs]

The day did not start good for some, when it was discovered that the Travelling Vee Dub could not give taillights to the van. The pilot decided to go and we all left the waterhole at around 7.45, and headed back out to the highway. More problems with the Travelling Vee Dub, as there was also a problem with the brake controller. After our resident sparks lent a hand we were soon on the way again, minus taillights on the van.

The rest of the trip was quite uneventful and we arrived at Bitter Springs around 12.30. Got booked in, but not together. Went for a walk later that arvo, down through the park to the little Roper River, and followed it along for a while and eventually got to the hot Springs.

The car park was full and so was the waterhole. We agreed that the best time for a swim would be early the next morning. So we returned to camp and had the happiest of hours. Deciding that a swim at seven and leave by at 10.00, was in order.

Day 27 – Mon. 04.07.16 Bitter Spring (Mataranka) – Katherine [Knotts Crossing Resort Caravan Park]

Not all were game enough for the swim, so it was only those of a very brave heart, and a reasonable amount of foolhardiness, that took up the challenge, which really means there was only four of us who got up and got wet this morning. We did and we enjoyed it very much.

After brekky it was pack up and we left at around the agreed time and headed for Katherine. Ronny had made the booking at the Knotts Crossing Resort, and we all had good sites with ensuites, but not all together. However, this was to be a five-night stopover, and therefore it was where we could sit back and relax for a while in a very nice park, and think about what to enjoy here and, after this, and before Darwin.

The afternoon was a time for a car-load to head to the information centre and do some shopping. This was a very good idea as I got coffee with scones and NZ cream for afternoon tea, "beat that".

The Auto-Sparkie was booked for 16.30 to fix the lights on the Travelling Vee Dub. It was found that the Pilot had turned a little tight at the Waterhole and pinched the wiring loom and actually cut a wire, so once again this gets logged under "Operator Error", becoming a habit don't you think.

Day 28 – Tue. 05.07.16 Katherine [Knotts Crossing Resort Caravan Park]

Info centre was the place to find out what was on and R & L went to check it out. They brought home a load of pamphlets and stuff to digest.

Went back to the info centre to book a trip up the gorge at 07.00 the next morning, (now that was to be a challenge)

Happy hour was a happy hour plus some, (as usual).

Day 29 – Wed. 06.07.16 Katherine [Knotts Crossing Resort Caravan Park]

Some of the group, (one in particular), could not sleep before such a big event, and was to feel poorly for the next couple of days. The morning came, and we all got away on time to get to Gorge in time for the trip.

To our surprise breakfast was supplied, so we all had another cup of coffee and half a muffin.

At 07.00 the trip kicked off, with the trip up the first gorge, then we had to disembark and walk approx. 400 meters to the next boat, then went up the second Gorge. All of this was very good, and after 35 years it was good to see the changes and improvements that have taken place. All enjoyed the trip and thought it was well worthwhile.

Later in the day, it was back down to the info centre, to get our permits for the Kakadu trip.

Day 30 – Thu. 07.07.16 Katherine [Knotts Crossing Resort Caravan Park]

Today was a look around day. Some did the thermal Springs, while R & L went off to check out Edith Falls. After lunch it was relax time then prep for tomorrow when we were to head North.

Day 31 – Fri. 08.07.16 Katherine [Knotts Crossing Resort Caravan Park]

An early morning swim, at the Katherine Thermal Springs, was the order of the day. Well, not that early, try 09.15. The swim was good and refreshing and enjoyed by all.

After the swim it was home to coffee with scones, jam and cream. Why not?

The afternoon was a time to do some shopping, fill up, empty out, and wash off, and generally get ready to leave in the morning.

Day 32 – Sat. 09.07.16 Katherine – Daly River. [Daly River Barra Resort]

Good trip, left Katherine 08.45 headed for Daly River, and some Barramundi. Wanted to stop at Emerald Springs for smoko, but a Road Train cattle truck beat us and the place was a mess, so we just used it as a drive through. We stopped at Hayes Creek

Coffee and toilets. A good spot, but the campground was a bit dusty. On to Daly River and camp. The camp was a little disappointing, mainly from the lack of green grass.

The fishing expert won't be back until Monday night. This place has not come up to expectations, and the girls are wanting more. We had originally booked for four nights but changed that to three at check-in.

After lunch, the girls all headed for town to find out if there is any more to this place. Came back after finding the Aboriginal settlement, but not much else.

Day 33 – Sun. 10.07.16   Daly River. [Daly River Barra Resort]

Time to have a communal breakfast, how good are they. Followed by a nice cup of coffee. All done at leisure. How good. Two cars went off to have a look around, found the river, and saw a few freshwater crocs lying on the river bank. Also, plenty of Barramundi (or Catfish, we don't know which) swimming up and down the river.

Day 34 – Mon. 11.07.16   Daly River – Adelaide River [Free Camp, Showgrounds]

07.45 saw the blokes head off for a look at the river down at the public boat ramp, the fog closed in and covered just about all. Did not see any lizards, so were a little disappointed.

After brekky, having a coffee, it was decided that we were moving on to Adelaide River showgrounds. So it was a mad rush to pack up and get going, to be there before midday.

This was achieved but it was not without some moments. I will leave it at that. The Dorat Road that we travelled on, from the Daly River Road, up to Adelaide River, is apparently a Heritage Listed roadway, as it is part of the very original Stuart Highway. It was a little ordinary, but that is to be expected with little maintenance.

Day 35 – Tue. 12.07.16   Adelaide River [Free Camp, Showgrounds]

A lazy morning, but the weather was still perfect, with very little wind and a clear sky, well not really, as the smoke haze was still with us because of the burning off of the bush. This is something that happens at this time every season up here.

After smoko, we all went to the Commonwealth War Cemetery. Very impressed with the way it is kept, in fact the appearance of the whole town is very good. Worth coming back to one day.

We are expecting some rain to get to Darwin tonight, whether it gets down this far is the question. Might have to pack up in the rain tomorrow.

Late afternoon found a new pastime, that of watching model aircraft. A fellow camper had a model powered glider that was flying with the eagles.

Day 36 – Wed. 13.07.16 Adelaide River – Darwin [Darwin Boomerang Motel & Caravan Park]

Rain overnight, at least some were smart, and packed up awnings and mats etc. the night before. Packed up for a 09.30 getaway, but were on the road by 09.15. heading for Berry Springs. We last visited this place in 1981. As usual with everything in the NT, it had changed a lot. The thermal Springs water holes were much the same, but the picnic grounds built around then was impressive. After smoko and a look around, it was time to head off to Palmerston and the Boomerang Park.

After checking in and setting up the van, we headed off to the shops for supplies.

Day 37 – Thu. 14.07.16 Darwin. [Darwin Boomerang Motel & Caravan Park]

Light wind during the day and evening, partly cloudy sky.

This morning was a trip for the blokes, with Mark, (son of Ron & Brenda), to the new Palmerston Hospital, which is under construction, by Lend Lease. Mark was able to arrange a site visit for us as he is a Project Manager with the NT Department of Infrastructure. It was very interesting to see the overall plan of the facility and the amount of progress they have made in a relatively short time.

While the blokes were donning safety clothing, hats, glasses, boots, and gloves, the girls were home doing those domestic things called washing and cleaning.

After lunch, we went over and had a look at "Jenny's orchid Garden" on the way out to East Point and the Darwin Military Museum. Did not go into the Museum, as the time was running out, and we would not have seen too much.

Called it quits and headed for a late happy hour.

Day 38 – Fri. 15.07.16 Darwin. [Darwin Boomerang Motel & Caravan Park]

Light wind during the day and evening, partly cloudy sky.
The girls had booked in for haircuts over at the Casuarina Shopping Centre. So, the guys dropped them off and headed for the Australian Aviation Heritage Centre. This was a good display of all types of aviation, an actual Boeing B52G on display.

This was backed up by a replica Spitfire, F111, Mirage, F86 Sabre, among a lot of others. Our good fortune was that some aviation exercises were being undertaken by the USAF and the RAAF, and a flight of FA18s took off from the air base and it happened that the flight path was over the venue we were at. Very appropriate.

After this it was back to Casuarina to pick up the girls, have a coffee, spend some more money, then head for town, doing Spotlight on the way, Spotlight, also turned into Anaconda and more money spent. It was then on to the water front, for a bite to eat, and a look around.

This included the tunnels dug into the surrounding hills, that was used for bunker oil storage during WW2. After it was some window shopping at the waterfront and a look at the wave pool, before heading home.

Just after five it was time to head off to the Palmerston markets. We went by Mark's pad and could then follow he and Karen (daughter of Ron & Brenda, who flew up to Darwin to have some time with the traveling family and Mark). On to Palmerston City Centre and the Markets. Plenty of good food and people. Had a bite to eat, then headed for home.

Day 39 – Sat. 16.07.16   Darwin. [Darwin Boomerang Motel & Caravan Park]

Light wind during the day and evening, partly cloudy sky.

Slower day today. Somebody had to try out the new washing machine, purchased for the van. With the trial deemed a success, it was off to do some more shopping at the supermarket and get some fuel.

Tonight, was a BBQ at Mark's pad. Damned good night with a lot of laughs, a good night was had by all.

Day 40 – Sun. 17.07.16   Darwin. [Darwin Boomerang Motel & Caravan Park]

Light wind during the day and evening, partly cloudy sky.

Sunday Morning, communal cook-up time. Ronny left early to pick up Karen, Mark was off on a pre-planned bike ride so couldn't make it. Cooking by 08.00, eating by 08.45, good stuff.

The Darwin Beer Can Regatta. An event that has been going strong since 1974. J & L remember them being held in Gove, in the late seventies.

It was off down to the beach at around 09.30, to have a look at some of the boats and the markets. The main event was not until 15.00 so only a few were on display, but got a good idea of what some good ones would look like.

It was decided to go into the city, have a look at the plaza, and get a coffee fix. After which we returned to camp so R & B could spend some more time with the children, leaving K & S back at the beach to see the race. R & L caught up with some friends who were staying at another Caravan Park, then went over to spotlight to do some more retail therapy, before going on a sightseeing tour of Darwin.

All were to return for a happy hour that we had not had for a few days.

Day 41 – Mon. 18.07.16   Darwin. [Darwin Boomerang Motel & Caravan Park]

Clear sky's light wind during the day dropping off in evening through to the next morning.

Very early start. Out at the gate at 07.15 to be picked up by the bus, for a tour out to Litchfield National Park. The bus was late and we were beginning to wonder if it was going to come at all, but it did at around 07.45. By the time we all got on the bus was full, so I think it was nineteen plus the driver.

Headed out along the Arnhem Highway, to a place called Window to the Wetlands Visitor Centre. Had a look around and watched part of a DVD called "The big Wet". This about how this part of the country is affected in the wet season. (I think I have this at home, so must remember to share it around when we get back there). From there it was down a dirt road to the Adelaide River to see some Croc jumping, all very good both Ross and I got some good photos.

Then it was back in the bus, and headed back along the Arnhem Highway, to the Stuart, and headed South. All the time of course being entertained by the driver who was giving a running commentary that never stopped.

Got to the turnoff to Batchelor and stopped the other side of town for a supplied lunch. After lunch it was off to the Wangi Falls for a swim, with more commentary. Karen, being the youngest, was the only game enough to take on the cold water. Ross and I when on a quick walk up to the top of the falls, just to get some photos. Along the way saw some piglets (not good), and flying foxes.

It was then on to the Buley Rockhole for another swim, with more commentary along the way. After a fruit smoko, (with no smoke) we were on our way back to Darwin, arriving at our park around 17.30.

A little late in starting happy hour, but we made up for it, as it was Ross' Birthday it was a real "Happy Hour". All said goodbye to Mark & Karen, as the next day we were moving again.

Day 42 – Tue. 19.07.16   Darwin – Mary River [Mary River Park]

Clear sky's light wind during the day dropping off in evening through to the next morning.

Late start, as we could not book into Mary River until around Lunch time. Move-out was to be 10.00, but we were early again, and made it by 09.50. Headed out along the Arnhem Highway and pulled into a roadside stop and called it smoko. With Mary River only 60Kms down the road, there was no rush.

After coffee we headed off and pulled into the wilderness retreat and got set up. Decided that the next day we would hire a couple of buggies and go for a drive on some of the tracks around the place.

Day 43 – Wed. 20.07.16   Mary River. [Mary River Park]

Clear sky's light wind during the day dropping off in evening through to the next morning.

Ten o'clock was the booked time for the buggies. Sue and Lesley were the nominated drivers, Lesley got the fast one and took off like a scolded cat. The tracks were very dusty, so it goes without saying really, that those on the back, got covered in dust, because for some reason the buggy in the front could not go slow enough.

The trip was around the outside of the camping area, and down along the river. On one of the sand bars we spotted four crocs, and another in one of the billabongs we went past.

After dropping the buggies back, we thought we might book a table for dinner in the restaurant, to celebrate the wedding anniversary of R & B.

Happy hour at 17.00, up to the restaurant at 18.15 for dinner. After a bit of a disagreement over the price, two having got their dinner 30 minutes ahead of the rest, the Barra that was ordered was overcooked and cold, we decided by mutual agreement that it was not much of a restaurant, and we would not be going back. So, it was home to bed.

Day 44 – Thu. 21.07.16   Mary River. [Mary River Park]

Clear sky's light wind during the day dropping off in evening through to the next morning.

Another lazy morning, smoko was to be at 10.30. When we arrived at the venue, it was found that Ron was taking tuition from Lesley in the art of knitting, and Ross was having his toe nail manicured by Brenda. I decided that it might be safer to go home for coffee.

Day 45 – Fri. 22.07.16   Mary River – Jabiru. [Kakadu Lodge]

Clear sky's light wind during the day dropping off in evening through to the next morning.

Eight o'clock start was requested and an eight o'clock start was delivered. The reason was to get to Jabiru early, as they would not take advance bookings. It was a 140 odd k's run from Mary River to Jabiru, so we were nice and early and got some good sites. Had a coffee break finished setting up, then went downtown before lunch. A lot of the town was closed thanks to the NT Show Day. Back for some lunch and to chill out in the vans air conditioning until sunset watching time. Approx. 35 Deg today.

Day 46 – Sat. 23.07.16   Jabiru. [Kakadu Lodge]

Clear sky's light wind during the day dropping off in evening through to the next morning.

Slower start today. With kick-off to be 09.30. We headed for Iburr Rock to see some rock paintings. It was a pleasant drive north along the escarpment. Got to the rock and spent about an hour walking around looking at all of the sites. I got up on to the top of one of the rock formations and got some good photos looking out over the wetlands.

After the rock it was time for coffee or tea. After it was back down the road to Cahills Crossing. We had been told of this event that only happens on a major high tide. Apparently, the incoming tide brings with it a lot of fish, and as the water flows over the crossing the Crocs have a bit of a feeding frenzy. High tide was still about one and a half hours away at 13.45, yet the viewing platform was packed with people wanting the best view. So we waited and waited and waited. (a bit like watching a cake cook, really).

The event came and went with no fish, and a few hungry Crocs and people, so we went back to the rock and had some lunch. It was then home to wait for the sunset watching. This was also the Northern part of the trip and the closest we would come to Arnhem Land (just across the East Alligator River at Cahills crossing).

Please note there has been no mention of the change of Navigator for this trip, with the original one spitting the dunny and handing over to an old Territorian, after being told he was on the road to Maningrida.

Day 47 – Sun. 24.07.16   Jabiru [Kakadu Lodge]

Clear sky's light wind during the day dropping off in evening through to the next morning.

Nourlangie Rock was the target for today. After an early morning tea at 09.30, we headed off down the Kakadu Highway to Nourlangie. Found the turnoff and headed in, we turned off the main track and parked the trucks. The walk across to Anbangbang billabong was only 250mts, we found all the grassy banks of the billabong had been rooted up by wild pigs, it was a bit of a mess, let's hope some of them became croc food during the night.

On to Nourlangie and the rock paintings. There has been a lot of work done in these parks over the years and now it is really good with viewing platforms, step and stairs to make the access very good and easy, even some rough stuff for those who want it. So rough in fact that one of the group claims he was attached by Rhinos and Bears when he sat on a log. (I think the truth was his attraction to gravity was so great that it overcame the strength of the log, so he wound up hitting the ground at high speed with his butt. In the process grazing his arm, and maybe other places that we were unable to see.

However, this did not detract from this being a very good mornings walk, finishing in a picnic lunch for all. It was then on to a drive around the track to the Muirella Park, and the Djarradjin Billabong, took a couple of pics' then it was time to head back to camp.

Another good sunset watch was had by all, well not all, as some, no, just one, deserved a little, and got a lot.

A vote was taken on the best way to start the Journey home, and it was agreed that two nights in Katherine was in order, with as much swimming in the thermal pools as we could stand, as well as stocking up for several nights free camping out towards Cape Crawford and beyond.

Day 48 – Mon. 25.07.16   Jabiru. [Kakadu Lodge]

A little cloud this morning, and the wind got up a little stronger around midday.

Great start to the day. It was time for the deferred cook-up for breakfast. (what a way to start the day, for a bunch on holiday. (extended holiday).

Some decided that it was a day to stay at home, and have a look around Jabiru, while a car load headed off, for a look at the Yellow Water Region. This was a trip of about 54Km from Jabiru, and heading for Cooinda Lodge, and to find the start of the boardwalk along the wetlands. Found all of that. And the boardwalk was very good, considering that it was now near midday. Then it was back to the Warradjan Aboriginal Cultural Centre. This was very good and consumed a fair bit of time. After a Ice cream on a stick (very nice, thank you very much). It was time to head for home, but taking time, to stop at the Mirral Lookout.

This was a thing for the blokes, 1.6kms, 50 minutes return, very steep, very rough, for a 360 deg view of Kakadu. 35 minutes later, we were back with all the photos we needed, and with somebody's ankle still intact. Time for home, and a cold G & T.

Another good sunset watch was had by all. (what a good habit this is).

Day 49 – Tue. 26.07.16   Jabiru – Katherine. [Riverview Tourist Village]

A little cloud this morning, and the wind got up a little stronger around midday.

Time to move, 08.00 for a 08.30 getaway, was the order, and it was achieved by all. Had a good run all the way, stopped for coffee just south of Pine Creek, then on to Katherine.

Got set up, and each went their own way, for the arvo.

Another good sunset watch was had by all.

Day 50 – Wed. 27.07.16   Katherine. [Riverview Tourist Village]

No cloud this morning, and the wind got up a little stronger around midday, and slackened off by evening.

A late start by most, except for two brave blocks who went for an early morning swim.

The order of the day was some washing, coffee at the Coffee Club because a certain member needed another fix.

It had been a week away from civilization, Civilization being, having access to a Coffee Club. After coffee it was time for shopping, filling up, and washing off.

Back at camp, it was pack away, and get some lunch. Although some thought that chasing a photo of "The Ghan" coming through Katherine was more important.

Sunset watching was set for Five, but after it was time to start packing up and hitching up ready for an early departure in the morning, so as to have an early arrival at Daly Waters, to be able to secure a park for the vans.

Day 51 – Thu. 28.07.16   Katherine – Daly Waters. [Daly Waters Pub Caravan Park]

No cloud this morning, and the wind got up a little stronger around midday, and slackened off by evening.

Left Katherine at 07.30, and headed straight to the Pub, to book in for the night. While we were waiting another three or four vans turned up, some just drove off, probably not liking what they saw. Anyhow, we got our booking and got directed into our allotted sites. The sites were very dusty, but I guess we are in the dry season. We had also booked for dinner, when we booked in, A Steak and Barra, for $32.00, you just have to try that.

It was off down to the Pub at 16.00 to secure a table for dinner, and to join in the "Happy Hour" that started at 17.00. The entertainment started at around 17.00, and was Country and Western, a chap by the name of Guy Maxwell, not bad. At 19.00 was dinner time and it was OK, certainly plenty of food.

An 08.00 start in the morning, although not a lot to pack up, as we stayed hooked overnight.

Day 52 – Fri. 29.07.16   Daly Waters – Cape Crawford. [Heartbreak Hotel Caravan Park]

No cloud this morning, and the wind got up a little stronger around midday, and slackened off by evening.

Left camp at 08.00, and headed for the junction of the Stuart and the Carpentaria highways, to top up with fuel. When the refuelling was complete, it was off to Cape Crawford. It was a good run apart from some idiot drivers going too fast.

Arrived at Cape Crawford around 12.00, booked in and then set up camp before lunch.

Had a lazy arvo, before we did the usual sunset watching, at 17.00.

Day 53 – Sat. 30.07.16   Cape Crawford – Borroloola, (Day Trip).

Another cloudless Territory day, with a light breeze.

It was decided that we would drive into Borroloola, for a look around. During our Sunset Watching evening, we had a visitor from another van, and was saying that they went and saw the "Lost City", this is on the road to Borroloola. Say no more we had to see this. So, the next morning we took two cars and headed for town. About 65 Kms. We drove about out we came to the Caranbirini Conservation Reserve. About half a k in we parked, and headed for the spectacle. It is not actually a Lost City but rock formations, that have been eroded by time and water. It was a great area to walk through, and to get some very good photos.

It was on from there, to town, into the Supermarket before it closed at 12.00. along with everything else in town.

(Actually, this is still the practice in the NT. Half a day Saturday, and no trading on Sundays. How civilised is this.)

We were going to have lunch at the Pub in Borroloola, but as it also closed, we headed back to Cape Crawford. Had a lazy arvo, before we did the usual sunset watching, at 16.30.

Day 54 – Sun. 31.07.16   Cape Crawford – Wonarah Bore. [Free Camp Wonarah Bore]

Another cloudless Territory day, with a light breeze.

Left at 07.30 this morning, with a full day ahead, with the target, Wonarah Bore, a free camp we stayed at on the way into the N.T.

The changes in countryside and the variation in the foliage, made up for the quality of the road. After leaving Cape Crawford, the road was reasonable, but got progressively worse, as it wound through the low hills, and climbed up onto the tablelands. As we went up the trees got smaller and more parse, and the small shrubs gave way to the grasslands. At times here was not a tree to be seen only dried grasses. The paddocks were divided by cattle-stops, with many kilometres in between.

Many times, it was a matter of coming to a halt to give way to the cattle, and their fat little calves. In all it was a great trip of contrasts. In the 377 Kilometres of the Tablelands Highway, we did not have anyone wishing to overtake us, and only ten vehicles coming towards us.

We got to the Barkley homestead at around 12.45. and all topped up, to give enough to carry us through to Camooweal, where the fuel was cheaper.

We arrived at the bore around 01.45, and started setting up while the girls prepared lunch.

Had a lazy arvo, before we did the usual sunset watching, at 16.30.

Day 55 – Mon. 01.08.16   Wonarah Bore – Mary Kathleen [Free Camp in old Town site]

Another cloudless Territory day, with a light breeze.

The plan for today, was the head for Mt Isa, and spend the night, as one of the mob wanted to visit the "out-patents "at the Hospital.

Left camp at 08.00, and headed for the border. After about 30 minutes we caught up to a couple of semis' carrying wide loads. With some good communication on our CB radios, and a couple of pilots' that knew their job, we were able to get buy. Not before another Idiot bloke (no not bloke, just idiot), in a Prado and pulling a van, dropped his bundle, and passed the wide load, going up a hill and over a white line. It would seem that he did not have any radio communication, and thought that if we were passing the wide load so would he. What a fool.

Back in QLD and stopped at Camooweal for a coffee and homemade, Vanilla Slice, (beat that). A change to the plan, stopping a Mt Isa was now off and the change was to head for Mary Kathleen, spend two nights, then move onto Cloncurry for one night. This was confirmed when we got a booking at the Caravan park, for the one night. This was to be the farewell night, as we were splitting up and Lyn and I were heading for Magnetic Island for a week, and the others were heading up to the gulf.

Arrived in the Isa with a need for fuel, and a little shopping, for all. This done it was off down the road to set up camp at the old Mine site, well the old town site actually. It was around 15.30 when we arrived, so a quick bite, set up camp, and wait for the sunset.

After dinner, it was time for a bit of stargazing, and spot the satellite. Until you have witnessed the night sky out here you will not understand just now bright it is, and how absolutely full it is of stars.

Day 56 – Tue. 02.08.16   Mary Kathleen [Free Camp in old Town site]

The wind started at around 01.00, from the south, and got so strong that, three of us got up and took down our awnings, to stop them from getting blown away. It was another cloudless day, but very cold, well to us it was, after coming down from Darwin with the temp in the mid-thirties.

Went for a drive up to see the old mine. It was time for Bengie to get down and dirty, and to see if she could do what she was designed to do. We saw the big hole in the ground that they had taken all the Uranium from, and now had a lot of water in it. Got some photos of the hole as well as the tailing dumps. Saw some Camels on the way in and thought we would get some photos on the way out, but it seems they had other ideas, and had moved on.

It was a cold sunset watching, just as well we started early.

Day 57 – Wed. 03.08.16   Mary Kathleen – Cloncurry [Cloncurry Caravan Park Oasis]

This wind has been blowing now for thirty hours, with no sign of letting up. In fact, it has been getting" worsera", (that means very bad), and still as cold as.

It was on to Cloncurry, about 60K's down the road, for a night in the Caravan Park, and a planned communal farewell dinner, before we parted company, with L & J heading for Magnetic Island for a week, and the rest going on up to Mornington.

Dinner has been cancelled, due to the wind and cold. We all got set up, had some lunch, then went downtown for essentials. We had to ring our local GP in Burpengary to get a prescription faxed to the local Cloncurry Pharmacy, for Lyn's infection. Then it was into the last happy hour for some time, well at least until we met up again.

Day 58 – Thu. 04.08.16   Cloncurry – Hughenden [Hughenden Allan Terry Caravan Park]

The dammed wind is still blowing and is still as cold as.

Got away this morning at 08.15, or there-about. Said our good-buys to the others. Had a good run to Julia Creek. It was much bigger than we thought it would be. Had ourselves a coffee, and got under-way again. At Richmond we got some fuel, and a pie for lunch, and went over to a park on the shore of this great little lake right in town, (great spot). It was then on to get checked in at Hughenden. A good clean park. The wind has died off a little now, but it made for some very bad economy figures during the trip today.

A note on the roads we encountered on today's trip, from Cloncurry to Julia Creek, not bad, but not good. From Julia Creek to Richmond, bloody terrible. From Richmond to Hughenden, absolutely bloody terrible, in other words it was pretty much shit really. The road builders of Queensland should go to the N.T. and find out how road building is done, because the roads in the N.T. are first class, compared to what we have to put up with.

Day 59 – Fri. 05.08.16   Hughenden – Charters Towers [Aussie Outback Oasis, Big 4]

The wind is still blowing, not as hard, and is still cool.

Got away at 08.00 and had a reasonable trip over to Charters Towers. Got checked in on a good drive through site, for a quick getaway in the morning.

Went down-town for so last-minute shopping, as we think the Island will be a little expensive. This was confirmed with a phone call to Annie, who had just spent some time there.

Also gave our little grub Benjie a wash. The disgusting little thing had not seen water since Katherine.

The camp is doing "Wood-Fired Pizza's" tonight, so have ordered one to save on the cooking and washing up.

Day 60 – Sat. 06.08.16   Charters Towers – Magnetic Island. [Island Palms Resort, time share]

No wind this morning, calm and mild, with cloud, I think the first time since Darwin.

Got away at 08.15, and headed for the ferry terminal at Townsville.

Had to do a quick stop to check if somebody had turned off the Battery and pump. On closing up the van, I did something to the door lock, and could not open it again. I tried several times, changed the key, still could not open it again. So left it as it was and kept going, to sort it out in Townsville. Got to the terminal at around 10.00, to find there was no room in the lock-up compound for the van, so had to park in the compound next door, which was not lockable. Then proceeded to transfer what we needed from the van, into the Benjie, and what we didn't need in Benjie, back into the van. All of this having been done we headed over to line up and wait for the ferry.

All was good, and the ferry got away on time at 12.35. The trip was thirty-five minutes, with the breeze getting up a little. When we arrived, we decided to go and see if we could get an early check-in to our unit. All worked out well and we were in at around 13.45, a unit on the fourth level, and overlooking the marina and bay, through the palm, and a giant fig tree down on the esplanade. After many trips up and down the stairs, ferrying all of our gear, going down again, for a walk out along the break-water, going down again, to go to the supermarket, we were buggered, and therefore slept very, very well.

Day 61-66 – 07-13.08.16   Magnetic Island. [Island Palms Resort, time share]

A light breeze started most days, getting a little stronger as the days went on.

Our unit is very central, with a supermarket, bottle shop, Pharmacy, and Thai restaurant only about 150 metres away, with the ferry terminal and marina about 500 metres. The Supermarket prices on the Island were not that bad for the very day stuff, so next time I don't think we would stock up to the degree that we did.

Sunday, we went for a drive around the place, saw some great spots. Horseshoe Bay seemed very popular. I guess because the breeze comes over the Island, and creates the offshore breeze on the beach, so lots of activity there. A lot of restaurants there as well, so made a mental note to return for that.

Today Thursday was one of those perfect tropical Island days. A very light breeze, cloudless sky, and around 26^0.

Got a reasonably early start, and went for a walk to the Forts, around 4km return. The track was a little ordinary, being very rocky, and very steep in places.

It was a good work-out, and from the top where the forts were it was a good view. These were observation posts and a couple of gun emplacements used during WW2. Saw a couple of Koala's up in the trees, one with a youngster.

Back home for and a bit more of the games, then over to Horseshoe Bay for a Barra lunch.

Went for a walk this morning, drove to Picnic Bay and the start of the Hawking's Point walk. This was good, certainly plenty of rocks to climb over.

This arvo (Friday) started packing as will be out of here tomorrow morning and start on the home-ward journey.

Day 67 – Sat. 13.08.16   Magnetic Island – Calen. St Helens Gardens Caravan Park.

A light breeze started most days, getting a little stronger as the days went on.

Caught the 9.55 ferry back to the mainland, drove off the ferry and around to pick up the "Brick" half expecting to see it with no wheels, or the door busted in and everything gone from inside, or just plain "not there", but no, there it was as we had left it. Started to do the change-over and repack the car and van.

After a cup of the coffee, we were ready to head off to our next camp at Calen. An uneventful trip down, but the wind got stronger as the day went on, and this knocked the fuel economy around

Wind something terrible, but we made it. A nice clean and tidy Park, a lot of road noise during the night, only small park, but would stay again.

Day 68 – Sun. 14.08.16   Calen – Childers. Sugar Bowl Caravan Park.

A light breeze to start, but got stronger as the day went on.

Decided to make a day of it and go through to spend the night at Childers. A long day of eight hours driving, but it was worth it as we would only have a short run home the next day. The Caravan Park seemed to full of Pack Packers, it must have been time to pick some produce or something. All of that was not a problem, but the park was a little run down, and needed a make-over.

Day 69 – Mon. 15.08.16   Childers - Beachmere

The weather was much the same as yesterday. Got away from Childers at about 07.15, hoping to get home at 11.30. Had a good run, stopped for a coffee at the Gympie Lake, then got some fuel, and headed for home.

Got home and uncoupled, so we could go down-town for some necessary food, then home to unpack and do the things one does at the end of a trip.

In Conclusion.

It was a good trip, I think we all enjoyed the time we had and the places we saw, either for the first time or to revisit something we might have some years before.

I must add that on this trip we were very lucky with the weather, had a little overnight rain at Sapphire, followed by drizzle for the day. We left Longreach in the morning, and that afternoon they had the start of what was to be around 75mm. We had very light drizzle overnight at Ormiston Gorge, but cleared very early the next morning. On the homeward journey from Childers about two very light showers, just nuisance value really. At Darwin the weather was very cool for the locals, but just right for us. At Jabiru we had clear skies, and light breezes, and this was to last all the way to Magnetic.

All vehicles and vans performed well, yes there were a few little things like flat batteries, but nothing major.

This is a journal of our Journey's journey. The other three vans also have their own stories to tell, after we had our planned split-up at Cloncurry and could be added to this one.

The next trip has now entered the last stages of planning so it will be off again soon. JB

Some Statistics of the trip for "The Merc on a Journey"
- Distance Travelled = 10,250 km
- Fuel used = 1388 l
- Average Fuel Cost = $1.27
- Total Fuel Cost = $1,783.20
- Average Speed = 74.04 kph
- Average ls/100Km = 14.02 l

Our neighbours Brenda and Lesley decided that Lyn and I would not get away with just letting the celebration of our 50 years of marriage just slowly drift by. They organised a party.

It was too big for any of the villas, so it had to be held in the Beach House. It was a a tremendous afternoon, with all of our friends there. Myra made a cake, as she usually does for occasions like this, and once again it was really good.

We got a fair bit of ribbing on several subjects, but that's what you expect from this mob. I just have to remember to give some back at every opportunity.

Lyn and me after 50 Years of marriage.

In May 2017, Lyn and I were talking to Warwick and Carole Kendall who said they were going up to Sapphire, to fossick for some sapphires again. I told them about our thoughts of going up to Cooktown to have a look. They said why not call in on your way back? This sounded all right, so I started some serious planning. Ronny and Ross were going off on their "Round the Island" thing, so we would head north in June before it got too hot up there.

On the 9th of June 2018, off we went. We stopped at Bargara the first night, made Sapphire the next day, and stayed for a week; another week trying to get that elusive big stone. We tried to leave Sapphire on Saturday 17th, but the lights on the van decided that they would not cooperate. I tried contacting auto-electricians to fix the problem, but nobody could help, so I rang a few in Emerald. Nobody. That was until the last guy said, "Bring it over." So away we went. I left the van behind, as I knew the problem was with the ML.

We arrived at this guy's house, and apparently he was getting ready to go to work. He was on contract to one of the coal processing mines around Emerald. Anyway, he looked at it, took out his multi-meter, and tested a few things, asked a few questions, did some Umm-ing and Ah-ing. He removed the control unit and took it into his workshop. When he brought it back, he said he had re-soldered a few suspect solder joints, and it now tested out ok. (Is it not funny how three or four techos can solder all the faulty joints on the same small PC board, but the thing worked fine?) We paid the guy $100 for his trouble and said our goodbyes.

I had been to see Mary-Anne at the caravan park in the morning to ask if we could stay an extra night, and that was fine. That night we went down to the happy hour spot with the big open fireplace,

I met a guy who had once owned a ML, and he had the same problem that I was having. He said he had been through it all and told me that the controller is just like a computer. If it does not do what you want it to do, reboot it. When I thought about it, that is what the mining bloke did. He disconnected it, waited a while, then re-powered it, and away it went. He must still be laughing, but that's ok. I got on my way the next morning with everything working fine. We headed off for Charters Towers.

We had a good run up the road. We got to the Towers and looked for the free camp spot. I said to Lyn, "I'm going to keep going, we lost a day with the lights, and if we go straight through to Mt Surprise, we will be on time again. After a bit of to-ing and fro-ing, that's what we did. We rang Mt Surprise and told them we would be late getting there. They could expect us around 18.00hrs. We spent a couple of nights there and asked about fossicking for the next time we came that way.

The next stop was Lake Tinaroo. We stayed a couple of nights. This a nice quiet place, worth a revisit. Next stop was Cooktown, and we spent 3 nights at the Big4. We had a good look around the old town. There is plenty of history there, and the museums are really good. From Cooktown it was back to Mareeba, to Carole and Warwick's, for another 5 nights and a bit of relaxation. Lyn had been on about going to see Paranella Park, so like a good bloke, I said okay. It was a bit far from Mareeba to do it easily, so we spent a night at Herberton on the way. There is a lot of history in this place as well. Next day it was off to Paranella Park. Got on to one tour that afternoon, another that night. The tickets also covered the cost of the caravan park, making sure the little girl was happy.

We made our way down to Mission Beach and stayed two nights too long at this place. It did nothing for us at all. We travelled on and stopped at a free camp for the night at Home Hill, then onto Cape Hillsborough for two nights. I think the Martians live there as the power supply is up the pole. For some reason, we could not get the power going. I can't remember what I did about it, but we stayed on. We saw kangaroos on the beach the next morning. Apparently that is a necessary thing to do. From here, it was a rush home with one stop at Calliope River free camp, not bad, then home.

Life slowed down a bit after that trip, and maybe I slowed down a little too much. It was around September that Jan came up and paid us a visit. The girls went shopping and all that stuff, but one night, after dinner, the girls were watching something on the tele that did not interest me much, so I went out and sat at the computer, and thought I would do a bit of something, I don't know what.

Anyhow it seems I fell asleep. I mean a sleep so deep that my heart rate slowed, my blood pressure went way down and I slipped into a coma. Because I was sitting up in the chair, my brain ran out of blood. After about half an hour Lyn came in to see how I was and got the biggest fright of her life when she could not wake me, not even by yelling in my ear. I cannot tell you her exact words, but apparently, they were not the ones she would normally use.

The next thing I can recall is just before they loaded me into the waiting ambulance. After that it's arriving at the Caboolture Hospital. It was then that the little blonde paramedic said, "You were very lucky, John. When we were trying to recover you, your heart rate was at 36 beats per minute. If it had gone down to 35, we would have had to hit you with the paddles, and that's like having me sit on your chest." I thought to myself, "And what would be wrong with that?" That's when I knew I would be OK. A day or so of tests and I was home again.

For quite some time I had also had a problem with numb feet. They felt like they were just blocks of wood on the end of my legs. I had it checked out before we left home, and they said it was peripheral neuropathy, meaning the nerves to my legs were being pinched somewhere in my spine. If I stood in one place for too long, my body would go numb from the waist down, I mean everything, the Old Fella included.

In the end, I went to an orthopaedic surgeon and he told me that the vertebrae in my lumbar spine were closing off on the spinal cord because of the growth of arthritis, and that was the problem. They called that spinal stenosis.

The best news was that there was an operation that had good results, with little risk. I joined the waiting list. We took a holiday to Tassie while waiting.

In the latter part of 2018, we did not do any travelling, but were lpreparing for an upcoming trip to Tasmania in 2019. Ronny was doing most of the planning and was in touch with the Tasmanian Tourist Bureau, who gave him a lot of info. With all the planning done, it was a matter of getting ready, as we would be away for around two-and-a-half months.

I began to keep a log of this trip, but I never seemed to have time to write it. A couple of times I jotted stuff down, but in the end, I gave up. There were ten of us on this trip; Ron and Brenda with a van, Ross and Lesley, also with a van, Rob and Sandy, yes, another van, Lyn and I, the same, then there was Duane and Wendy, no van this time, they were in their SUV and stayed in cabins all the way.

On the morning of the 5th Feb 2019 we were off, heading for the first night at Goondiwindi. All went well. Next morning it was off to Coonabarabran, for the second night, then two nights at Forbes and Finlay before arriving in Melbourne, at the Crystal Brook Tourist Park. We spent two nights there to get sorted for the crossing to Tassie. There was much to do as, during the ferry crossing, we were unable to keep the fridges on. We could not use gas, as the bottles had to be off and sealed during the voyage and leaving them on would have flattened the batteries.

On the 11th of Feb, we had a very early start to get to the ferry terminal at 6am and start loading for a 9am departure. It was a good crossing, with the sea reasonably calm.

After disembarking at Devonport, we headed straight for Ulverstone Big 4, west of Devonport. Ron had planned that we would stay there for 3 nights, to give us time to shop and fuel up.

On the 14th, we went further west to stay for 7-nights at Crayfish Creek. From there, we did day trips out to Stanley, the Nut and Smithton, then to the Tarkine forest and the Trowutta rain forest walk and Australia's largest sinkhole. We travelled down to the Arthur River. We all took a cruise up the Arthur River on the "Little Red Boat". It was a very good trip with lunch included. I think we all agreed that it was a better cruise than the Gordon River Cruise that we were to do later. We went back and spent a day at Burnie, as we had passed through it towing the vans and therefore did not see much.

On the 21st we left Crayfish creek and headed for Zeehan Bush Camp and Van Park for a 5-night stay. There we looked at all the stuff they offered around the place. Then it off to Queenstown for 2-nights. From here, it was a day trip to Strahan, and the Gordan.

From Queenstown it was an early start to make it to Snug, with a couple of stops on the way. One stop was Derwent Bridge. Before crossing the bridge, we turned left and headed to the visitor centre at Lake St Clair. The centre was very good, but we could not go any further without permits.

Back to the Highway and over the Derwent River, we turned left to go and see "The Wall". The Wall is in a big shed, and consists of slabs of Huon Pine 3metres high, and 2 metres wide. These are joined to form a wall about 30metres long. On this wall is carved the story of the pioneering days of the timber workers and their communities. One walks down one side and back up the other as it is carved back and front. It is still a work in progress.

The artist was there on the day. There were other things carved, like a coat hanging on a peg. At first glance it looked like a leather coat, but it was actually carved from Huon Pine. The "Wall" was one of the must-see things of the trip.

From there we went down to the other side of Hobart to Snug, for another 7-night stay. From Snug we did day trips to all the places south of Hobart, all the way to Southport, until we ran out of sealed road. Geeveston was a great little place, with a good museum. They had statues of people carved and placed on corners or at a shop entrance and a great little restaurant that we visited twice.

We left Snug and went on to Triabunna, for another 7-night stay. From there we visited places like Richmond, Seven Mile Beach, and Sorell. Lyn and I had decided that we would not go to Port Arthur, as we had done it before. However, some others did.

From Triabunna, it was off to Scamander. Based in Scamander, we did the trip back down to Bicheno for a good look around and up to St Helens, a good spot.

My hands were giving me a bit of strife. They felt tingly, especially the tips of my fingers, and mainly on the left hand. This became worse as the holiday progressed until it would wake me in the middle of the night with pain I had not experienced since the heart attack. When we found that St Helens had a good-sized hospital, we paid it a visit. There was not a doctor on duty, but they could call one in an emergency. I was not in that class so I saw a duty nurse, who could not do much at all.

She suggested that I go and see the local chemist, as they might help. The chemist was very helpful and suggested I use some gloves designed for arthritis. I did this, and by wearing them to bed I had a much better night's sleep.

We did the end of the road trip up to the Bay of Fires, and all places in between. We visited Derby, the mountain bike capital of the world. This town is all about mountain bikes. They are everywhere, and so are bike shops.

After 7 days, we packed up and moved to just north of Launceston to a place called Legana and booked in for 11-nights. Once again, it was the day trip thing to see all the sites. We did the trip up one side of the Tamar River and down the other, then out to the mouth of the river, on both sides. It was a good trip. Another trip was over to Scottsdale, on the Tasman Highway, and then up to Bridport. That was a good trip through some beautiful country.

After a good look around the Launceston area, we headed once again for Ulverstone for 4-nights this time. Ulverstone is one of the closest parks to the ferry, therefore a good place for early starts.

It was an early start on the morning of the 6th April. Time to head back to the mainland. We had made the decision that, when we hit the mainland, we would go our own way, as we were all going to do something different.Lyn and I headed for Seymour and a park on the Goulburn River. It was a good park and worth a revisit some day.

From there it was up to Jan's in Howlong. She had moved into a new house in town, but there was room to park the van on the street without hindering anybody. A couple of days was enough time for the two girls to exchange all the gossip they needed. It was time to head north, so the next nights were at Karuah and Woolgoolga, then it was home, arriving on the 11th April. It was a great trip and I would recommend it to anybody who has the will.

On 27th June, I had the operation on my back. They wheeled me into the theatre at 11 o'clock on that Thursday and I walked out of hospital at 11 o'clock the next day, after the surgeon had chiselled out the very compacted L4 and L5 vertebrae. Most of the problems are now fixed. The blocks of wood will take a long time to come good, as the nerves are very slow growing. However, all is well, and will get better.

Epilogue

Here I am in 2020, 74 years of age.

I have been married to my little girl for 53 years, with more to come. We have done so much together, and when I think about it, I realise that I could not have done a fraction of it on my own, but only in our loving partnership. We have had a full life, moving around this vast country, all the time doing the best for the boys, giving them adventure at every turn, but also giving them something to learn from, and to think about.

I think about the wonderful gift we were given in our daughter, who gave us such pleasure every day of her 11 years. Her handicap was very severe, but she didn't know this and so made the best of everything. She touched everybody who met her and left them with a lasting memory.

I also feel very fortunate to have had wonderful parents who allowed me to explore and experiment, to find out for myself. There was never any push from them to follow a particular path in life, just that I should learn from the mistakes, and not forget the correct choices.

Unfortunately, in my early years, I missed out on the fundamentals of learning. Whether I didn't listen, or just plain did not understand, I don't know, but it was a big handicap to my learning. I tried to make up for it later, by using my memory to increase my knowledge, but I was always that little bit behind where I could have been.

We have three wonderful sons and daughters-in-law. They have produced four lovely grandchildren, who are at the top in their schooling, and I know they will all go on to great things. The world is theirs, to go and experience as much as they can, while they can.

We do not know our future, and I think that's a good thing.

My brother Hilton was still living in Eltham, in the same house that he and Leone moved into when they married, back in 1967. It was sad to learn that on the 20th November 2019, Hilton passed away in the New Plymouth Hospital, one week past his 77th birthday.

I have written these words down on paper while I am still able. I see the counter on the Word file is now over 103,000 words and that is quite enough!

Four More Good Ordinary Blokes

The Barra   Marc   Tony (with Rohan)   Geoff (with Brendan)
& Friend, David Marven

*I have enjoyed writing this story,
and hope that it provides a little entertainment
to all who read it.*

www.ingramcontent.com/pod-product-compliance
Ingram Content Group UK Ltd.
Pitfield, Milton Keynes, MK11 3LW, UK
UKHW061223180426